JOHN E. (JACK) CAMPBELL, born in London of Scots parents and reared in Govan, left school at the age of 15 and joined the infant *Scottish Daily Express* as a copy boy. He was its first (and only) cub reporter when he was 16, and six years later was transferred (unwillingly) to a sub-editorial desk.

At the outbreak of the war he was deputy chief sub-editor. He joined the Navy's rescue tug section (manned by merchant seamen) as a 2nd mate, and served six years at sea, latterly in command of one of the vessels.

Demobilised as lieutenant RNR, he rejoined the paper as night editor, then became news editor and managing editor. He edited the *Evening Citizen* from 1957 to 1961, resumed his post as managing editor until 1974, and edited the *Scottish Sunday Express* until retirement in 1978.

After leaving the *Express* he edited company newspapers and during this time wrote *The Fairtry Experiment*, the story of the world's first factory trawler whose plans were deviously secured by the Russians to spawn their powerful ocean fishing fleet.

He is now retired, allegedly finally, at Prestwick. His grandson, Donald Martin, is editor of the *Aberdeen Evening Express*.

A Word for Scotland

*To Gerald
with sincere good wishes —*

JACK CAMPBELL

Jack Campbell.

Luath Press Limited

EDINBURGH

www.luath.co.uk

First Edition 1998

The paper used in this book is acid-free, neutral-sized and recyclable.
It is made from low chlorine pulps produced in a low energy,
low emission manner from sustainable forests.

Printed and bound by
Bell & Bain Ltd., Glasgow

Typeset in 10.5 point Sabon by
S. Fairgrieve, Edinburgh, 0131 658 1763

Photographs reproduced by kind permission of Express
Newspapers plc, unless otherwise stated.

Contents

Foreword

WHEN JACK CAMPBELL WAS summoned on to the set of *This Is Your Life* in October 1997, he pointed an accusing finger at me: 'I have never forgiven this man,' he said, 'for stealing away my best reporter!'

It took me back, I can tell you (it took me aback as well!). It took me back all of 44 years, to my first visit to the editorial department of the *Scottish Daily Express* at 195 Albion Street, Glasgow. I had just returned from five rather self-indulgent years at Oxford. I was young, brash, brimming with quite unjustified self-confidence and stony-broke – and I had come to proffer my services as a journalist to the legendary *Scottish Daily Express*. 'Mr Campbell' was the Managing Editor. I think he was so amused by my effrontery that he decided to give me a chance to sink or swim. He had no idea (nor, indeed, had I) that, a year later, I would marry his star feature writer, Mamie Baird, who would cheerfully abandon her journalism in order to become a full-time wife and mother.

He was not a bit like the newspaper editors I had seen on American movies: hard-bitten, cigar-chewing, snarling and caparisoned in shirt-sleeves and green eye-shield. He was quiet, courteous, patient and considerate. He looked younger than his 40 years except for a couple of deep furrows on his forehead (which I now suspect had been there since birth), which made him look interestingly world-weary.

I was soon to learn that the *Scottish Daily Express* was his pride, his joy, his very life. He told me that I was joining the greatest newspaper in the world – and I believed him.

From him I learned that The Story was all: that he expected his reporters to be first on the scene, first to get the key interview, first to reach a telephone. We were of course expected to write the best story - the most colourful, the most concise and, above all, the most accurate.

The enthusiasm was electrifying, and I fell in love with it all - the excitement, the camaraderie, the stories, the loyalty, the determination to put one over on the *Daily Record* or the *Daily Mail*, our great rivals. The *Scottish Daily Express* was a broadsheet in those days, but the legendary Arthur Christiansen was charting a way which would lead to a shotgun marriage between the 'responsible' broadsheets and the brash tabloids. We used to work all the hours 'the job' required (there was no overtime in those days), and afterwards there was the carousing with colleagues and rivals alike, telling taller and taller yarns about the scoops we had engineered and the tricks we had got up to in order to beat the opposition.

These were halcyon days. And they were privileged years. Through the *Scottish Daily Express* I found myself living through history in the making. I was sent all over Scotland in pursuit of the telling tales, the epic dramas and delicate lyrics of a great nation, day by day and year by year.

And now Jack Campbell has brought it all to life again. He was never one of the roisterers and revellers, never a teller of impossible tales. But he knew it all. He knew it all from the very beginning, in November 1928, and he would be at the centre of things through all the 46 years of the *Scottish Daily Express* in Albion Street.

Long after I had left for pastures new, and had read about the demise of my beloved 'Scottish', I used to think what a great story a chronicle of these times would make, if only someone who had lived them and helped to shape them would undertake it.

But Jack did not just sit down and reel off his memories on to paper. Consummate newspaperman that he always was, he tracked down every survivor of those golden years he could find; painstakingly, he milked us all of our memories and then spent endless months in the Mitchell Library in Glasgow checking and rechecking the facts. For Jack, facts were always sacred.

What a gallery of eccentric, colourful and occasionally brilliant characters he has drawn! They are all here: the reporter who became a Secretary of State for Scotland (Hector McNeil), the girl reporter who became Scotland's second woman QC (Isabel Sinclair), the legendary Ben Allison and his uncanny knack of getting a story, the gentle and gentlemanly Gilbert Cole of the Edinburgh office, Jimmy Henderson who became Editor of the *Northern Times*, the enterprising Drew Rennie who signed up top international sports stars of the 1960s such as Muhammad Ali and Arnold Palmer, photographer Albert Barr who scooped the world with a photograph of Princess Margaret at an alfresco 21st birthday at Balmoral with Peter Townsend....

And what an evocative collection of unforgettable, warm, human stories Jack has conjured up: the discovery of Dr Buck Ruxton's victims by a *Scottish Daily Express* reporter, the sad last days in 1946 of world boxing champion Benny Lynch, the Glasgow smallpox outbreak, the Knockshinnoch mining disaster and the theft of the Stone of Destiny (all in 1950), the sinking of the *Princess Victoria* ferry in 1953, 'Operation Snowdrop' in 1955 when the north of Scotland was beleaguered by the worst blizzard of the century, the strange story of Sheena Govan and her sect of 'Nameless Ones', the lurid career of serial killer Peter Manuel (hanged in 1958), the Cheapside Street fire of 1960 which cost the lives of 19 Glasgow firemen, the Longhope lifeboat disaster of 1969 and the loss of the Fraserburgh lifeboat the following year, the corruption trial of the top civil servant, 'Gorgeous' George Pottinger...

I could go on and on (and frequently do!). Suffice it to say here that I am intensely proud to have played a small part in those pioneering journalistic years, and to have been given the privilege of contributing this Foreword to *A Word for Scotland* – despite having stolen Jack Campbell's best reporter.

Magnus Magnusson KBE (*Scottish Daily Express,* 1953-61)
November, 1998

Preface

WHEN THE RESIDENTS OF 195 Albion Street, Glasgow, lost their home in March 1974, there were those who said they had been unfairly evicted and others who said they had only themselves to blame; but whatever the truth of it, almost all of them remember the old place and the old times with nothing but affection. For 46 years they made the *Scottish Daily Express* there and, for much of that time, the *Evening Citizen*, too.

I was one of them. So, too, was Jack Webster, author and columnist. He insisted that since I was the only one left among those who had attended the birth of the paper, and was still there on the day of the exodus, I should set down the story of those momentous years.

I was reluctant. Certainly, I had been there, at the chaotic and tragic events of the last night of printing in March, 1974; but I had not been one of the midwives at the birth on Thursday, 8 November, 1928: I had arrived, aged 15, in time only to fetch the midwives their cups of tea.

Besides, although scraps of notes and jottings survived from my collaboration with the writer Theo Lang on the in-house publication for our 25th anniversary, they would have provided a rather flimsy basis for a proper history of the paper.

I was finally spurred to take up Jack Webster's challenge, however, after I found an item in an issue of the *Scottish Daily Express* in June 1994 reporting the death of Gilbert Cole, for so many years the Chief Reporter of our Edinburgh bureau. It was contained, dismissively, within a six-line paragraph tucked away on an inside page. Truly, a generation had grown up which knew not Gilbert Cole! He had been my first mentor, one of the most gifted and most loved of that talented corps of journalists who served the *Scottish Daily Express*, and I was distressed not only by his death but also to find that someone like Gilbert Cole had not been accorded a more generous memorial in his old paper.

Younger readers should note that throughout the Albion Street years, the *Scottish Daily Express* was a large-format broadsheet newspaper. It was not until January 1977, three years after the end of the Albion Street enterprise, that the *Express* changed to its present tabloid form.

What I have written in this memoir is an account of how the people at Albion Street brought to their readers the drama and colour of those stirring years. It is essentially a personal account, but I hope that it has been redeemed from too heavy an emphasis on the first person singular pronoun by the help of the many good companions along the way who have added texture to the story with their own recollections.

Jack Campbell
November, 1998

CHAPTER I

A Word for Scotland

I MIGHT NEVER HAVE KNOWN Albion Street at all had it not been for my mother. I was one of a family who came 'home' to my father's native Govan because Father was too ill to go on working for a company building bridges in England – although this did not prevent him, before he died, from leaving Mother pregnant with a sixth child and loving memories, but with little else with which to nurture her brood.

I went to school (at Copland Road Elementary, originally) unwillingly, because Mother did not appreciate that to be sent to school dressed in Norfolk jacket and Eton collar was not considered acceptable in Govan society.

To Govan High School I also went unwillingly, and on some occasions absented myself, until its diminutive but formidable headmaster, Daddy Maclean, offered me the choice of 16 of the best (eight on each hand) or expulsion. I have been grateful to him ever since. He did not tell my mother, and he also let me sit the Day School Leaving Certificate, which probably equated with the present-day Standard Grades.

I had no idea what to do with the certificate. I had once tried to sign on as a cabin boy with the Anchor Line, but Mother went to see the Marine Superintendent and told him that I had falsified my age and was not even 14; she had then extracted from me a promise not even to consider going to sea until I was at least 17. I certainly had no ambition to enter journalism. Apart from having had the strict discipline of grammar, and an ability to communicate understandably in English in a world outside the playground, instilled in me by a Miss Mackinnon at Copland Road Elementary, there was nothing to justify such an aspiration.

However, on discovering that a requirement of prospective apprentices at Barr and Stroud's works at Anniesland was an ability to write in comprehensible English, I wrote an essay spuriously entitled 'Why I Want to Be a Scientific Instrument-Maker'. For two months I used a simple engraving machine and managed to deface a proportion of the metal identification plates on their range-finders before I learned about the coming of a new newspaper and applied to throw in my lot with it.

Since it was impossible to request leave of absence to attend the interview, Mother went in my stead, and so impressed the chief commissionaire at 195 Albion Street that I was awarded the job of office boy at 10s 6d (52p) per week. Barr and Stroud were happy to release me.

I reported for duty on the morning of Monday, 12 November, 1928. By then the infant paper had made three public appearances, but some of the 380 staff had already been there for two months, and Jimmy Moran, its first sports editor, always said that those last weeks of pregnancy had been even more painful than the birth itself.

None of us would have been at 195 Albion Street at all, however, if a Presbyterian minister named William Cuthbert Aitken had not emigrated to Canada over a century earlier from the little village of Torphichen, in West Lothian.

Lord Beaverbrook with the second Lady Beaverbrook, pictured during an Aitken family reunion at Silvermine Farm, Torphichen, the old family home from which his minister father emigrated to Canada

His third son, William Maxwell Aitken, was then, in 1928, the first Lord Beaverbrook, a self-made millionaire, political king-maker and press baron. He had taken the title of Beaverbrook from the stream in which he had played as a boy in the little town of Newcastle, in New Brunswick province. His friends called him Max; his public foes called him 'The Beaver' or 'the little Canadian adventurer'. We came to refer to him as 'The Beaver' as well – irreverently, but never disparagingly, as his enemies did.

He had come to Britain in 1910. Although then only 31 years old, he had already made a considerable fortune from financial deals; the largest and most controversial of these had created the amalgamation of all Canada's cement mills.

In London he became private secretary and friend and adviser to the Canadian-born Conservative politician (later Prime Minister), Andrew Bonar Law. Bonar Law persuaded him to contest the Liberal-held seat of Ashton-under-Lyne in the General Election of 1911. It was a bastion of Free Traders, but Max defiantly proclaimed in it his message of Imperial Preference and sensationally snatched the seat with a majority of 196 votes.

The year 1911 was also the year in which he entered Fleet Street. He did so only in response to a plea for financial help from the editor of the then ailing and endangered *Daily Express*. Within five years he had control of it. He then started, in 1918, a companion *Sunday Express*. By 1923 he controlled the *Evening Standard* as well.

The deals he brokered in politics, as skilfully as he had done in business, are said to include manoeuvring his friend Bonar Law into leadership of the Tory Party, and displacing Asquith as Prime Minister in 1918 in favour of Lloyd George; but his acceptance of a peerage in 1916 curtailed his own political ambitions: no longer a commoner, the way to the highest offices of state was effectively barred to him.

Until now he had seen his newspapers as subsidiary to his political ends, or as a mean to those ends; now he applied his formidable energy to them with skill and purpose and real journalistic flair. He had found (or rediscovered) the zeal which had prompted him, as a 14-year-old, to establish a paper called *Leader* in his home town of Newcastle in Canada. Max Aitken's youthful *Leader* had been predictably short-lived; but now, despite Lord Northcliffe's dire warning that 'You'll lose all your money in Fleet Street', the grown-up Max Aitken's newspapers prospered, and by the 1920s he was on his way to making the *Daily Express* the most widely-read newspaper in the world.

Now, in 1928, he was setting his sights on Scotland. In that first issue of the *Scottish Daily Express* on 8 November 1928, he wrote that he had fulfilled 'a dream that I have always carried in my heart, that as my father went out from Scotland to speak to the Canadians, I might return from Canada with a word for Scotland.'

No doubt the competition for readership among national newspapers of the time had something to do with his decision to invade Scotland. But the Torphichen connection always mattered a great deal to him. A later incident from October 1961 underlines the point. Lord Beaverbrook, who was then aged 82, had just disembarked from a liner which called at the Clyde at the end of a voyage from America. With him was the future second Lady Beaverbrook, Marcia Anastasia, Lady Dunn, the widow of his boyhood friend Sir James Hamet Dunn. Lord Beaverbrook came to lunch with some of us at the Central Hotel and afterwards pleaded a need to rest. But instead of resting, he left the hotel with Lady Dunn and instructed his driver, Charlie Armstrong, to take them to Torphichen. At the village from which his father came he took his bride-to-be into the churchyard where, in the old Scots custom, he plighted his troth and considered himself married.

He certainly could not have started the *Scottish Daily Express* with the idea of making a quick financial return. It was scarcely a propitious time to enter into hazardous new business enterprises. In 1928, when a figure of even a million unemployed was considered unacceptable, there were two million people out of work, and the Great Depression and the Wall Street crash were just around the corner. Beaverbrook's friend and confidant, Ewart J. Robertson, advised him to delay. His counsel went unheeded.

Gladys, the first Lady Beaverbrook, to whom he had been married for 22 years, had died on 1 December, 1927. Beaverbrook immediately took his two boys, Peter and Max, on a cruise to America and the West Indies. With them, as additional company, went three of his closest London newspaper aides – Brigadier 'Mike' Wardell, director of the *Evening Standard* (and later a publisher in Canada), the columnist Viscount Castlerosse, and the Scots-born journalist John Gordon, who at that time was an Editor Without Portfolio.

I have no first-hand knowledge of this, but I was told by Sandy Trotter (my editor for many years), who heard it from John Gordon, that the final decision to invade Scotland was taken by Beaverbrook during talks with his three aides on board *SS Leviathan* during that voyage to New York.

John Gordon was no less dismayed by the decision than E.J. Robertson, but for a different reason – he could see himself as the logical choice as editor of the Scottish newspaper, whereas he had wider horizons in mind. His fears only increased when he was deputed to go, like Joshua, to spy out the promised land.

Since someone of his stature could not conceal his presence in Glasgow from rival newspapers, he installed himself grandly in the Central Hotel and from there looked for somewhere to establish the paper. He also recruited his first members of staff; they included H.V. Morton, the author of *In Search of England*, who then added *In Search of Scotland* to the list of books which brought him his literary fame.

After two months John Gordon reported that Scotland was ready for deliverance into their hands. He was also much relieved to receive a summons to go south immediately to take up editorship of the *Sunday Express*, in which post he was to prove the truth that someone of large ambition could not be contained within his native land.

John Gordon, however, had been unable to find a base for the invasion – the right premises in which to house the new paper. He had coveted the noble building in Gordon Street opposite the Central Hotel, which housed the Grosvenor Restaurant, but its price was as daunting as its marble staircase entrance.

So the search for premises was taken up by Sidney Long, OBE, a man of as many talents as his ample chins. In London he had been Father of the Caseroom Chapel (that is, the chairman of the men's representatives in their dealings with management) until Lord Beaverbrook, impressed by his forthrightness and honesty, appointed him his production manager. Two years earlier, when the General Strike had silenced all newspapers, he had worked under the editorship of Winston Churchill to produce the Government's official *British Gazette,* almost single-handedly typesetting its entire contents.

It was Sidney Long who found 195 Albion Street; but it was E.J. Robertson, who had been so hesitant earlier, who committed his master irrevocably to the enterprise, because Lord Beaverbrook could not be contacted at the time. 'E.J.R.' signed to pay a little over £30,000 for the building in which F and J Smith, a subsidiary of Imperial Tobacco, manufactured and stored Crown Roll and Glasgow Mix tobaccos and a variety of cigarettes with improbable names like Wild Geranium and Harvest Moon and Morning Gallop.

Albion Street was a few blocks away from High Street on the one side and the City Chambers and George Square on the other, but it was a far cry from the ambiance of the prestigious Grosvenor Restaurant. It was a poor area, at times reduced almost to squalor by the presence of unfortunates addicted to cheap liquor. All too often they spilled out of a corner pub to prop up – momentarily – the outside wall, before slumping into the Ramshorn Churchyard, there to sleep as profoundly as its occupants. The wall came to be known as The Wall of Death.

The first front page

Sidney Long and Edwin Trotter, the works manager, had to break down the entire front of the Albion Street building to introduce the presses. They chose to house these behind a plate-glass facade. It proved an unfortunate choice, because a few years later I watched the unemployed 'hunger marchers' diverge from their route in order to throw stones at people who lived in glass houses.

The linotype machines and page trolleys were being manhandled up the narrow spiral staircase entrance, or hoisted by block and tackle through the windows, when the Dean of Guild refused a certificate of worthiness, maintaining that the floors had not been designed to carry such loads. Thousands of tons of concrete had to be poured into iron cages around the slender pillars on each of the four floors. To the sports editor, Jimmy Moran, it seemed that they would meet the starting deadline only with the help of divine intervention.

Whatever doubts anyone else had, at least one outsider had none. Tom McEntee, whose pub was sandwiched between 195 and the Salvage Corps next door, repainted his sign and changed the name to the Express Bar (although to this day no one has ever referred to it as other than 'Tom's').

The head printer was Herbert Spencer. He wore a black jacket and pin-striped trousers, and if he had carried an umbrella he could have passed as a City gent, although it is doubtful if he would have been accepted in polite drawing rooms. I was to see him join battle every night with John McAdam, the Chief Sub-editor, and to hear words which made my hair stand on end.

Herbert Spencer did not reserve his invective for sub-editors. I was told that on the several nights of dummy runs before the paper actually hit the streets, he would stand on a page trolley, gather his men around it, and tell them roundly, 'Gentlemen ....gentle...men... you are making a b***** a*** of the paper.'

In the last three days of rehearsal, the pages were actually cast and installed on the presses. The presses turned, and then stopped. The few copies were spirited away, perhaps even destroyed, to prevent them falling into the hands of the opposition. No trace of even a single one of them was ever found.

Jimmy Moran's call for divine intervention turned out to be unnecessary. So also was the precautionary duplication of the print at the Manchester office. On the night the *Scottish Daily Express* marched in, it did not need a crutch.

Some of the 380 original staff had common identity. Many of the printers came from the Dundee Courier. When the General Strike had ended they had been offered their jobs back on condition that they renounced their union, but they had loyally chosen to join the dole queue. Others were Scots exiles from the London and Manchester offices, and a chosen few Englishmen were officially on loan. In the case of a beloved little Geordie named Albert Tulip, who later ran the caseroom, the loan extended for more than 30 years. The English among us – and particularly the photographer, Bernard (Bill) Sykes – became more fervent Scots than the natives.

There was a general manager named Henry Franklin, and an editor, Bert Gabb, who had launched the Manchester-based *Express* the previous year; but during my first weeks on the paper, neither was as important as Mr Mitchell, the editorial commissionaire.

In comparison with today's high-tech age, the operation at 195 Albion Street belonged to the Dark Ages. John Gordon used to recall that in his days as a junior with the Dundee Advertiser (which he joined at the age of 14 for 4s 6d (23p) a week) he had used carrier pigeons to send in the football results. We had progressed beyond that, but not all that much. Correspondents out in the country, and sometimes staff on 'out of town' assignments, were provided with prepaid Post Office forms to telegraph reports which were not sufficiently urgent to be sent by telephone.

The telegraphed messages – strips of tape gummed to Post Office flimsy sheets – arrived by instalments, sometimes suspended in mid-sentence. Two youths, Edward Fenna and Douglas Machray, who were designated Head Boys by virtue of being aged 18 and 17 respectively, sat at one end of the sub-editors' horseshoe-shaped table, and pieced the messages together before passing them to the Chief Sub-editor.

Stories reached the caseroom for the printers (sometimes!) by 'the Carrier'. This was a contraption of wires and pulleys which clanked on an endless cable through every department. The cable had iron clamps with jaws which snapped open and shut at stations to receive and deliver messages along the system. Unhappily, the jaws always contrived to do this at the wrong stations, so that stories could land anywhere other than with the printers, or they could became entangled in obstructions on the way and arrive in a state of mutilation which owed nothing to the normal attention of sub-editors. There really was no substitute for us boys.

The telephoto room was buried deep underground to protect it from daylight. It was sited at the end of a dimly-lit tunnel which ran from the tobacco factory under the courtyard of the Salvage Corps headquarters on to what had been a loading bay in George Street.

The room was tiled all round like a railway station's superloo, and its only light was the diffused glimmer of a red electric bulb. The apparatus was the first of its kind in Britain, but Alf Piper, who was in charge of it, had to set the starter going with an engineer's brace before the engine took over. The first picture which came from London – the sketch of a hen for the Beachcomber column – was in negative form. It took 30 minutes to send.

There was no nonsense about how late boys could work, and sometimes we hunted rats in the tunnel. At one time there was warfare between two sets of us, and we even resorted to makeshift weapons. The wonder is that none of us became a juvenile delinquent

Perhaps we were saved from that by Bill Nicholson. Bill Nicholson, who was to become the first secretary of the Scottish Tourist Board, was the late night reporter. He used to set weekly essays, offering as reward to the winner half a crown (12p) and the opportunity to sacrifice one's weekly night off in order to join him on his round of calls at police and fire stations and hospitals.

The Scottish edition had inherited a circulation of 86,000 copies, previously printed in Manchester, with which to sound the trumpet around the walls of Jericho; but at first the walls showed little disposition to fall. It was natural that the established press in Scotland would resent the intruder. But no one had foreseen the extent of hostility from the general public. It seemed that if Lord Beaverbrook had 'a word for Scotland', few wanted to hear it. In the first two months, only 2,000 more copies were sold, and soon afterwards 1,000 of these were lost. Sales staff were told depressingly often, 'But you're just another English paper'. One salesman who called on a newsagent in Dumfries responded to this remark by throwing his visiting card on the counter: 'Call ME a Sassenach?' he said. The name on the card was MacEwan; but MacEwan forbore to tell the newsagent that he had been born and reared in Wigan.

After the initial setback, for a brief and tantalising period sales soared to 160,000. In a rush of blood to the head a challenge was issued to the *Daily Record* to publish its sales figure, which had been estimated at 183,000. To everyone's chagrin, the Record triumphantly claimed sales of 215,000.

MacEwan and his colleagues had more to worry about before the year was out. Lord Beaverbrook called his editors and managers together and told them he planned to launch his Empire Free Trade crusade. The response was unenthusiastic. A daring few told him that the people in the towns would never countenance a 'stomach tax', since his plan for free trade within the Empire entailed duties on foreign foodstuffs. Nearly all the salesmen predicted a slump in sales in urban areas.

There was little enough in the way of important or exciting news with which to enhance the circulation, except for the union in October, 1929, of the Church of Scotland and the United Free Church, or Jenny Lee winning North Lanark for Labour to become Britain's youngest MP, or Ramsay MacDonald telling the Commons that he would consider giving Scotland the right of self government.

But for Gilbert Cole the year was marked, and forever remembered, by a photograph.

(Hugh) Gilbert Cole was a 22-year-old reporter who had come from the *South Wales Echo* and was surprised and delighted to be paid seven guineas a week. He was on duty on New Year's Eve, 1929, when a telephone call brought him what he later called 'the most heart-rending day of my life'. The call was to tell him of a fire at a children's matinee show in a cinema in Paisley. He arrived in the town to find that even the tramcars had been commandeered to ferry injured children to hospital, and to witness a pathetic procession of mothers at a hastily improvised mortuary.

The fire itself had been only a minor outbreak. A film had caught fire in the projection room of the Glen Cinema; the flames had been quickly doused and the burning reel had been hurled out of the building – but not before someone had shouted 'Fire!', and thrown 500 children into panic. When the firemen arrived they found a stairway – just ten steps from the outside door – piled high with dead and dying boys and girls. On top of the heaped bodies was an 18-month-old child. Other children were found beneath seats, huddled in one another's arms. Some in panic had even tried to climb the screen to look for a way of escape.

The headline on Gilbert Cole's story next day said '69 Child Victims of Appalling Cinema Panic'. The toll became 70 on the next day, because another child in hospital did not survive.

The picture taken by Bill Sykes, who accompanied him, was printed on the front page alongside the story. It was a simple enough composition – just the wall of a cloakroom, a window high above and a chair below; but the floor was piled with the coats and scarves of children who had tried in vain to reach up to the window and to safety outside.

CHAPTER 2

Keep your nose out of it

NOTHING IN THE CONTENT of the newspaper of 1930 seems more remote
from today than the 'Around The Courts' feature – a ragbag of pathos
and humour recorded as minor miscreants passed through the courts. It
occupied more than half a page, at some remove from other pages
wherein were to be found, from time to time, reports of the trials of
more newsworthy sinners in the higher courts. Even the local district
police courts did not escape attention.

Bill Nicholson's half-crown essay prizes helped to cover the fee for a
morning business-school class in which the embarrassment of being the
only male pupil was compensated by the acquisition of shorthand. The
speed of the shorthand was derisory, but it provided sufficient confidence
to present myself at the Glasgow Marine divisional court and claim a seat
on its non-existent press bench. Superintendent McLaren, the officer in
charge of the division, although surprised, was tolerant and helpful; he not
only arranged a place for me on one of the side benches, and ensured the
accuracy of my reports, but often shared his morning tea with me.

One day he confided that he was particularly worried about a young
girl from Lanarkshire who had run away from home. He knew that she was
living with some Lascar seamen in Glasgow docks, but he had no authority
to restore her to her family against her will. Without telling Superintendent
McLaren I went to the address in dockland, pretending to be her brother. I
did not find the girl – I doubt if I would have known what to do if I had –
but I met her 'protectors', and I also encountered another girl who was
cooking and cleaning for 26 pedlars in a neighbouring hovel.

The story I wrote owed much to youthful fantasies about 'white slave
traffic', but the News Editor, John Kennedy, seconded me to Gilbert Cole
to ensure a more measured report. No matter the restraint in the
subsequent account of what could happen to girls who drifted into
dockland, enough of the original overtones remained to cause an
enthusiastic sub-editor to give the report ('By Our Special Representative')
the lurid headline treatment:

Terrorised Girl Slaves of Glasgow's Dockland.

Mystical Powers of Black Seamen.

Police Powerless to Interfere.

Superintendent McLaren, tolerant as ever, forgave me, but he made
it clear that it was good manners to wait to be asked; his actual words

were that if I stuck my nose in like that again he would kick my little backside all the way from the police station down to the Broomielaw. So much for investigative journalism! Years later the late Lord Clyde, Lord President of the Council, was to say something of the same sort – but he went much further, threatening editors with jail for contempt if their reporters got in the way of police enquiries.

It would be pleasant to think that this misguided initiative prompted John Kennedy to appoint me as his first cub reporter, but it is more likely that he needed additions to his staff and could not afford the full penny. Anyway, in February 1930 I exchanged 10s 6d (52p) a week as an office boy for two guineas (£2.10) a week to become the junior colleague of Gilbert Cole, Bill Nicholson, Dave Smith, Pat Grimley, Joe Hogan and Betty Watt.

Mother need not have worried about my going to sea: I had forgotten all about that early ambition. On the other hand she might not have approved of some of the things I was doing now, or was pressed into doing by my superiors, such as begging in the street – a stunt intended to disprove a charge someone had made that the proverbial generosity of Glasgow people was a myth.

Douglas Hewat, the Pictures Editor, whom I remember as a man of Falstaffian proportion capable of consuming three suppers at a time each night, provided two of his own paintings as props. I sat on a pavement in Exchange Square with the paintings and a cap at my feet. The money in the cap, destined for charity, was enough to vindicate Glasgow's reputation for generosity, but it was rather less than Douglas Hewat felt that his paintings merited.

At this time our first editor, Bert Gabb, returned to Manchester. His successor was with us too fleetingly to make much mark on the scene. I knew only that he was a Scot (not surprisingly, with a name like MacDougall), and I also knew that he was an ex-soldier because I recognised the regimental tie of the London Scottish which my Uncle Jack always wore.

Mr MacDougall was followed by Tom Innes. He not only filled the editorial chair, he overflowed it, so rotund was he. He was reputed to have been involved in films as well as in newspapers, and he certainly could have played the part of a newspaper editor in a Hollywood movie if he had been asked. He shouted a great deal, although I never heard him actually cry 'Hold the front page!'. His face was permanently adorned with a huge cigar, and topped by a green eyeshade, and every sentence was uttered in staccato.

He was also a martinet. When Dave Smith and I were on night duty and missed a small fire at Carntyne greyhound stadium, he suspended us without pay for two weeks and would listen to no explanations.

No one, least of all I, was sorry when during an editorial outing he stumbled into a burn and had to have his trousers changed at the Bailie Nicol Jarvie Hotel in Aberfoyle. Douglas Machray and I were entrusted with the task of drying his trousers in the hotel boiler room, and we scorched them so badly that he was never able to wear them again.

Office football team 1929/30... first in back row, the team's centre half, Chief Sub Editor John McAdam, (later sports columnist in London); first in front row, 16 year old inside right Jack Campbell

Those early 1930s were unkind years – except for a 16-year-old too absorbed in his own exciting future to give thought to the fortunes, good or ill, of his employer, much less those of the nation.

The decade started with a glimmer of hope amid the economic gloom: in May the Cunard company awarded to John Brown's shipyard at Clydebank an order for a liner which was to be the largest in the world, larger even than one on their stocks which was waiting to be launched (the Prince of Wales arrived next month, setting maidenly hearts a-flutter as he named the ship the *Empress of Britain*). But the glimmer amid the gloom was to prove illusory. The giant new Cunarder was given the number '534'; but in 1932, lack of finance forced work on her to be abandoned, and '534' was to haunt the Clyde as a national symbol of the slump for two despairing years.

By the autumn of 1930 the only happy news to report was the impending arrival of the first royal baby in Scotland for centuries. John Kennedy sent me to join a posse of reporters and photographers gathered outside Glamis Castle, in Angus, the family home of the Earl of Strathmore, whose daughter the Duchess of York was awaiting her second baby. I might as well have stayed at home. The assignment called for little more than standing watch outside the castle in order to alert the news desk to the approaching moment.

Protocol demands the presence of the Home Secretary immediately after a royal birth in order to testify that the infant who might be an heir to the throne is no changeling. The Home Secretary at the time was Joseph Clynes. He had been staying for two weeks at nearby Cortachy Castle, the home of Lord and Lady Airlie, awaiting a telephone summons to perform his ancient ceremonial duty.

Eventually we saw him speed into Glamis Castle at 9 pm on the evening of 21 August with, as it proved, just 25 minutes to spare. But we knew that neither he nor anyone else would reappear to let any one of us be the first to impart the joyful news in our public prints. That was circulated by the Press Association, as expected, in a bulletin issued by an unnamed official at Buckingham Palace, announcing that 'Her Royal Highness the Duchess of York has given birth to a daughter'. The Home Secretary was quoted later as saying that he had been conducted into the room where the child was, and saw 'a fine chubby little girl'. Even that quote came from the Press Association, courtesy of the Palace.

The chubby little girl was to be christened Margaret Rose. The enterprising John Gordon commissioned an astrologer, R.H. Naylor, to cast her horoscope; he then projected this into a regular feature called 'What The Stars Foretell' – the first of its kind to be published in the British press. And what did the stars foretell for Princess Margaret Rose?

Princess Margaret's horoscope

'[Her] basic characteristics are loyalty, pride, an intensely affectionate nature, in turn depending on affection, but with a strong will. There is a love of the beautiful, great frankness – a scorn of restraint. From Venus... will come a vivid emotional nature, which insists on following the dictates of the heart rather than those of the head, but this royal child, when she reaches maturity, will be essentially a woman of the New Age.'

The stars may have been a bit blurred, but the horoscope which John Gordon published was remarkably prescient.

What the astrologer failed to foresee, however, was that both he and John Gordon would be charged with being rogues and vagabonds and telling fortunes; they were acquitted only because it was held that the statements made were so vague that they did not come within the terms of the Vagrancy Act.

If we had expected our Hollywood-style editor to transform our fortunes dramatically, something must have gone wrong with the script, for we were prospering no better than before. The unfortunate sales staff in Scotland found little in the content of the paper to help them repudiate the charge of London orientation. True, the 'London Diary' became 'The Diary of a London Scot' (unidentified), and from time to time there were 'Highland Notes' and 'In and Around Edinburgh' and 'Along the Borders'; but these were no more than token oases.

Christmas boxes given away to the needy who could not afford to buy the paper, and festivals of song organised for those who could afford it but had to be persuaded, helped to generate a little goodwill in those hard times. But the thaw in our public reception was slow. Nor was honest bribery getting us very far. A promise to take the paper for six weeks could secure a dictionary, a set of china perhaps and, after thirteen weeks, flannels and a sports jacket, a gramophone, or a nest of tables, or a dinner service. The return was often nullified because other newspapers did the same, and the recipient could, and often did, sign up to take the offer of a rival paper as soon as the contractual weeks had elapsed. The wits maintained that if you took every national paper for long enough you could furnish a house and clothe yourself from head to foot.

The free gifts did not last long enough for that, but the circulation 'war' which had been started by Joseph Elias, Lord Southwood, the owner of the *Daily Herald*, was to last for a few more years before he and his rival owners decided there was no profit in throwing their money away.

There were free insurance policies, too, which became invalidated only by the outbreak of the War. The last claim I can recall was a payment of £5,000 to the victim of a rail crash near Paisley.

Perhaps we had no right to expect editorial miracles from Tom Innes. It was a time only for crying. The islanders who had been scraping a life on the bare rock of St Kilda (which we inevitably called 'The Edge of the World' – what else?) were evacuated to share the amenities of the mainland, and the two and a half million unemployed on the mainland reckoned they would have been better off staying where they were.

At No. 195 there was despondency. Even the copy boys knew that the situation was precarious. When Lord Beaverbrook sent Sidney Long and Brigadier 'Mike' Wardell up to Glasgow we all thought the writing was on the wall. The brigadier, whose eye-patch gave him a piratical appearance, was grim and morose, and I reflected that my career as a reporter was going to be a brief and inglorious one.

One of the good things about newspapers is that when battles are being lost it is often the generals who are shot first. Whether or not Tom Innes, as editor, was a candidate for the bullet (and it was rumoured that he was), in a theatrical gesture which could have been a pre-emptive strike he telephoned Lord Beaverbrook one evening and said, 'I hear I've been sacked'.

'Who told you that?' Lord Beaverbrook asked.

'The night porter at the Central Hotel,' he replied.

Although Tom Innes kept his post he was not to know that he had been given a mere stay of execution. The emissaries from London did not carry a big axe after all; but they did have a surgical knife, and it was said they wanted ten per cent of our flesh. The knife hurt, most of all in the mechanical departments, and one Friday night there were many sorrows to drown in Tom's.

Small fry that I was, I escaped. One casualty in the editorial, however, was reporter Joe Hogan, who was on his honeymoon in Ireland when he learned he had no job to come back to.

While the patient survived (if only just), the wounds inflicted on production caused havoc in the circulation department. Three quarters of Scotland's population lived within a fifteen-mile radius of Albion Street. But Glasgow and Lanarkshire were the strongholds of the tabloid *Daily Record*, which spoke to its predominantly working-class readers in their own idiom. The *Scottish Daily Express* had accordingly made a concentrated effort to woo the parts of Scotland less susceptible to our rival's influence, such as the north of Scotland.

The key to the north was the 10 pm train from Glasgow's Buchanan Street Station. It was the last train which could deliver supplies in time to provide papers on breakfast tables beyond Perth. But thanks to the stringent economy cuts, production often stuttered and the vital train was missed. It was still possible to catch it at Perth, because it stopped there for an hour to load more freight; but (again because of the cuts) there were not enough vans to take advantage of this, and reporters with cars of their own which were mechanically sound were pressed into service to rush supplies of papers to Perth. Sidney Long's son Jasper, driving his second-hand Bentley, held the record for the race to Perth. Eventually John Norman, the circulation manager, persuaded the management to subsidise a special train to Perth, and a locomotive and guard's van left Buchanan Street station nightly at 11 to catch up with the regular service train at Perth.

In 1931 an economic blizzard blew away Ramsay MacDonald's Labour administration and a National Government was formed, led by

MacDonald and Stanley Baldwin, 'to save the country from bankruptcy'. The first thing the new government did to save us from bankruptcy was to abandon the gold standard – an action welcomed by the *Express*, alone among the nation's newspapers, as 'Good News... Nothing more heartening has happened for years'.

It did nothing to mollify the angry unemployed, however. Dole money was cut, as was the pay of all State employees, 'to stop us living beyond our means'. Strikes and riots erupted in every city. In two fraught nights in Glasgow there were 49 arrests.

The trouble even spilled over into the Royal Navy. Some ratings had been left with as little as 25 shillings (£1.25) a week, but when the Fleet set sail they were unaware of that as yet: news of the cuts was withheld until the ships were at sea. Thus it fell to one of our occasional and little-known local correspondents to report, on 15 September 1931, what was afterwards described officially as a mutiny in the Fleet at Invergordon on the Cromarty Firth.

While the term was officially correct, it must have been the most low-key in all the annals of naval mutinies. The sailors prevented their ships from sailing for two days while they held meetings on a recreation ground and in a canteen which they occupied. They broke a few windows, and one of them threw a beer glass at an officer, before they ended their protest by marching in order back to their ships singing 'The More We Are Together The Merrier We'll Be'.

In such a climate Lord Beaverbrook chose to bring his Empire Free Trade crusade to Glasgow. The doubters among his sales staff had found little reason for conversion. For nine months he had stomped the length and breadth of England preaching his gospel, and everywhere he went his newspapers had faithfully recorded his progress. Since the formation of his United Empire Party in February 1930 we had recorded the progress of that, too, while privately questioning whether promoting the paper in Scotland was helped by printing his speeches at length, or by printing long lists of subscribers to his party, often devoting a whole page (at the expense of news coverage) and even recording offerings of the merest coppers.

His political opponents prepared a rowdy reception for him at Glasgow's City Hall. His sales staff, loyalists all whatever their reservations, prepared a heartening welcome, with a mammoth display of posters and contents bills all the way up the A74 road from the Border. Unfortunately, he chose to arrive by the east coast route, crossing the Border at Carter Bar.

On his arrival at Albion Street he complained he had never seen so many pots of tea, and so many little offices within a building, and he ordered all partitions to be removed. (A year later, in conversation with the manager who possessed the only curtained recess, he was to ask, 'Isn't there ANYWHERE we can talk privately?)

He was pleased, nonetheless with his visit, taking comfort that he had won a battle with Communist hecklers at his meeting. One riposte was to be famously repeated: 'Yes, my friend, it is true there are no unemployed in Russia. There are none in Barlinnie prison, either.'

He could not have been so pleased with the progress of his Scottish paper. Morale was as low as it was among the unhappy shipyard workers at John Brown's, who were told that Ship Number 534 had been halted by Cunard because of lack of money. There were rumours of our own impending closure, and no lack of Jeremiahs to give currency of them.

The riots went on with monotonous regularity throughout those years of the early 1930s; and all the while (despite incessant pleas to the Prime Minister, privately and in the House of Commons, by David Kirkwood, Clydebank's fiery Labour MP) the skeleton of '534' lay by the bank of the river, a silent symbol of despair.

Our reporters' assignment book all too often carried a note for the night-shift reporters: 'Watch for trouble, rally at Glasgow Green'.

Glasgow had acquired a military-type new Chief Constable named Captain Percy Sillitoe. The fact that he had once been a big game hunter was as manna to the demonstrators. When they marched to a rally, flanked by a posse of police, they sang:

A hunting we will go,
A hunting we will go
A hunting baby elephants
With Captain Silli... toe.

The marchers always seemed to us to be as orderly and as good-natured as were the police. Trouble usually only flared at the centre of the rally itself, when the police had to struggle with some elements inflamed by the speeches. It is fair to say that the confrontations on so-called Red Clydeside did not compare with the mayhem in London. The only serious clash occurred on Glasgow Green in late 1932 involving injuries to 15 people and indignity for one officer who was thrown into the Clyde (and promptly pulled out).

The 1930s

The moment of football tragedy, 5 September 1931

Hundreds of anxious people telephoned Glasgow Victoria Infirmary during the night of 5 September 1931 to ask about John Thomson, Celtic's young international goalkeeper.

Five minutes into the second half of an 'Old Firm' derby game at Ibrox Park, 80,000 spectators had seen Sam English, the Rangers centre forward, chase a ball through the Celtic defence. The goal was at his mercy. John Thomson came out and, as Sam English shot, the keeper bravely threw himself at the Rangers player's feet.

The shot went wide. Sam English rose, limping. But John Thomson lay ominously still. His head had crashed into his opponent's knee and his skull had been fractured.

Thomson's parents rushed to Glasgow from their home in Cardenden in Fife, and arrived at the hospital just minutes before he died.

On the day of the funeral, three special trains left the city packed with both Celtic and Rangers fans. On the previous evening, those who could not afford the train or bus fare had started walking the long road from Glasgow to Bowhill in Fife. The pits in and around his home town of Cardenden stopped work, and all the shops closed as 30,000 people gathered to pay tribute to the young man who had been hailed as Scotland's prince among goalkeepers.

CHAPTER 3

Go in on tiptoe

IN NEWSPAPERS, ONE SOON becomes well acquainted with tragedy, for so much news is of that commodity; but I had never seen a dead body before I stumbled on the story of Mr Giuseppe Pasquali.

Mr Pasquali, who used the English equivalent 'Joseph' as his forename, was an Italian immigrant who, while rummaging among bric-a-brac in Glasgow's 'Barrows' market, came upon a scrap of copperplate which he thought might be of value, because when he scraped its blackened surface he glimpsed colour. With the help of a chemist friend he cleaned it all to reveal what seemed to be a representation of Christ in his tomb. He wrote to art experts in London asking them to inspect it; in the meantime his chemist friend exhibited the find in the window of his shop, and it was there that I saw it.

The chemist provided the address of Mr Pasquali – two stairs up in a tenement in Park Road, Kelvinbridge. I assumed that the woman who came to the door was his wife. I told her I would like to see Mr Pasquali, whereupon she ushered me into the room which people in tenements usually called 'the parlour' and closed the door. I found myself alone with a coffin, looking down at a face which was as ancient and cracked as an old parchment or painting.

It was perhaps just as well that Mr Pasquali never discovered the worth of his find: they say you can't take it with you, but no matter – the 'treasure' he found at the Barrows would have added very few pennies in Heaven.

At least Mrs Pasquali had INVITED me into her home. All too often the newspaper reporter is required to call uninvited. It is not a welcome requirement, and the appalling death toll in the pits at that time made the requirement all too frequent. He goes in as a stranger, conscious that the moment he steps over the threshold of a house of sorrow he may be accused of taking a step too far.

There are too many instances of excessive zeal in newspapers these days, whether or not they are merely symptomatic of the declining standards of society. But where there is sorrow there is a lot less intrusion than some would have us believe. More often than not, the bereaved are grateful to be able to talk about their loved one, and often to provide a picture from the family album to appear with what they want to say in print.

Bill Young, now retired as a pictures editor, knows that. He once went to the home of the victim of an explosion. The widow spoke lovingly of her husband, and then said, 'But I'm grateful that at this time I am not alone'. Bill thought she meant that she was glad of his company, and was only brought to comprehension when she added, 'Will you join me in a wee prayer for His mercies?' And this cynical, hard-bitten journalist (oh, you know we are all meant to be so) sank to his knees and joined her not only in prayer but in tears.

When I hear people equate the excesses of a section of our tabloids with the profession as a whole, I remember Dave Smith and Gilbert Cole, both of whom had no need of codes of ethic from any Press Council but wore their honour like a suit which never suffered stains and never became threadbare.

Although Gilbert Cole was my first mentor, it was Dave who became my closest friend and confidant and counsellor. David Given Smith was our first crime reporter. It seemed a strange role for such a sensitive and gentle man. He could hardly have been 40 years old then, but he had read widely and travelled far and knew the world and its ways, and he imparted to me much more than the principles of our craft. I remember when I first confided to Dave my concerns about entering the homes of the dead, he said, 'Go in on tiptoe, feel for them, and you will leave as a friend'.

For those of my generation Dave Smith epitomised 'The Old Soldier'. Doubtless this was because as a legacy of the First World War he had an artificial arm. It served to cradle a telephone while he wrote with the other hand, and it served once, as I also saw, to incapacitate a thug who accosted us, by the simple expedient of tapping him with it on the chin.

He had left the lower part of his arm at Chemin des Dames in 1918. He was stumbling away from a field which had been set alight by liquid flame throwers, and he was wondering how lily of the valley could stink so vilely, when a shell burst. He might never have survived to tell me the tale, because the French medical orderly passing along the rows of victims with a lamp attached to his waist paused only to feel each pulse and to pronounce 'Mort'. But as the light of the lamp flickered over his face, Dave touched the hem of the orderly's coat, and when he woke later it was in a room awash with what he thought was a slush of water but was really blood.

He survived to take the stump with which he was left all around the world, finding temporary relief from gnawing pain only from a black medicine doctor in Papua, before returning to his native Fife, there to report for the *Dundee Courier*.

Our friendship – one might almost say our father-son relationship – endured for more than forty years. I saw him for the last time in August

1972 in a ward of Dundee Royal Infirmary just before he faded away, as old soldiers are supposed to do. By his bedside was Bert, his old wartime comrade who had come up from Devon and spent every day with him for a week in silent vigil.

There being no other cub reporter to indulge, I was spoiled not only by Dave and Gilbert but by others, too, like P.A. (Patrick Aloysius) Grimley, who had abandoned a career as a schoolmaster in Lanarkshire, and who would occasionally ask the News Editor, before setting out on an assignment, 'If the boy isn't doing anything in particular, can I take him along?'.

Pat Grimley's habit was to introduce me as 'My young assistant'; steeped as I was in the exploits of the fictional detective Dixon Hawke, who used that very phrase to refer to his aide, Tommy, I accepted the description with pride.

In March 1932 the baby son of the aviator Charles Lindbergh was kidnapped. The drama was 2,000 miles away, but it was heightened for us because the baby's nursemaid was a Scots girl called Betty Gow. It was she who found the cot in the nursery empty, and a ransom note on the window sill.

Pat and I were the first to call at her family's home in a tenement in Pollokshaws Road, Glasgow. Pat was a huge, charming lump of a fellow with a persuasive tongue, and we left Pollokshaws Road with snapshots of Betty Gow wheeling the baby in his pram, and another of her with the family pet dog, and with an assurance of a welcome if we wanted to call again.

Colonel Lindbergh flew all over the country lured by false underworld 'leaks' about his baby's whereabouts, while Betty Gow, despite her protestations of innocence and despite the family's declared faith in her, was subjected to merciless questioning by the police as a suspected accomplice. After eighteen weeks, when a dead baby was found in woods near the family grounds, it was Betty who was called on to identify her charge. She collapsed in shock.

The kidnapper was a German illegal immigrant named Bruno Hauptmann. He was tracked down in September of the following year and sentenced to death.

Throughout Betty Gow's long ordeal her mother admitted no reporter into the family home other than Pat Grimley and his 'assistant', and when Betty was finally cleared by the police the only transatlantic telephone call she would accept from a newspaper was one from 195 Albion Street.

Exciting as it was to be Pat Grimley's 'young assistant', one disadvantage of being the only cub reporter was automatic selection for any task beneath the dignity of my superiors. So, when complaints were made about the conditions at the old Barnhill poorhouse (later named Foresthall), I was dressed in old clothes, given a few coppers in my pocket, a false name and address and a hard luck story, to seek refuge for the night.

I presented myself at 3 am, huddled into my coat against a sly autumn wind, so chilled I could almost persuade myself I really was the waif I purported to be. I then spent sleepless hours in a house-full dormitory until it was time to take communal breakfast of skilly porridge (gruel) and bread and tea. I went home on foot and by tram because Douglas Hewat, who had delivered me by car, did not turn up to bring me back.

The story which appeared in the *Scottish Daily Express* was a paradigm of early 'yellow' journalism:

INSIDE STORY of a Great City Poorhouse
A NIGHT WITH THE CHILDREN OF POVERTY
The captain who could not get a job....
The men who never want to work....
The tragedy of the stricken dancer....

'The people who live there from time to time and have eaten its porridge call it Skilly House. It is not advertised, though it is no exclusive residence.....'

Miss Mackinnon would have given me a 5 and a scolding; Randolph Hearst would have given it a VG+.

The officials at the City Chambers did not rate it much, either; they threatened to prosecute both me and the paper for using their shelter under false pretences. I don't blame them but I felt at the time that they had exacted quite sufficient retribution for their bed and skilly porridge and tea – because whether it had been needed or not, I had been given a bath liberally doctored with disinfectant, and scrubbed vigorously until the flesh was raw.

At this time we acquired a new regime. Our fatherly News Editor, John Kennedy, was replaced by Hardie Stewart, a 25-year-old from Dundee, the city famed at the time as the home of jute, jam and journalists. The Editor, Tom Innes, made way for Reginald J Thompson (always known as 'R.J.T.'), one of John Gordon's deputies. Tom (later Sir Tom) Blackburn came as circulation manager, and he brought with him Lord Beaverbrook's son, Max Aitken.

Max had served an apprenticeship in the London office during vacations from Cambridge. He assumed the post of classified advertising manager in Glasgow, though that was to be only a stepping stone to a managership itself. He had evidently not come as an armchair general.

He had learned from his father: Beaverbrook had once (but only once) sold advertising space personally, to Gordon Selfridge, the stores magnate. Max now went out himself to seek advertising revenue, and he persuaded the drapery magnate, Hugh Fraser, to place the paper's first full-page advertisement. Hugh Fraser (who became Lord Fraser of Allander) displayed a framed copy of that advertisement on a wall of his office for many years.

Max and Tom Blackburn also got involved with one of the notorious Glasgow gangs – on its own patch. Glasgow gangs were essentially territorial; they warred only with one another. You could walk home through Glasgow in the dark hours and never fear molestation. The gangs did not interfere with newspapers, either, even those which not only reported their lawlessness but also condemned it.

But one of them, in Garngad, in the north of the city, did take umbrage over an *Express* report of their activities. When their complaint was summarily dismissed by Hardie Stewart, they formed a picket outside 195 Albion Street, so menacing that the News Editor was unable to leave the office for two days. Inconvenient as this was for Hardie Stewart, they also threatened to waylay and burn the supply of papers to street vendors in their patch.

Tom Blackburn was quite prepared to regard news editors as dispensable, but sales were sacrosanct. He and Max Aitken followed the supply van into Garngad and when it was duly ambushed, they parleyed with the gang leaders and made peace.

The bargain cost the paper a full kit of football gear, but they could have spared themselves the expense of that if they had left the matter to Eddie McKenna.

Edward (Eddie) McKenna was a Glaswegian of Irish descent and rock-solid build. His physical attributes were equalled only by his (admittedly streetwise) business acumen. Eddie would drive anywhere for us, at any time, even for a derisory fee. His attachment to us began when he offered to drive a supply van overnight on Sundays to Oban and back for a fee of £1. He once drove all the way back again to Oban when it was discovered that five contents bills had misspelled a name. Perhaps the fact that the name was that of our owner added urgency to the journey.

The reward for his enthusiasm was the street-vending contract and the bill-posting contract, for the fulfilment of which he acquired a second-hand motorcycle and a sidecar in which he carried his pot of paste and a brush.

Eddie was most likeable, but not if you did not like him; when some of his street rivals objected to the presence of his men on pitches in the city they found he could take good care of his own interests.

CHAPTER 4

The Graduate Gang

THE NEW EDITOR, 'RJT' THOMPSON, was given no pot of gold to let him add to his slender staff resources. He introduced a number of graduates from Glasgow University without straining his budget, and three young reporters from weekly newspapers, whose wages did not break his bank: Bill Grant, Bill Johnston and Ben Allison. Ill-assorted as they might seem, Bill Johnston and Ben Allison became inseparable comrades.

Ben Allison was an eccentric who revelled in his eccentricities. Many legends were to attach themselves to him; it was always suspected that if he did not generate them himself he did everything he could to foster them – such as the story that he had woken up one night in his lodgings with a cry of 'Fire!' ringing in his ears, and only just time to light a cigarette from the burning sofa on which he had fallen asleep before helping to carry it outside.

He then inserted an advertisement in the window of a West End newsagent's shop on behalf of himself and two colleagues: 'Three Christian gentlemen seek quiet congenial lodgings', and was soon ensconced in the home of two unsuspecting maiden ladies. What is undoubtedly true is that he behaved towards them with such gallant old-world courtesy that they thought the world of him.

He could have gone on stage in the role of a playwright or poet, affecting as he did a long black coat and a black slouch hat. He said he had been taught by the Jesuits, and at the drop of the said slouch hat he would indulge in debate on any topic, so free-ranging was his mind. Unfortunately, the range was such that he would flit like a butterfly, until in a mist of metaphysics both he and his protagonist would forget what the matter of debate had been.

It was Bill, rather than Ben, who was the poet. If he ever wrote a sonnet it could only have been in mockery, but with or without excuse he could always conjure up an impish rhyme. He had a most fertile mind. Once, when he was re-writing a correspondent's report to fit into a general weather story, he invented a railway to Tomintoul which, situated at 1160 feet (353 m) above sea level, is the highest village in Scotland. The correspondent had reported that after the village had been isolated for days by blizzard, a rail-plough had managed to reach it, so Bill added a cheering crowd at the railway station to lend colour to the drama.

'Well, it WAS a rail-plough,' he said. 'How was I to know it had been mounted on a lorry?'

The station was tactfully removed from the following day's reports, and it is only right to say that this was an exceptional lapse in Bill Johnston's reputation for accuracy. But that was to be proved later.

They were an exuberant gang, that class of graduates of '33 and '34. A fortunate few were assigned as paid trainees to the sub-editing table; the others joined the newsroom desks as freelances, paid according to the number of lines of print which appeared by merit or by chance in the paper.

The mob included Hector McNeil (later MP for Greenock and Secretary of State for Scotland), Archie Lee (later a BBC producer in Glasgow), Bert Williamson, and two others to whom I became particularly attached – Andy Ewart and Malcolm Livingstone. We three took over, for a pittance, a squalid little room off the waterfront in Anderston to write short stories in the manner of Damon Runyon and William Saroyan, until we were forced to give up because we couldn't pay the rent.

One other among the graduates was a girl with an enchanting smile and a warm natural charm. There were few women in journalism in those days, and such as there were belonged to the gentle tribe who wrote of gentle things. In male conceit, hard news reporting was a game too rough and raw for girls to play; Hilde Marchant had still to make her name as a war correspondent and Kate Adie had not yet been born.

But Isabel Sinclair was thrust among the other freelances to scratch a living and claw out a career, and it was not surprising that on one of her first assignments her report contained a passage which betrayed a certain innocence. In the middle of a story about the annual Clydesdale Horse Show, she wrote, 'So I said to my escort, 'What exactly is an entire horse?' ' She was saved the embarrassment of its appearance in print by a more worldly-minded sub-editor who tactfully deleted that particular paragraph. Nowadays such a sentence might not raise an eyebrow in a nunnery.

In a little more than a year our lovely ingénue could (and did) undertake any news assignment, and began to edit a so-called Women's Section to boot. She could have become as noted as anyone in the profession; but during the latter years of the Second World War, when newspapers were reduced to four pages which gave no scope for writing talent, she began to study law, and she went on to become, in 1964, Scotland's second woman QC (the first was Margaret Kidd).

There were other imports for the newsroom. Jimmy Gray was a ship's draughtsman, a victim of the recession, who started to report cases at Glasgow Sheriff Court. He claimed to have trained for the priesthood in the Church of England for a time, and he frequently coloured the somewhat salty language of the newsroom with ecclesiastical invective from the Bible. His own bible was *Jane's Fighting Ships*, for ships were in his blood. He was an urbane, gentle person, with only one boast - that he lived opposite the only tree in Argyle Street (it still stands there opposite what used to be Jimmy's flat). It is having known the likes of Jimmy Gray that makes me glad that ours was such an open profession in those days.

Peter Saunders came too, to write theatre gossip, in the hope of making his way to a larger theatrical stage in London.

Finally there arrived Ian McColl, who was later to take the editor's chair not only in Glasgow but also in London. As an 18-year-old boy wonder with the Young Liberals, he had delivered a conference speech which won a standing ovation and the attention of the media, prompting 'RJT' to send for him 'because I wanted to see what you are like'. He liked the young man well enough to offer him a place among the freelances at the reporters' table.

His earnings were not likely to be advanced by the mischievous advice of a fellow freelance who told him that it was the practice in newspapers to take one's reports directly to the Chief Sub-editor, placing the offering carefully on a spike which stood on his desk. The Chief Sub-Editor of the time, Charlie MacNicol, was a formidable character who ate cub reporters for supper, and since the spike was in fact his repository for rejected 'copy' he watched bemused as young Ian carefully impaled his latest offering on it.

'Excuse me,' he said, 'but what do you think you are doing?'

'I'm spiking my story, Sir,' said our editor-to-be politely.

'Well,' he was told, 'you may have guessed its destination correctly but you really must permit me that privilege.' Mr MacNicol carefully removed the story, glanced through it, and put it back on the spike.

It is nice to think that after the War, when Charlie MacNicol exchanged the stressful Chief Sub-editor's chair for that of the Assistant Editor, and had lost the need to roar, he and Ian McColl would sit side by side on the 'back bench' (the top tier of editorial executives), and when they were not discussing the contents of that night's paper they would argue on theological matters from the standpoint of their respective faiths (Ian McColl was a staunch Presbyterian, while Charlie was a Roman Catholic) and politely agree to disagree.

Ian McColl, my dear friend of so many years, is one of the most painfully honest people I know. This became evident early on. One Sunday afternoon 'RJT' called him to his desk and told him he wanted him to interview Sir James Lithgow, the Clyde shipbuilder. He then gave Ian a slip of paper on which he had written three queries to put to Sir James.

Our 18-year-old telephoned Sir James at his home and said that he had three questions he would like to ask him. Sir James said he had not the slightest intention of answering. Ian, who was more in awe of his editor than of any industrial magnate, was taken aback. 'You mean you refuse to answer?' he said. 'I shall have to report back to my editor. He will be most displeased.'

'Tell me,' said Sir James. 'How old are you, boy, and for how long have you been a reporter?'

'I am 18 years old, Sir,' said Ian, 'and I have been a reporter for three months.'

'Tell me your questions and call me back in fifteen minutes,' said Sir James. The interview made the front page and RJT ordered a payment for Ian of seven guineas. When Ian received the cheque he took it back to the editor and told him he was returning it because his father had said it was too much and that there must have been a mistake.

'Tell your father that his son earned every penny of it,' said RJT.

Not that Ian earned too much after that, any more than the other freelances did. Peter Saunders, for instance, was so badly off that he could not afford to eat in the office canteen; he subsisted on marmalade sandwiches provided by his landlady, and he ate them out of sight in the office lavatory.

Dave Smith gave him a pair of new shoes and he never forgot the kindness. Years later, when he was a London impresario, known as 'The Mousetrap Man' because he produced Agatha Christie's plays and she had given him the rights to her most famous stage work, Peter acknowledged the debt in his autobiography. He also ensured that Dave had a free seat at the theatre whenever he visited London, although Dave himself always regarded the gift of the shoes as a simple act of friendship.

CHAPTER 5

All at sea and upside down

PERHAPS BECAUSE OF HIS TRAINING at D C Thomson's in Dundee, where juniors often started their careers in comics and boys' and girls' papers, Hardie Stewart, the News Editor, had strange notions from time to time – such as sending me to a Highland Games wearing a straw boater to record people's reactions. He then wanted to send me to Glencoe, openly declaring my identity as a Campbell, and whereas I am sure I would have been accorded the obligatory Highland courtesy whatever my origin, I am glad that wiser counsels prevailed on him to abandon the project.

That clan memories die hard, however, was clear when I was given a list of people injured in an explosion on the Lochaber power scheme. The list included one with my surname. I telephoned the police station in the village of his stated domicile to be told, 'Ach no, man, there must be some mistake. There is no one here of that name'. When I repeated that the name and address had been supplied by the power company, the police sergeant was equally insistent: 'No, no, man, I am telling you. There are no Campbells here. Once we had Campbells, but we did not encourage the buggers.'

Happily Hardie Stewart found other things for me to do. He sent me to Dundee to work for several months with the very good-natured Arthur Menzies in his office in Seagate, so that I might appreciate that there were other cradles of civilisation in Scotland besides Glasgow.

He also sent me to Scapa Flow, where the German High Seas Fleet of the First World War had lain sunk and rusting for 25 years until the arrival of a scrap merchant who was too stubborn to accept the received wisdom that they lay too deep to be raised from their grave.

Ernest Cox had no text book. He also had no prior knowledge of salvage. Nor had any of the motley crew of crofters and country blacksmiths and Clydeside shipyard workers whom he assembled at Lyness Bay. All he had was a theory: that if he could pump enough compressed air into their steel skins they would become like submerged balloons and rise to the surface. Over eight years they managed to raise thirty of the ships which the German sailors had scuttled rather than hand over to their victors.

I watched the cruiser *Prinz Luitpoldt* rise, upside down, the compressed air chambers stuck to her hull like monstrous barnacles, and 'the Guvnor', as his men called him, allowed me to go down into her

The German battle cruiser Von der Tann passing under the Forth Bridge
on her way to the scrapyard. On her upturned hull, the hut in which I lived with 13 others

innards and walk – and crawl – along decks which were really ceilings. I then joined the team of 13 men on board the salvaged 2,000-ton battle cruiser Von der Tann as she was towed, upside down, for 230 miles to the breakers' yard at Inverkeithing on the Firth of Forth.

We travelled in a large hut perched on the upturned hull. Fortunately the treacherous Pentland Firth behaved itself, and the North Sea was comparatively kind, too. It was an eerie voyage for all that. Beyond Duncansby Head all we could see by day were the three powerful tugs ahead of us, and the salvage tug Ferrodanks shadowing us astern (she was there to save us if we had to abandon ship), and by night the lights of our escorts.

In the ponderous monster below us were a million and a quarter cubic feet of compressed air keeping us afloat, some of it spilling with every wallow on her creaking and clanging way, so that the engineers manning the pumping power house had to be constantly vigilant. Luckily we did not need to call for help from our rescue ship; the only cause for alarm was on one occasion when the dynamo took a fit of the sulks.

'RJT' made much of the story, and gave me my first by-line. He gave me another one over an article on the leader page; but I fear he must have acquired an exaggerated notion of my talents. He conceived the idea of celebrating the centenary of the death of Sir Walter Scott by publishing several of the famous novels as short stories, and he commissioned John Carvel (who wrote under the name of Iain C Lees) to write them – all, that is, save two: I was given *Ivanhoe* and *Castle Dangerous*. How a teenager could have had the effrontery even to attempt this task I now do not know; nor, for that matter, can I understand how RJT could have been so crazy.

In 10 May, 1933, John Lawrie, the dog-watch sub-editor, whose habit was to play the bagpipes after the paper had gone to bed, was able to play them for the first time, without protest, when Max Aitken announced a record net sale of 216,000 copies and an advertising revenue increase of fifty per cent. But if the Daily Record was down, it never heard the count, and for years afterwards it continued to claim the highest net daily newspaper sale in Scotland.

We had a Racing Section (copying the concept from Manchester where it had been initiated by Arthur Christiansen) and a children's Saturday Section, and we expanded Isabel Sinclair's Women's Section to eight pages.

You could almost feel the wind of our going places. We had not won the war, of course, but we now called ourselves the *Scottish Daily Express* and in October the Beaver pinned on his personal medal by authorising the title banner on our front page to bear the words 'Founded by Lord Beaverbrook'.

Almost anything was an excuse to take to the air. This was when noted aviators of the time were flying the Atlantic as a matter of course. Jim Mollison and Amy Johnston fell in love and, after a honeymoon at Kelburn Castle in Largs, they flew the Atlantic together and were feted in New York; and the Marquis of Douglas and Clydesdale (the son of the Duke of Hamilton) and Flight Lieutenant David McIntyre flew over Mount Everest for the first time.

In that year we flew papers on the first flight to Tiree, and it hardly mattered that it was small beer compared with the Atlantic – it was done at a hundred miles an hour, no less; and I travelled with Captain Edmund Fresson when he started a service between Inverness and the Orkneys.

More often than not the plane was a Fox Moth, in which the pilot sat in an open cockpit, with the reporter and photographer ahead in an enclosed cabin with sliding windows. Usually my companion was a huge square-sided fellow called John Millar, known affectionately as 'The Mad Millar' because of his recklessness. He had climbed with steeplejacks, he had sat atop the dome of the City Chambers in Glasgow, and he was the only cameraman who had scaled the frightening Glomach Falls which lurk unseen at the top of a precipitous ravine in Ross-shire and drop further than Niagara.

All the photographers took their pictures hanging out of the sliding windows while we reporters held their legs, but the Mad Millar would lean out so far that I could only pray that we would not both fall out. I was often ill in these planes, using my hat to protect the pilot in his open cockpit astern.

The Mad Millar and I flew to Campbeltown when there had been an explosion on board a submarine. As we arrived there was a second blast, just when it was thought that all danger was over. The Mad Millar persuaded the doctors at the cottage hospital to let us see and talk to all the less seriously injured; I doubt if we would have been allowed over the threshold today. The *Daily Record* team had arrived by car hours earlier, and had set off for Glasgow unaware of the second explosion, and there was no radio link in the cars to allow their frantic News Editor to turn them back.

The tables were turned, however, in November when we flew in search of a runaway trawler called *Lucida*. The *Lucida* had been caught fishing (allegedly illegally) in the Irish Sea off Barra. The fishery protection vessel Doon put a naval guard on board her and ordered skipper Bert Jenks to make for Stornoway, where he would face charges. But as soon as he was out of sight of the cruiser the bold skipper headed off south with his disputed catch and with the guard as well. The destroyer *Viceroy*, anchored in Campbeltown Bay, was ordered to go in pursuit of the *Lucida*. So too were navy planes. They failed to find her. The *Doon* eventually located Bert Jenks snug in his home harbour of Fleetwood, and ordered him to steam for Stornoway – under escort.

Hardie Stewart had been uncharacteristically dilatory when the story broke. The *Record* had already hired the only plane large enough to be licensed to fly over water, and we were left with only a little two-passenger Fox Moth. Since it would not be allowed to land in Stornoway, our only hope was to be able to find the *Lucida* and photograph her en route.

With the pilot's connivance we dodged back and forth from the land out to sea all the way up the west coast without catching a glimpse of her. Perhaps that was as well; I was becoming fearful that the Mad Millar would have to be dissuaded from desperate measures, for he had hinted at them before taking off. As it was, the fuel tank began to empty rapidly, and the pilot said we would have to abandon the chase. We made a forced landing in a field at Ledaig, north of Oban. Only then did I learn from the pilot how near we had been to falling out of the sky. He handed me a flask of brandy – the first hard liquor I had ever tasted. 'Here, son,' he said, 'drink some of this. You were very nearly shaking hands with your Maker.'

But Hardie Stewart and pictures editor Douglas Hewat were not going to accept defeat easily. They arranged with a local photographer in Stornoway to take pictures of *Lucida's* arrival and then give the film to another contact, who concealed the roll inside a red grouse. The contact then persuaded the *Record's* plane crew to take the bird to Glasgow, where someone would collect it and deliver it to a 'sick friend'.

Unhappily, when the parcel eventually arrived at an address in Byres Road in Glasgow, the film was blank. The suspicious *Record* photographer had opened the parcel, located the film and exposed it before putting it back. So the *Record* got the exclusive pictures and all we got was the bird.

That year of 1933 had begun with the emergence of Adolf Hitler as ruler of Germany, but it was a monster of a different kind which engaged our attention towards the end of it.

No one can discount the possibility that there are mysteries hidden in the depths of Loch Ness; amid the lights and shades over its waters many people have genuinely noted a presence. But how the Monster managed to reappear after having vanished for fourteen centuries has never been explained, and I blame it all on Arthur Boyne.

Arthur Boyne came to us in 1938 from the *Press and Journal* in Aberdeen, where he was a luminary among the local literati, with a reputation for sartorial elegance to which his bow ties and fancy weskits testified. He came of a newspaper family. As schoolboys, he and his brother Harry used to take their father his tea and sandwiches at 3 o'clock every Monday morning when the *Inverness Courier* went to press. He had earned distinction as an upholder of editorial freedom: while acting as caseroom sub-editor on the *Press and Journal* he had ordered Oswald Berry, a member of the owning family, to leave the caseroom, on the ground that he was interfering with the production of the paper; but since the point he had made to Oswald Berry had been reinforced with a well-aimed punch, his position at the *Press and Journal* was rendered untenable, so he left to become one of us. It also made him one of the few journalists ever to have been acclaimed by members of the typographical union.

The first recorded sighting of the Loch Ness Monster was in 545 AD, the correspondent being an old abbot, Adamnan, who wrote a biography of St. Columba. The chapter was headed 'How the Holy Man Drove Away the Great Water Beastie'. It was quite a lengthy report, which in modern times would have earned a great deal of lineage.

The Monster was not seen again until, as Arthur said, an *Inverness Courier* correspondent reported a new sighting, 'and I just followed it up'. It is not at all clear whether it was the *Courier* or Arthur Boyne who unearthed all the people who then remembered having seen the Monster, but it is not without significance that its re-appearance coincided with a circulation drive by the *Press and Journal* in which Arthur and a companion reporter, David Malcolm, were required to provide 'at least two good stories a day'.

Once the monster had been drawn from its lair, it rapidly shed its Greta Garbo image and showed itself to an astonishing number of people; an expedition which went fishing with legs of mutton as bait even alleged that the beast had chased them. Even the medical officer of Fort Augustus reported that the beast had shown itself to him on 26 December – and who could doubt the testimony of such an eminent man of medicine?

CHAPTER 6

To Mecca and back

ARTHUR CHRISTIANSEN THEN CAME to see us. He was already a Fleet Street legend. While still in his twenties, as deputy editor of the *Sunday Express*, he scooped all Fleet Street on the night of the R101 airship disaster. He was editor of the *Daily Express* in Manchester when he was 28, and editor of the national daily at 29. He was revolutionising newspaper presentation techniques, tossing all accepted concepts of typographical design into the dustbin, and elevating sub-editing to the level of a creative art.

When 'RJT' introduced me to him, 'Chris', to my astonishment, offered to take me to Fleet Street. I was 20 years old and I had a world to learn, yet this princeling would introduce me to his court at Mecca! Had I foreseen that within a little over a year I would be chained to a desk I might have hesitated.

In London I shared lodgings in a flat in Norfolk Square with Gilbert Cole, who had been sent south as 'our man in London'. Gilbert was now 29. He was urbane, he had impeccable manners, he had *savoir faire*, and he drove a Lagonda. He took one look at my Fifty Shilling Tailors' suit and introduced me to Hector Powe's, which was as far as I was ever likely to get on the road to Savile Row. He also introduced me to elegant women who scared me to death, and to musical alternatives to favourites like 'Stormy Weather' and 'Night and Day', which were the pop hits of the day, leaving me no choice – since it was HIS gramophone – but to listen to Bach or Schubert or nothing. If he failed to transform a gauche youth he was always kindness itself, never betraying disappointment.

I was neither lonely nor homesick. I could explore the city, and I even sought out the address of what had been the family home. Whatever it had been like in Father's and Mother's day, the street was now very run-down and bore little resemblance to how Mother had remembered it. No, I was not lonely, even if Chris once said that at the age of 20 he had thought London the loneliest place on earth. No, it was not that.

I certainly did not set the heather on fire in Fleet Street. It might be said that there was no heather to set on fire (although I do not plead that in extenuation). The trouble was that Chris had apparently failed to consult the venerable News Editor, J. B. Wilson, before inviting me to come south, and had even forgotten to mention that I was coming. So J.B. Wilson behaved as if I did not exist. He totally ignored me.

In 1934... 'Our poor little Scots boy' was 21 years old, the paper was six and called itself for the first time the *Scottish Daily Express*, and his London supper companion was about to become its editor

On night duty (which was when JB did not need to see me) I would take supper in Lyon's Corner House at Ludgate Circus, where I was often joined by the political sub-editor, Edinburgh-born Sandy Trotter. One evening John Gordon came in (he must have been slumming – surely he dined habitually at the Savoy Grill?) and both he and Sandy Trotter tried to persuade me that the only road to success in newspapers was via the sub-editorial table. It was the only time I ever met the great man, and I seem to recall that he left Sandy Trotter and me to pay for his sausage and mash.

No, I wasn't lonely or homesick. It was something Dorothy Secker said which convinced me that I had no place in Fleet Street. Dorothy was J B 's secretary, and a motherly soul. I overheard her in conversation refer to 'our poor little Scots boy'. I went straight to J B and asked him if I could transfer back to Glasgow. He said he thought it might be possible to arrange, if that was my wish. It was.

I did not attempt to say goodbye to Chris. I hoped he would understand. And I know he forgave me, because soon after the war ended he repeated the invitation to join his staff.

It was with no heavy heart that I left. Mecca could wait. I went back to Hardie Stewart and hoped he had forgotten all about Glencoe.

While I had been away someone had at last listened to Davie Kirkwood, MP, who had led the fight by the 'Red Clydesider' MPs to get the shipbuilding industry going again – particularly the promised giant Cunarder. The Treasury gave a loan of £9 million to merge the Atlantic interests of the Cunard and White Star companies and to complete contract No. 534. More than that: Clydebank could look beyond '534', because the loan allowed Cunard to order another of the same, which became contract No. 552.

Among the flags and bunting which hung from tenement windows in the celebrating town, one proclaimed 'Happy Days Are Here Again', and that was the one we featured in the paper, hoping (like everyone else) that it would be so.

Soon after the workers at Brown's had begun to clothe the skeleton which had languished on the stocks for two years, the Prince of Wales decided to pay another visit. That visit was made memorable for us by the inimitable Eddie McKenna. He decided that the occasion was as much to celebrate our Racing Section and Women's Section as it was to welcome the Prince, so he spent all one night decorating with posters and boards the entire route which the royal visitor would take as he entered the city.

On a last-minute patrol in his little van he was dismayed to find that all his work had disappeared. He backed his van into a little side street which, being a cul de sac, had not been barricaded off like all the other streets, and there he harboured dark thoughts. Were his *Daily Record* rivals responsible? (As a matter of fact they were not – the police had asked the council cleansing department to remove the offending posters). A few moments before the entourage was due to pass, his rage overcame him. When the police motor-cycle outriders appeared, a little green van, festooned with advertising boarding, thrust itself, seemingly from nowhere, between them and the royal car.

All efforts by the police guards at the kerbside to shunt it aside were in vain, its driver conveying by signals of feigned dismay his inability to comply because of the barriers along the roadside, and in this manner the royal procession conveyed Eddie McKenna's defiant message right into the heart of the city.

Eddie McKenna's attachment to our cause was absolute. When the publicity staff could find no one to assume the role of a Crusader knight in a pageant at Prestwick, Eddie volunteered. A horse of goodness knows how many hands had been hired from a farm and duly caparisoned. After Eddie had donned his chain mail and visor, his doubting helpers watched him mount, handed him his shield and lance, and backed away to a respectful distance in anticipation of the noble animal's reaction.

The horse reared up, alarmed by the unaccustomed weight. But its intrepid rider brought the cavorting steed under control, raised his visor and with an accent which belonged to no medieval gentle knight he said, 'You buggers didn't know I'd been in the Scots Greys, did you?'...

CHAPTER 7

The Sultan of the Alhambra

'RJT' THOMPSON WAS RECALLED to London in June, 1934. So was Tom Blackburn, while Max Aitken went to Manchester to take over the management there. Our new manager in Scotland was to be Frank Waters, a Cambridge rugby blue and Scottish international,

RJT had claimed the right to nominate his successor as editor and insisted he had to be a Scot who would continue his policy of emphasising the Scottish identity of the paper. He had named Hardie Stewart. But when Lord Beaverbrook interviewed the nominee he withheld approval; it was his custom to heed his instinct, and he said (quite illogically, for Hardie Stewart was a handsome fellow) that he did not like the look of him.

Christiansen then looked around the Scots in his London office and chose Sandy Trotter, his political sub-editor, for the editor's chair in Glasgow.

Alexander Cooper Trotter was born in an Edinburgh tenement and always made the most of his humble origins. He would say that each Sunday his father betook himself to the stairhead landing, there to sharpen the kitchen carving knife on the stone steps with such furious purpose that neighbours might observe and take envious note – even though the family was only having mince as usual. Sandy would tell this story in whatever society he found himself, and he was to find himself at times among the most distinguished. But there it is: in all newspapermen, no matter how eminent, there is apt to be a streak of plain, honest yellow journalism.

It is normal, or politic where it is not fashionable, to profess that one's entry into journalism was caused by an innate compulsion to express oneself in print. Sandy Trotter had no time for such pretension; he said he had come into it for the money.

The money was a lot different in those days, particularly if you had left school at 14 years of age, when eight shillings a week in a newspaper office was a few pence more than what was offered by the local brewery. When Sandy joined the Edinburgh *Evening News* as an office boy, the news editor was Walter McPhail, who alternately praised him and castigated him as a ginger-haired whelp, which he no doubt was. Later, in further proof that he was only in it for the money, he accepted 30 shillings a week (£1.50) from the *Daily Record's* local circulation manager, and Mr McPhail told him: 'You have your 30 pieces of silver. It may interest you to know Judas Iscariot is also reputed to have had red hair, and that I consider your acceptance of this offer as a triumph for incompetence'.

From Edinburgh, Sandy went to the *Statesman* in Calcutta (where he said he did not relish the curry), and eventually by way of the *Sheffield Independent* and the *Nottingham Guardian* to Fleet Street, where most of the money was to be had.

In London, while he was working as the Press Association's late-duty sub-editor, he was on his way back to his lodgings on a January morning in 1928 when he noticed the normally placid River Thames lapping the embankment. Although he knew that the Press Association frowned on frivolous expenses, he hailed a passing taxi and told the driver to take him to Horseferry Road, where he found ambulance men taking away the victims of the worst London flood of the century. Sandy telephoned his story from a kiosk behind the House of Commons. Fleet Street slept in, but the *Yorkshire Post* and other provincials took the PA story. He was rewarded with a bonus and an increase in his wages – and some searching questions about his expenses claim.

Sandy then joined the *Daily News* (which became the News Chronicle), where he stumbled across the second great scoop of his career. Early in the morning of 15 February, 1933, he volunteered to stay late and monitor the radio commentary on the Test Match in Australia, and from this assemble a report on the day's play. As he was doing so, a newsreader broke into the commentary to announce that there had been an attempt to assassinate President Roosevelt in Miami.

A British women's golf team were in Florida at the time, and Sandy tried desperately to telephone their captain, Diana Fishwick. He was unable to locate her, but a helpful telephone operator connected him with the presidential train itself. A voice from the train said, 'I am sorry, but the president cannot speak to you. This is Lieutenant Colonel Manning, Governor of Florida.'

Governor Manning then told him the entire story. President Roosevelt had only just stood up in his car to address a crowd of 100,000 people in a park in Miami. Among the crowd was Giuseppe Zingara, who had vowed 'to kill ANY president'. The would-be assassin fired five shots. They all missed the President, but others were hit, including the mayor of Chicago, before a woman caught the man's wrist and deflected the last shot. The mayor died later from his wounds.

Through this exploit Sandy Trotter came to the attention of Arthur Christiansen, who had just arrived in London from Manchester to be deputy editor of the *Daily Express*. Chris offered him 16 guineas a week, which was considerably more than he had been earning with the *News Chronicle*, and he took the money.

For three long weeks after his nomination as the next editor of the

Scottish Daily Express, Sandy Trotter wore his Sunday best suit until it was almost shiny, awaiting a summons from Lord Beaverbrook's lair at Stornoway House. When it came he passed the test, and was given £25 a week and a one-way rail ticket to Glasgow.

So we were given Alexander Cooper Trotter; and after our bewildering succession of editors he was to hold the post for 28 years and then to be our chairman until his retirement. During his editorship he boosted the paper's circulation from 201,837 to more than 600,000. Whatever conceit we had already acquired, he boosted that too. He also gave some among us ulcers, but that could be considered an inevitable corollary.

True, he arrived at a fortunate time when the days of the leaky lifeboats had passed; but that in no way detracts from his achievements. He also arrived when momentous events were happening, both at home and abroad, to stimulate the sale of papers. Within days we were recording the murder by armed Nazis of the Austrian Chancellor Dollfuss, the death of Hindenburg and the elevation of the former house-decorator, Adolf Hitler, as chancellor and president of the German Third Reich.

The immediate event at home, however, was the launch of No. 534 at John Brown's yard in Clydebank. The Queen came to name her, and to no one's surprise she christened her the *Queen Mary.* Sandy Trotter commissioned the author George Blake, former editor of the Glasgow *Evening Citizen,* to describe the event, while several of us were deputed to act as supporting players, taking up various vantage points to feed the great man with our observations. Thankfully my post was not at the ringside, on the periphery of the opposite bank of the river, because when the great ship slid into the river a wall of water, ten feet high, swept over the wall and sent dozens of spectators retreating in alarm.

In that year the Government moved the Scottish Office from London to new headquarters in Edinburgh. As a native son, Sandy Trotter was as conscious as any of the status of our capital city and, in recognition that it would acquire even more importance than he already assumed it to have, he brought Gilbert Cole back from London to head our editorial staff in Edinburgh.

The office in Edinburgh's India Street housed just three reporters and an office boy at the time. For the first few months after Gilbert's arrival the only typewriter in the office was his personal property which everyone used in turn. Hardie Stewart, the News Editor, sent him a girl cub reporter from Glasgow, working on the theory that if babies are thrown into the water at the deep end they will automatically swim. Little Winnie Glen had barely time to say 'Hello' to anyone in Albion Street before he had sent her away with an instruction to produce a column of Edinburgh 'copy' every day – which she did, biting her fingernails to the quick and wondering why she ever abandoned her place at teacher training college.

One day a visitor who was crossing the Gardenholme Linn bridge near Moffat chanced to see what appeared to be a human hand in the rocky ravine below. He phoned the *Express* in Edinburgh, and thereby uncovered the infamous Ruxton murders.

Gilbert Cole was the first reporter to arrive on the scene. He had with him a newly-recruited young photographer called Peter MacVean. Together they scrambled down into the ravine and thrust their way through rank grass and bramble bushes until they saw a parcel. It was bound in linen and from it there hung a slender arm. Beyond it were what appeared to be other parts of a human body.

Lest they should obliterate any vital clues, they clawed their way back up to the bank, jumped into their car and drove to Moffat to report their find to the police. Many more pieces were found in the following month, adding up to the bodies of two women, identified as the wife of Buck Ruxton, an Indian doctor in Lancaster, and their family nursemaid. The doctor's caution had led him even to remove a bunion from one of his wife's feet before dismembering her body. But he was traced because he made one mistake: he wrapped the pieces in a blouse and a child's rompers, bits of bedsheets and newspapers, not realising that one of the newspapers was featuring details of a local carnival in Lancaster. It was the vital clue the police needed to direct their search for the murderer.

Professor John Glaister of Glasgow University and other forensic experts put together the human jigsaw, and their evidence sent Dr Buck Ruxton to the gallows in March of the following year.

(Hugh) Gilbert Cole, most talented and loved journalist... he was to serve the paper for 34 years, and in retirement to remain adviser and friend to many, till his death in 1994 at the age of 87

Gilbert's bureau grew mightily until eventually it was more than 20 strong, and under his tutelage it produced many who went on to occupy high office in newspapers and television and radio.

Meanwhile, I was happily doing whatever Hardie Stewart saw fit to assign to me until, one day, my roof fell in: Sandy Trotter had not forgotten our conversations in the Lyon's Corner House at Ludgate Circus.

I had just come back from Skye, where as one of a search team I had been reporting on what was known as The Coolins Mystery. A shepherd had found Barbara Nicholson dead in a burn in the hills, but there had been no trace of her fiancé, Stanley Moore. (The mystery was not solved, indeed, until three months later, when three women climbers found him dead in the dark depths of rock-strewn Coire Nan Creache; it was assumed that when he had fallen there his bride-to-be had left him with whatever shelter was possible in order to go for help, only to fall from a crag into the burn and die there of exposure in the stormy rains.)

Sandy Trotter called me into his office to tell me that he was transferring me to the sub-editors' table. I did not share his enthusiasm for the sub-editing role. There is no doubt he had my best interests at heart (I truly believe he always did for all the time I knew him), but I said that I preferred to stay on the reporting staff and, daringly presuming on our previous acquaintanceship in London, I said I had no wish to grow up to be an editor. Sandy replied that while it was unlikely that I would grow up to be an editor it was time I grew up anyway and learned what newspapers were really all about – and would I kindly report to the Chief Sub-editor, Charlie MacNicol, the following week.

So I left the reporting table to sit at a desk on the other side of the editorial floor. Ian McColl sat on the opposite side of the desk for he, too, had been transferred. There we began to learn this arcane trade, with scraps of agency copy to be butchered into one, two, or three paragraphs, and to accord to the results headlines in descending order of importance, coded as p's, and f's, and h's.

We were also given the preparation of the fish prices. These were the lists of average prices which the various types of fish fetched at daily auction in ports throughout the country. In those days their preparation was the first discipline a junior sub-editor had to master. Was this 'learning what newspapers were all about'?

A few years ago, while on holiday in St Andrews, I met John Blackwood, the former editor of the *Scottish Daily Mail* who had bought the Central Bar in Market Street on his retirement. I remarked on the distinctive tie he was wearing. On a navy blue background it carried a £ sign, intertwined with a silver fish. John said it was the insignia of the Fish Price Sub-Editors' Association, a club whose membership was reserved for those who had sub-edited the fish price reports in earlier days. So reserved was it that even his best friend, the columnist Vincent Mulchrone, was excluded – or rather, he HAD been. Vincent was nothing if not persistent. During a holiday in Ireland, after much Guinness had been consumed, an exception was made for him by the formation of the Clarinet Players' Section of the Fish Price Sub-Editors' Association.

When John learned that I, too, qualified as a member, he sent me a tie. Unfortunately, it went missing in the post. So if you ever see someone who is obviously under middle age at least, wearing a tie with a £ sign intertwined with a silver fish, know well that he is an impostor, the sort of bounder who would wear the colours of a regiment in which he had never served.

Arthur Christiansen's concepts for producing newspapers are no longer revolutionary. His techniques are now basic not only to popular newspapers but to the quality press too, and even if there are a few quality papers still presenting the news in a dull way and a few tabloids still running down the street screaming with their throats cut, there has been a process of polarisation.

Important news, even the dullest and most complicated, Chris would say, can be made palatable with a recipe of 'sugar with the cascara', this by projecting the people involved as the basis of the news, by introducing description and atmosphere and background, by explanation and interpretation, and by writing simply so that everyone could understand it.

Those of us who had known no other school of learning had absorbed this, the reporting part of the technique, as if it were our mother's milk. But the corollary of the technique was the presentation of this amalgam of the important and the entertaining in a package which called for attention on every page and yet was simple enough for someone to read, 'even if', said Chris, 'he is hanging on to a strap on the bus'.

There was to be more. then, to sub-editing than the preparation of the fish prices.

Sandy Trotter was strawberry blond, and pink, and round; his appearance conjured up the image of a jovial Benedictine monk disguised in civilian clothing. If sub-editors were the new aristocrats of journalism, he was of the blood royal. He was affectionately known as 'Sandy,' and more formally as A.C.T. To that was added (behind his back, of course) the title of 'the Sultan of the Alhambra', because it was his custom, after the first edition was well under way, to repair to the Alhambra Theatre and the company of its manager, Bert Lumsden, who was his special friend; but he always returned in time to countermand for succeeding editions any misguided directions which his deputies might have taken.

If the motive for Sandy's posting to Glasgow had been to impose an even more definite Scottish imprint on the paper, Chris had chosen well. One of the ways in which the new editor emphasised this was to initiate a series of 'slip editions' – one-off runs of the main editions containing at least one page-change for distribution in targeted areas. Thus, coinciding with the main editions, we had slips to Inverness and district, to Aberdeen, to Dundee and Fife, to Edinburgh city, to the Borders, Lanarkshire and Paisley, all devoted exclusively to local news and gossip. Ultimately there were 13 such editions.

Ian McColl and I filtered on to the local pages desk. It nurtured many

Sandy Trotter (right) with Arthur Christiansen

others. James Cameron, who later made the world his province, cut his milk teeth on these local pages, as did Jock Mowat (one of two young trainee solicitors who worked part-time as sub-editors), who became a sheriff in Fife and later presided over the enquiry into the Lockerbie air disaster. Another was A.I.B. (Ian) Stewart, who followed his father as procurator fiscal at Campbeltown. Sandy Trotter not only taught us young fry: he jollied us along and convinced us it was all great fun and that we were lucky even to be paid for it. When we joked that we were Slaves of the Sultan of the Alhambra, there was more than a modicum of truth in the jest.

The local page unit was a hard school. No one suspected that a working week was anything less than seven days, never four, as it became later by union decree. Days off were allotted on a rota devised by Chief Sub-Editor, Charlie MacNicol, who did not believe in days off at all, and whose rota in any case was as unpredictable as was his temper, which was awesome. He could – and frequently did – bellow. Robins Millar, our theatre critic, likened it to the sound of the Bulls of Bashan, a description whose source most of us had to look up in Cruden's Concordance of the Bible. There was no recognised supper break. We ate – usually sandwiches from home – on the run.

In this period of learning we owed much to the tolerance of the printers. In the floor below, where people spoke an esoteric language, Davie Coupar and Jimmy McNaught and Willie Hawson, who had been accustomed to working with their professional equals, found themselves nursemaids from time to time to a gaggle of raw intruders who could neither tell Ruby and Pearl apart nor distinguish between one type face and another, nor even know how many points made an inch. But they sheltered us as they would have cared for their own urchins.

Over a time we came to make friends with the different printing tribes – the powerful families, some fat and ponderous, others lean and gentle and graceful. We learned to know which among them would be comfortable with, or even capable of, marriage to one another, and which would scream in horror to be in the same room. We also learned to design pages for Sandy Trotter, and to write headlines for him which were compelling, never ones he would reject as 'mere labels'.

So that we might profit beyond his hands-on guidance, our editor adopted Chris' practice of issuing daily bulletins in which he analysed the contents of each issue, dispensing or withholding commendation. Since he was as tolerant of our frailties as would have been the jovial monk he so resembled, few resented his judgments.

But while he was moulding us he kept at hand an instrument of correction. By his side on the back bench, where reigned the editor and his chief lieutenants during the long night, sat a wise old bald-headed eagle named George Taylor ('GT') Brown.

GT had digested the *Encyclopedia Britannica* and much more besides. No error escaped him, no possible libel and no *double entendre*. Of the latter there was a devotee among the subs who was compiling a dossier of howlers and misprints and was suspected of being not averse to trying to intrude his own contributions for the benefit of his book. His most prized items included one misprint which recorded that 'The royal party then pissed over the bridge'.

G T's wrath upon finding error was normally preceded by a call as he digested a proofed item: 'WHO did this?' ('this' being identified by the catch-line which had been attached to the item). When he had located and interrogated the offender he would thunder for all to hear: 'You great ignorant bohunk!'

The worst crimes which could be committed were failure to check previous cuttings relating to the subject, or failure to consult the appropriate reference book, whether it was the Bible or the *Book of Quotations* or *Who's Who* or *Burke's Peerage* or the *Gazetteer* or whatever; but the most heinous offence was to identify a place-name in his native Kincardineshire as belonging to the neighbouring county of Aberdeenshire (and once someone unforgivably misplaced his native Stonehaven).

At times one could have said fairly, had one but dared, that the appropriate reference book was not available (GT having already sent for it, not so much to verify his own normally infallible knowledge but to produce it if need be from under the flap of his desk and confront the accused with it).

The only sub-editor who never ran foul of GT was a fellow native of the north east: George Ritchie, who joined us from the *Aberdeen Press and Journal*, was so knowledgeable that he could always be depended upon without recourse to the library.

I only once saw GT non-plussed. On the night of 11 December 1937 two express trains crashed in a blizzard at Castlecary Station, killing 33 people and injuring more than 90. Bill Johnston was the reporter at the scene. When he telephoned in his report, the death toll he gave conflicted with the figure supplied by the Press Association.

'And what makes you think you are right and not the PA?' demanded GT.

'Because,' said Bill, 'I've been into the waiting room where they have taken the dead and I've counted them.'

'Well,' said GT, 'Go back and count them again.'

Grim as the task was, Bill did so, and telephoned the same answer.

Most newspapers in those days had what was known as their Prodnose, whose specific task was to seek out gaffes and to sniff out libel, as GT did as a matter of course, and all newspapers also had a staff of 'Readers' to pick up any typographical mistakes. Thirty or more of these sat in teams of two, side by side; one, the copyholder, read aloud the wording of the original article to his companion, the reader, who held and corrected the printed proof – this in a room isolated from other noise, in which the resultant whispering chorus sounded like an exclusive social gathering of the Church Woman's Guild.

Their occupation had an illustrious pedigree: learned scholars, among them Erasmus the philosopher, acted as 'correctors of the press' for early printing houses. In the 18th century it is said that some printers hung up page proofs in public places and invited people to find errors. In the absence of Readers' Departments in newspapers nowadays it is as well the custom never survived.

As further protection against legal complaint or error, a team of five part-time lawyers, headed by the erudite John Neil, sat in the editorial department on nightly rota. One of them was John McCormick, founder of the Home Rule movement Covenant. If a sub-editor sent for a particular volume of the encyclopedia, there was a fair chance that it, too, would not be readily available. This was not because of GT, but because John McCormick would take one volume at a time and try to read its contents through to the end between bouts of proof-reading. Ernie Knox, the librarian, told me that John McCormick ultimately managed to get through every single volume of the *Encyclopaedia Britannica*.

The most noted example of black-listing in our trade belonged to the *Dundee Courier*, which by decree of its family owners, DC Thomson, would not refer to Winston Churchill directly by name, even when he was Prime Minister. We ourselves had no Black List; but there were people on a 'White List' whom the Beaver disliked for various reasons, and there were others on it to be avoided because they were litigious.

There were also 'Advices from Lord Beaverbrook' which came to be known as The Edicts from Mount Sinai. One was 'Cry not down the pleasures of the people'; but, it added, 'generally, however, be on the side of the angels'. It was easier in the 1930s than now to be on the side of the angels.

Newspapers have always reflected the culture and manners of their time, and these were sternly moral times. On Mondays we published excerpts from what had been preached in the pulpits on the Sabbath, and we printed 'The Midweek Sermon' on Wednesdays, usually by the noted preacher, the Rev Dr Lachlan McLean Watt.

When I joined the paper there had been a furore in Montrose over a local sculptor's exhibition which contained the statues of two boys. The local council told him: 'Unless they wear kilts they must be removed'. It was 1930 before Renfrew's Victory Baths lifted a ban on mixed bathing, and even in 1934 the council in St Andrews decreed: 'Every bather must wear full regulation bathing costume when bathing or sun-bathing', only relenting later to concede that 'Male bathers may undo their shoulder straps'.

Even the prettiest girl was not supposed to have a bosom. A team of retouch artists saw to that. The principal task of the retouch artists was to enhance the reproduction of pictures: if, for instance, a background was too dark, they lightened it. But they also painted out any suspicion of a cleavage, and if a skirt was too short they lengthened it.

One of our photographers on a pit explosion story took a picture which, in the light of his flashbulb, clearly showed, beside a wagon, an unfortunate fellow who had been overtaken by the call of nature. I saw retouch artist Davie Sharp remove his manhood with one deft flick of a brush.

We weren't alone. The old *Sunday Graphic* is said to have painted out the testimonials of a prize-winning bull, and to have been sued by its outraged owner. The old Glasgow *Bulletin* was said to have printed a picture of a proud woman owner holding the halters of two champion cows at a farm show, and to have headlined it 'Prize Winning Cows'; unfortunately the caption writer had not been told that for space reasons one of the animals had been cut out of the picture.

We had our own taboos. No one in a divorce case was alleged to have 'committed adultery'; offenders were said to have been 'guilty of misconduct'. Contraception and abortion were never mentioned. When we daringly ran a contest headlined 'Choose Scotland's Prettiest Bathing Girl', we felt compelled to print, in oblique justification, an article 'By A Barrister' which said: 'The Inspectors of Decency recently appointed at a number of seaside resorts have no power whatsoever. There is no law by which they can interfere with or dictate to anyone using a bathing dress which they think 'indecent'. Only a threatened breach of the peace caused by the scantiness of a costume would justify police or an official interfering.'

The bathing girl contest was won by a Miss Dora Fullerton of Perth. Her prize was £20. She was to be only the first of many. After her came a plethora of beauty queens chosen at holiday resorts – and of bonny babies.

One time Bailie Mrs Jean Mann, the forthright MP for Airdrie and Coatbridge in the 1950s, who was famed for her imposing repertoire of Commons questions which ranged from bombs to the price of butcher meat, was invited to judge a bonny babies contest and she banned every infant wearing rubber panties. We all thought it hilarious. But Jean Mann had made the point in her speech that she objected to rubber pants because they were concealing soaking nappies, which good mothers ought to be changing. The story, written by Mamie Baird (of whom more anon), appeared on the front page. In his bulletin on the day's paper, Sandy Trotter complained that the thought of all those wet nappies would put readers off their breakfasts!

It was never an easy matter, trying to define what was, and was not, good taste.

CHAPTER 8

No fiery cross for Prince Charming

KING GEORGE V DIED AT five minutes to midnight on 20 January 1936. His end was hastened peacefully and mercifully with drugs administered by Lord Dawson, the King's doctor, so that the death could be announced in the 'respectable' morning papers such as *The Times* rather than in the next day's evening papers.

The dashing young Prince of Wales took over as Edward the Eighth. For eleven months he was more than just a figurehead, not someone simply to acquiesce and sign papers, not just a silent onlooker of the plight of the unemployed. But one day he spoke too much and went a step too far.

If Sandy Trotter received any brief from above (or from down south) towards the end of those eleven months, he never issued any instructions to his staff to submit to his scrutiny any reference to the impending divorce of Mrs Ernest Simpson, much less about her relationship with the King; but perhaps there was no need, for the conspiracy of silence among the newspapers which Beaverbrook and Lord Rothermere had brokered was faithfully observed until the Bishop of Bradford chose to voice his concern about the King's attitude to duty. But we knew, although the general public did not, that the King sought to marry Mrs Simpson, née Wallis Warfield, ex Mrs Erle Spencer. Secrets are no secrets to newspapermen, and in any case we could read all about it in American and continental papers and magazines, wherever cautious wholesalers had not cut or blanked out the references.

When the newspapers finally ended their self-imposed censorship, the news was announced in the *Daily Express* in solemn and portentous words: 'A grave constitutional crisis has arisen...' Grave though it was, Bill Johnston and other backroom poets had already contributed to a host of ribald rhymes and slanderous ditties.

The young men of my acquaintance had adopted Edward's bowler hats and tied their ties with the Windsor knot, and all the girls had adored him, but there were few among us who would have gone to the barricades for our Prince Charming to keep him on his throne. Wasn't he supposed to marry a fairy princess or at the least a glamorous aristocrat? It wasn't as if the lady was even good-looking, unless one conceded she was handsome in a severe kind of way. Her looks reminded me of our old school's maths mistress, who was put together in angles, and had a caustic tongue forbye.

One result of the abdication crisis was, of course, a massive surge in newspaper sales for everyone. Our circulation soared in that month of December 1937 to a dizzy 290,717, and when we published that figure and with it an average figure for the year of 260,142, we finally toppled the *Daily Record* from its perch. Our rival had never published monthly figures as we did, but it now acknowledged an average for the year of 250,000, and so in effect hauled down the flag.

Once I had been promoted out of the local pages class to a higher grade, it was possible to contemplate that maybe – just maybe – Sandy Trotter had been right and that it had been time for me to find out 'what newspapers are really all about'. Or it would have been so, had there not been so much cause to envy my former brothers.

Ross Kennedy was one. He was given a column to write entitled 'I Cover The Waterfront' (the title of a popular song of the time). Now THERE was a posting to covet! All the length of the Clyde from the Tail o' the Bank to the Broomielaw, not becalmed as it is now but with the ships of all nations along its quays, the Anchor liners still sailing from Yorkhill Quay, America-bound with their cargoes of human hopes, children scrubbed and tidy and dressed to carry with them the pride of their nationality, the boys in kilts, even though most would not have known a skean dhu from a Boy Scout camp knife, and all the liners bringing back people with tales to tell him for his column.

And Ben Allison...

Benny Lynch, the tragic boy from the Gorbals who rose to the pinnacle of boxing fame and sank to the gutter, crashed a car in Ayrshire and was arrested on a bus on his way back to Glasgow. Ben Allison paid his bail to get him out of jail, and he was able to file, exclusively, Benny's own story. He became the boxer's confidant. And when, after that, in preparation for the defence of his world title against Peter Kane, Benny took refuge from drink and temptation in Mellory Monastery near Clonmel, the county town of Tipperary, Ben Allison went with him.

Ben is on record as saying that he boarded the train at Glasgow's Central Station 'on impulse'. He never said that, as a result, no one knew for two days where he was. He eventually telephoned – to ask for an advance on expenses. Benny, he reported, was 'in really good shape'. When asked where the boxer was, Ben said 'He's right here beside me'; and although 'here' was the local inn, he insisted that Benny was rigorously following his declared regime of monastic simplicity.

Benny was indeed in great shape when he went into the ring to defend his title. He won his fight handsomely. But he never won his fight with the demon drink. One miserable night in August 1946, shambling, penniless, desperately ill and alone, the little man was found wandering in Govan's dockland. Benny Lynch died that night in the Southern General Hospital.

He was just 33 years old. His son, 'wee Benny', was later given a job as a lift-boy at 195 Albion Street.

And Gilbert Cole... Gilbert's telephone line was being flooded with calls from all over the world after his exclusive story about the Curse of the Pharaoh. It arose out of a conversation with Sir Alexander Seton, the noted archaeologist. During a visit to Egypt, Lady Seton had acquired a little finger-bone from the tomb of the pharaoh Tutankhamun. Since then, Sir Alexander said, the family had been haunted by the curse of the pharaoh.

The bone was displayed in a glass cabinet at their Edinburgh home, Prestonfield House (now a prestigious Edinburgh hotel of the same name). A series of mysterious happenings ensued which could not be explained away as coincidences. Sudden illnesses attacked the family and also the staff. Two fires broke out. Staff and visitors said they saw at night 'a robed figure' wandering through the house. Objects in the same room as the bone were found smashed. One morning the glass case itself fell and broke into splinters just two feet away from a table, but the bone itself was undamaged. Eventually maids refused to stay in the house at night.

Sir Alexander gave the bone to a surgeon friend. That night the surgeon's maid broke a leg as she ran in terror from the robed figure. Next day the surgeon returned the bone and Sir Alexander and Lady Seton took it back to Egypt. But before they did so, Gilbert Cole, undaunted by the surgeon's experience, borrowed it and kept it in his flat for two nights. Late one night a week later he was rushed to hospital to undergo an emergency operation for peritonitis, caused by a perforated ulcer, and he almost died.

Yes, I had plenty of cause to feel nostalgic for my reporting days. But as compensation, there was now, in sub-editing, to be found this larger, wider world in which there were happenings of far greater import even than what befell princes and kings and doomed romance.

The shipyard workers of Clydebank were furiously hammering into shape Ship No 552, the future *Queen Elizabeth*; time was short, for it was increasingly obvious that by the time of her completion she, like the *Queen Mary*, might be required to carry non-paying passengers on voyages which would be anything but luxury cruises.

At the King's Theatre, the comedian Dave Willis created a comic caricature of Haile Selassie. In this sketch a telegram arrived purporting to have been sent by Mussolini. His puzzled feed protested, 'But there's nothing on it!' 'Yes, I know,' replied the pseudo Haile Selassie. 'We're no' speakin'.'

When Mussolini did speak it was with bombs, sending the Abyssinian monarch fleeing from his palace in Addis Ababa minutes before it erupted in flames. During his subsequent refuge in Britain, Haile Selassie came to Glasgow in the summer of 1937, and it was a tragic real figure we saw clinging pathetically to his battered dignity.

Spain erupted in civil war, and the fascist dictators could not forbear to keep out of it. Twenty thousand others – 2,000 of them from Britain – could not keep out of it either. George, my best friend since schooldays, wanted to be one of them. Neither he nor I had any political affiliations, except for a brief spell as members of the Independent Labour Party, but that had been many years before, and only because the nicest girls were to be found at the Saturday night dances at the Mosspark ILP hall. But we subscribed to Victor Gollancz's Left Wing Book Club and to the *New Statesman and Nation*, so perhaps we did list a wee bit to port. George listed more to port than I did. He was also more idealistic than I was. Perhaps neither of us knew himself at all.

One Saturday morning when we met, as was our custom on Saturday mornings, in Reid's downstairs coffee room in Gordon Street, George was carrying a copy of the newspaper in which he had read a report of how Franco's Moors and foreign legionnaires had herded their unarmed prisoners into the bullring at Badajoz and massacred them all.

He said, 'We've really got to try to find out how we join the International Brigade.' But I was due to go on holiday, and in a seaside boarding house I found myself sitting at the communal dining table opposite the cheekiest little face I ever did see, and on the Saturday after I came home, when we met again in Reid's coffee room, I said, 'George, I'm sorry, I really don't want to go to Spain.' Whereupon George, who was known to be keeping trysts with a trainee hairdresser in Anniesland (and it wasn't to have his hair cut), said, 'That's alright, old son, I don't believe I do either.'

The Empire Exhibition of 1938, our last excuse for happy celebration before the Great Blackout, brought the Beaver back to Glasgow. He was delighted to converse with our theatre critic, Robins Millar, and to discover that he, too, was a son of the manse, and with Hector McNeil, who had studied theology at university; but he was scathing about some of the others who were introduced to him, and I was glad that I was on holiday and was never brought to his notice.

The Beaver took Hector McNeil to dinner, and afterwards wrote to Sandy Trotter suggesting that Hector might be sent to join the London office leader-writing staff, adding that 'if he proves immature he can always go back'. Hector did not tarry long in London, but that was in no wise due to immaturity. He was already not only a town councillor but a bailie too. He had fought two Parliamentary campaigns in Galloway, he had failed by only 149 votes to topple the formidable Walter Elliot from his seat in Glasgow's Kelvingrove, and he had doubled the Labour vote against Malcolm MacDonald in Ross and Cromarty. He knew well the path he intended to follow, and it did not lie with the Beaver.

By September, when the men of Clydebank had readied Cunarder contract No. 552 for launching, Queen Elizabeth came on the 26th to give the liner her own name. Four days later Neville Chamberlain returned from Munich waving a little bit of paper and declaring (it is said, under persuasion) that it was 'peace in our time', and everyone hoped it was – even those who feared that he had merely fed the appetite of the beast.

We carried the slogan on the front page then: 'There will be no war this year, or next year either'. No doubt Lord Beaverbrook believed it. He was certainly optimistic enough to order a Mark 2 version of 195 Albion Street for the future. By the end of 1938 our circulation had risen to 317,145. The old presses were wilting under the strain. They were relieved a little by a second-hand press dug up from somewhere, which we called the Flying Flea. But the old tobacco factory was just as venerable, and the Beaver ordered it to be pulled down and rebuilt. The new building was intended to house the *Sunday Express*, too. But it was not to do so in peacetime. On 7 August 1939 we dropped the slogan 'There will be no war', and three weeks later Chamberlain intoned over the radio, 'And so I have to tell you that a state of war now exists between ourselves and Germany'.

CHAPTER 9

The Athenia and U-boat lies

ON THE DAY WAR BEGAN the thoughts of so many young people turned to marriage. Ten days afterwards my little Cheekyface (Doris Janet), for whom I had travelled every weekend to Dundee throughout a three-year courtship, had her 21st birthday, and we became engaged that day. Being determined on the Navy rather than the Poor Bloody Infantry I enrolled in off-duty hours in the school of navigation at the old Royal Technical College. Tom McEntee refused to sell German beers although he still had some in stock. Marjorie Hird, who ran a 'Glasgow After Dark' column, painted her fingernails red white and blue. And naval reservist Andrew McLean, who had been writing the 'Henry Cockburn' diary column, slipped away from among us to join his ship.

Despite the instant night-time blackouts and the daylight scenes of tearful mothers saying goodbye to hordes of evacuee children, for us at Albion Street the real horrors of war were at first only in far-off anguished Poland, reaching us only as agency tape spilling from 'Creed' machines, until the horror arrived with rude suddenness on our own news patch.

Just six hours after the declaration of hostilities, as passengers in the Anchor Donaldson liner *Athenia* on the way from Glasgow to New York sat down to dinner, Kapitanleutnant Fritz-Julius Lemp in U-boat 30, disregarding the fact that the *Athenia* was unarmed and that she was carrying 1400 civilians (some of whom were neutral Americans), aimed a torpedo into her side. He sent 112 people to their deaths that evening.

Those who survived were picked up by two ships in the vicinity. Some were landed at Galway, but most were brought back to the Clyde. They landed at Greenock. Among them were children snatched from bed in their night-clothes, mothers parted from their infants and wives parted from their husbands; mothers happily found their children again among the 250 youngsters whom waiting buses took to Glasgow, but there were separated wives who scanned the faces in the crowd in vain. All of them had stories to tell of heroism and of harrowing hours in open boats – stories which were to become an all too familiar norm.

Kapitanleutnant Lemp's masters in Berlin alleged that a British submarine had been ordered to sink the liner in order to inflame American public opinion, and an Illinois travel agent said he had been told on board about arms in the hold for the defence of Canadian ports. In the ensuing MI5 inquiry into this canard, our own 'On the Waterfront' Ross Kennedy, who knew the agent personally, was able to testify to the agent's German sympathies. Meanwhile his entertaining column went into cold storage for the duration.

A lot of other features did so too, and Marjorie Hird had to find something to do other than patrolling the city dance halls for items in 'Glasgow After Dark'. We then learned that Lieutenant Andrew McLean RNVR, our 'Henry Cockburn' columnist, had been killed by an exploding mine on board his ship.

In October the war came to our patch again. Goering sent his bombers to seek out the warships in the Firth of Forth and to destroy the Forth Bridge. He thought there were no fighters stationed in Scotland; he was wrong – 603 Squadron shot down one of the bombers. The others fled after inflicting superficial damage on three ships. When they came back once more to seek out the prey they had missed, Ben Allison didn't miss THEM. He had been seconded to Gilbert Cole's staff in Edinburgh by then, and from his station at the Hawes Inn under the shadow of the Forth Bridge he shot down – on paper – more daylight raiders than Goering had sent over.

The feat was made possible because our censors deleted from reports only whatever was calculated to be helpful to the enemy, while permitting anything else which contributed to public morale – and Ben Allison contributed most handsomely to public morale.

Gilbert Cole's own wartime was spent at his bureau in India Street. So extensive had been the surgery in his 'Pharaoh's curse' operation that he was rejected as unfit for military service. But during what some called the Phoney War, or the Sitzkrieg (which lasted while Hitler and Stalin digested their meal of Poland and Hitler pondered what should be next on the menu), Gilbert was at the dockside in Edinburgh's port of Leith to meet HMS *Cossack* and to tell a stirring story which needed no embellishment to boost public morale.

There never was a phoney war at sea. The *Cossack* had brought back 300 merchant seamen who had been captives of the German pocket battleship *Graf Spee*. They had been shut up in the dark hold of the *Graf Spee's* supply tanker Altmark, on their way to a prison camp in Germany, when the *Cossack* sighted the tanker skulking along the coast of neutral Norway. The Altmark scurried into a narrow fjord to hide alongside two Norwegian gunboats; but under cover of darkness the Cossack edged into the fjord, and a boarding party stormed the tanker and prised open the hold with a cry which became famous – 'The Navy's here!'

During the so-called Phoney War everything seemed to mark time and it seemed a good time to marry, which Cheekyface and I did on 7 February, 1940.

The *Queen Elizabeth*, incomplete as she was, and still with some of

John Brown's men on board, stole secretly away from the Clyde in March. Except for an anti-mine device, she was unarmed. At a speed which in peacetime would have given her the Atlantic Blue Riband, she raced to New York, where she was received with tumultuous acclaim. She was just in time. Within weeks the Phoney War ended. Nazi troops poured into Denmark and Norway and soon afterwards into the Low Countries, and into France, encircling our men, and finally leaving us with the pride of their miracle escape from Dunkirk and the knowledge that we now stood entirely alone.

So great was the demand for newspapers that our circulation had risen to 345,128, exceeding the combined sales in Scotland of the *Record*, the *Mail*, the *Daily Herald* and the *News Chronicle*. The *Sunday Express* had now moved into the act, and somehow the old presses were coping with a seven-day week. We still awaited the replacement building, and with its completion the arrival of the *Evening Citizen* – Glasgow's oldest paper, which had been taken over in March of the previous year in a 50/50 deal between ourselves and George Outram and Co, owners of the *Glasgow Herald* and *Evening Times*.

In September 1940 the *Express* bought the controlling interest in the *Citizen*, and the whole evening newspaper operation moved from St Vincent Place into the shining black steel and glass Albion Street Mark 2, bringing with it 90,000 more copies to print.

But newsprint was becoming more and more scarce. Contents bills disappeared. They could have been phased out but there was no thought, as an economy measure, of reverting to the occasional issue of 'double bills'. This practice had been abandoned in disrepute since January of 1938. A clever night circulation clerk was alleged to have decided that the issue contained no story of outstanding selling merit, and he sent out a two-header bill which said:

JULIANA
– A BABY
GIRL

HITLER
BLAMES
MUSSOLINI

I say 'alleged' because there is no evidence to identify authorship. The only named suspect denied it and no one ever confessed.

The last contents bill, in April 1940, was devoted to the London staff's daring and darling Hilde Marchant. It said: 'Front Page Girl Sends War Despatch'.

The size of the *Express* dwindled by stages (it finally fell to only four pages). However expert in condensation the sub-editors might be, they were required to become even more so. Long before the size of papers reached their nadir, Christiansen in London directed that ideally a front page should be contrived to accommodate at least 30 items, and that is what he sometimes got – or even more (the Express was a broadsheet in those days, not a tabloid). Eventually, in the continuing austerity period after the war, no fewer than 48 stories were counted on the front page on one occasion.

One, two or more of the staff at a time left to join the Forces. They included our general manager. Frank Waters fitted his six foot four inch frame into a Royal Marine uniform and was succeeded as manager by Sandy Bruce from Circulation. I went into the Navy – thanks to that crash spare-time course at the 'Royal Tec' and being able to bluff my way through a Board of Trade exam which gave me a ticket into the ranks of the merchant seamen who served the Navy's rescue tugs section.

I did not meet any of my newspaper colleagues for five years after that. On the only leave which gave the opportunity to visit Albion Street I learned that Ian McColl was in RAF's Coastal Command, Bert Williamson was in an Army Intelligence unit, Bill Johnston was a naval gunner on board a merchant ship, and Ben Allison was in the RAF, where it was assumed he would be trying to rewrite the King's Regulations. No one could have said that the members of the old brigade were not coping, but if one popped into the office during a leave it was no surprise to have a pencil thrust into one's hand.

Hector McNeil became Labour MP for Greenock, unopposed under the wartime electoral pact between the parties, and it was said that on Friday nights when he came back from London to his constituency he always dropped in at Albion Street on the way to help out. It became such a habit that even when he had reached Cabinet rank, if his visit coincided with a big news break he would automatically sit down at a desk, dump his despatch box on the floor and grab the nearest telephone.

Tommy Muirhead, the famous old Glasgow Rangers player and football reporter, took his turn on the night news desk. Isabel Sinclair sub-edited. Night after night everyone took turns on rooftop fire watch, and almost never resorted to the shelters.

Lord Beaverbrook had been wont to refer to his reporters as 'young eaglets', so one of Sandy Trotter's business contacts with a story to offer asked for 'one of those young eaglets' to be sent to meet him. He was greatly taken aback by the arrival of Sandy Mowat, our farming correspondent, who was stubbornly refusing to retire although he was over 80 years old.

The censors did not allow publication of the names of towns targeted by the German bombers; so in the spring of 1941 all that the papers could headline was 'Scots Tenements Hit' when whole streets had been engulfed in flames in the blitz on Clydebank and Glasgow and almost 1000 people had perished. Nor should it be forgotten that all the cleaners turned up for duty on the mornings after the raids – and all of them on time.

Every Friday was 'Comforts for the Troops' night. Veteran sub-editor Teddy Coutts and Archie McCallum ('Old Mac', the editorial commissionaire who taught us as boys to swear in Spanish, having been an engineer in the copper mines of Chile) went round the departments rattling collection cans and calling out 'Alms....Alms for the love of Allah!'

Rudolf Hess, Hitler's deputy, parachuted from his crashing Messerschmitt on to a field near Eaglesham in May 1941, seeking the Duke of Hamilton to ask him to convey a peace-offering message to the Government, and since that time almost every newspaper in the country has boasted about its part in the event. The *Daily Record*, for one, claimed to be the first to speak to the ploughman who had 'captured' Hess as the German landed, and the *Glasgow Herald* claimed that it knew the identity of the mystery airman before anyone else, because the Renfrew police had asked for – and been given – biographical details and pictures of Hess from the *Herald's* files.

The *Scottish Daily Express* certainly did not have the news first, but it is just as certain that no one else did. We all published a picture of the ploughman, David McLean, brandishing the pitchfork with which he held the airman at bay until the police arrived. Years afterwards he said, 'Someone just stuck a fork in my hand and took a picture'.

There is, however, one exclusive we COULD claim. One day Sandy Trotter was told, 'There's someone on the line from Largs asking to speak to you. Says he knows you.' The 'someone' was John Howard, whose brother Peter wrote the 'Crossbencher' column in the *Sunday Express*.

'Would you be interested in pictures of our little do?' he asked.

'Our little do' turned out to be the Lofoten Islands raid. Five hundred Commandos, together with some Norwegians, had landed on the islands at dawn on 4 March, 1941, destroyed a number of fish factories which had been making glycerine for explosives, and blew up shipping and a power station and fuel tanks. They brought back with them 200 prisoners, ten Quisling traitors, and 314 Norwegian volunteers anxious to fight the Germans.

The censors could scarcely see John Howard's pictures as other than helpful to public morale, and they were duly passed for publication.

At the end of the war the old guard ungrudgingly made room for the returning servicemen. It was May 1946 before I myself returned. My demob group number came up and went by, and went by again, because there were not enough of us in our section to deliver back to the USA the ships which they had built for us under Roosevelt's Lend-Lease deal. But when I eventually reported at 195 as available for duty, Sandy Trotter gave me a place on his Back Bench as Night Editor, alongside himself and Charlie MacNicol, who had become Assistant Editor

Several close comrades never came back at all: Donald Henderson, Bobby Thriepland, Bert Williamson (who could easily have stayed at his desk in Intelligence but chafed over inaction and lost his life in the RAF), Maurice McKenna (who was one of the unfortunates mistaken as enemy by our own planes as they ran out of prison camp), and my young brother Douglas, lost over Sicily in a bombing raid.

Isabel Sinclair, our girl among the graduate class of '32, carried on her career in law after the war and became Sheriff of the Lothians and of Lanarkshire. Andy Ewart continued his career in London, and Archie Lee became a BBC producer. Hector McNeil was appointed deputy to Ernest Bevin at the Foreign Office and latterly Secretary of State for Scotland.

Ian McColl might not have come back to Albion Street at all. He would surely have become Ian McColl, MP, if he had learned, or had the inclination, to play political poker. He was chosen as Liberal candidate for the Dumfriesshire seat in the first post-war General Election, and was given leave from the RAF to contest it. The seat had belonged to a National Liberal whom the local Tories found incompatible. Ian was asked by them if he would stand as a National Liberal, which would have guaranteed him Tory support and certain victory. When he refused to change his allegiance, the National Liberals summoned from Madagascar a Black Watch officer named Niall Macpherson, who won the seat.

Ian's tempters did not give up, however. There would be another occasion....

The 1940s

The U-boat commander who sighted the 15,000-ton liner Arandora Star through his periscope at 6 am on 2 July 1940, 75 miles west of Bloody Foreland, had no thought of who his victims might be – any more than had Kapitan-Leutnant Julius Lemp when he sank the Athenia on the day war broke out.

The torpedo which ripped open the hull of the Arandora Star sent 143 of the U-boat commander's fellow-countrymen to their deaths; she had been carrying 1178 Germans and Italians bound for internment camps in Canada.

The British troops guarding them had had to maintain constant vigilance to contain the hatred between the two groups. In the panic which followed the torpedo's explosion there was savage fighting between the Germans and the Italians to reach the lifeboats. Scores were forced overboard.

470 Italians and 143 Germans lost their lives; 91 British troops and 57 of the 300 crew also perished.

We saw the survivors landing two days later at Greenock, the town to which came most of the sea's human wreckage throughout the war years.

CHAPTER 10

White ankle socks to nylons

MOST PEOPLE WERE HAPPY to say goodbye to 1947. It had been a year of misery in which we had frozen amid power cuts, and we had thought food rations could fall no further – but they did. Yet it was the year when Edinburgh chose to sound a triumphal fanfare to herald the city's first International Festival of Music and Drama.

It was also a year of achievement for us, because on top of the 100,000 our Dad's Army had added to our circulation, we had piled on even more to go over the half million mark for the first time.

My time on the back bench had been rewarding and I was flattered to receive from Christiansen another invitation to join his staff in London, but I still felt more at home on the Newsroom side of the house. Sandy Trotter knew that I was restless, and when the News Editor, Donald Brown, was appointed assistant editor of the *Evening Citizen* at the beginning of 1948, I was given charge of the *Scottish Daily Express* news desk.

The reporting staff bequeathed by Donald Brown included a thrusting gang of old comrades not long back from the Forces – Bill Johnston, Ben Allison, Adam McKinlay, Jimmy Gordon and Jack Coupar (Davie Coupar's son). And among post-war crop of new recruits was a girl named Mamie Baird.

Mamie had an irrepressible sense of fun, and an engaging personality which gave her an immediate and unfair advantage over her male reporting rivals. The advantage extended to a disproportionate measure of talent, and for that assessment you need not take my word alone.

One morning towards the end of the war Mr James Cowper, the English master at Rutherglen Academy, came into his classroom carrying a pile of exercise books in which his pupils had written their essays, and he took one from the top of the pile and said, 'Sit up and listen to this.' Without identifying the owner of the jotter, he read aloud from it. At the end, he put it back on the pile and said, 'That, ladies and gentlemen, is writing. For that I'll forgive her anything. When I come into my room and find her tap-dancing on my desk, when I see her hurtling down the banisters in the school, I'll look the other way, because Mamie Baird can write.'

In her last year at school she wrote an indignant rebuttal of an article in the *Sunday Post* which had argued against raising the school leaving age to 16. Her five-page reply was printed as a very, very short Letter to the

Editor. While this provided a first object lesson in writing for newspapers ('Be brief, or the sub-editor will do it for you'), it also led to an interview with James Borthwick, the *Sunday Post*'s editor in Glasgow.

Mamie went to his office, dressed in the Rutherglen Academy uniform of light-blue skirt, blazer, blouse and tie, and wearing white ankle socks, and it was no surprise to us to learn that on the way she jumped over a litter bin on the edge of the pavement in busy Buchanan Street and was rebuked by her despairing mother, 'For goodness sake, try to behave like a lady!'

When Mr Borthwick asked her to submit a sample of her work she sent him the school essay, duly sub-edited by herself (having absorbed the primary lesson about writing for newspapers). It was printed in the Sunday Post's stable companion, the Glasgow Weekly News, earning her 15 shillings and an offer from Mr Borthwick of a post on both papers at a wage of £1 a week.

She did not graduate from white ankle socks to nylons (so she says) until the autumn of 1947, which was when she had come to us at Albion Street. She promptly ruined her nylons on the first assignment which she was given. She was sent to Balmoral to report the arrival there of Philip Prince of Greece, newly betrothed to Princess Elizabeth. Prince Philip had been invited by the Royal Family to join them there for the celebration of Princess Margaret's 17th birthday.

Mamie, arriving by bus from Aberdeen, parked herself outside the gates of Balmoral, prepared to wait there for however long it might take before Philip's arrival; but the only arrival was a detective on a bicycle who told her that although the road was public, she should be aware that her presence (for he knew that she was a reporter) was preventing the King from leaving to go out shooting on his estate.

The only place she could then find to 'see without being seen' was a field which, unfortunately, could only be approached from the opposite bank of the River Dee. The Dee did not seem too deep to wade across, but it was deep enough at one stage of the crossing to cause her to sink up to the armpits, and she had to lie in the field to dry with only Princess Margaret's pet pony Jock as company. That evening she was told on the telephone that there was no longer need to obstruct the King's shooting because Philip was arriving next day at Dyce airport. So off she went by bus to Aberdeen.

At the airport everyone stood back deferentially, but our young reporter was determined to interview the prince as he stepped from his plane. Unprepared as she was with questions, all she could think to ask was what plans he had for Princess Margaret's birthday party. Unprepared as he also was, he said, 'Oh, I have no doubt I shall wish her many happy returns of the day.'

Mamie Baird and her friend 'Jock',
Princess Margaret's pony

The deferential reporters (as all reporters were in front of Royalty in those days) were delighted with Philip's snappy reply, and eagerly recorded all his answers to Mamie's ingenuous questions on his way to his car. It was his first interview with the Press. In no time at all he would learn how to put nosey reporters in their place.

Mamie went back to Deeside in December after the royal wedding. The happy couple were to spend the second part of their honeymoon at the royal residence of Birkhall. All the Scots newspapers agreed with the Palace authorities that in exchange for one posed picture they would not disturb the couple thereafter. But there was nothing in the agreement concerning prior reporting, so Mamie was sent to Birkhall to describe the setting for the honeymoon.

There was no police officer guarding the driveway when she walked up to the massive front door and pushed the button of its electric bell. The noise it made was loud; but it became ever more clamorous when she found that the fur glove she had worn in the freezing cold was clinging tenaciously to the bell-push. Although she managed to wrench the glove free, some of the fur adhered and kept the bell ringing. One of the staff eventually came to the door, and when she identified herself and asked to be allowed to view the house she was courteously conducted through all the public rooms, 'just like a client sent by the estate agent', enabling her to write an exclusive description of the honeymoon retreat.

The bell only stopped ringing as she thanked her guides and prepared to leave. A Post Office repair van was already in the driveway, dealing with the broken bell.

Some years later she met Prince Philip and told him of the incident. 'What do you mean, a Post Office van?' he said. 'We had our own repair van'.

It was an unimportant detail as far as Mamie was concerned. She never wrote about the broken bell. She had been trained to write, impersonally, about what happened to others, and never to include herself. The scrapes she often got into in her determination to get the story she had been assigned were reserved for after-dinner speeches. Sandy Trotter always said that she was a reporter born and bred, and although she became a feature writer towards the end of her newspaper career, she maintains that she always tried to keep the word 'I' out of her articles.

Another in the post-war intake of staff was Andrew (Drew) Rennie, who joined as our staff reporter in Fife after service in the Guards. He was brought over to the Glasgow office in 1949, and proceeded to write his name large among us for the next 20 years. Drew, a native of Fife, brought with him the story of the fabulous 'Talking Dog of Ceres'.

Bubbles was a Pekinese with a throat disorder which caused her to answer questions with sounds like a human saying 'Yes' or 'No'. The story aroused country-wide interest. Surprisingly many people claimed, on reading of the Talking Dog, that their pets, too, were able to communicate intelligibly with them.

The story also aroused the curiosity of MacDonald Daly, the editor of the *Sunday Express* in Scotland, who happened to be a dog breeder and a judge at Cruft's Dog Shows. He asked Drew to bring Bubbles to meet a panel of his fellow dog judges, but when Bubbles was placed on a table before them and commanded to answer their questions, the poor animal became dumb with fright.

Fortunately, in the comfort and friendly atmosphere of her cottage home in Fife, Bubbles recovered, and we were able to record a conversation between her and another talking dog which we located in Sheffield.

But however one favours the good, the happy, news stories, tragedy is never far away in newspapers. The most horrendous fire since the Glen Cinema disaster in Paisley happened on 4 May, 1949, in Grafton's Gown Shop in Argyle Street where so many Glasgow brides-to-be shopped and young girls chose dresses for special occasions. It took 13 young lives.

The horror of the Paisley Cinema fire on New Year's Eve, 1929, had been imprinted on Gilbert Cole's mind by reason of a particular picture. But I remember the Grafton's Gown Shop fire most because a picture was missed – and no one regretted it. Thirty young assistants were taking a tea break in the stockroom when one of them opened a door leading to a stairway and a moment later the room was engulfed in flames. Twelve of the girls never got out of the room.

The photographer at the scene was 23-year-old Bill Johnston, who was primarily on *Evening Citizen* rota duty (when paired in the same team with reporter Bill Johnston he was distinguished as (W.M.) Johnston and the other Bill as (W.T.G.) Johnston). Argyle Street was no more than a few blocks away from our office, and Bill was in time to take pictures of two men and four girls crawling along a narrow ledge towards safety on the roof of the adjoining Argyle Cinema, which had been cleared when the alarm was raised. But he arrived just after a young girl had leapt to her death from the 60-foot-high roof of the shop in a despairing bid to escape.

Perhaps it was as well he had not seen her. It is the instinct of all photographers to keep shooting pictures in all circumstances and to worry

One girl is rescued from the gown shop blaze,... 13 of her colleagues died

afterwards if need be – or ask his editor to worry. Mercifully, we were not faced with the question of whether or not to print the picture that never was. Nowadays, as we all know, it is not unusual to see on television death-leap pictures in fires or other disasters. These are seemingly considered acceptable so long as they have happened in Shanghai or Manila or Tokyo or in some other far-off parts. But could we some day find that Argyle Street, Glasgow, is no further away than Tokyo?

Throughout all this time I was not being missed from the Back Bench, my absence being more than compensated by the presence there of Ian McColl. Ian, however, was once again almost lost to us. In the General Election of 1950 he was invited by the Liberal Party to contest the Greenock seat. That seat was held, of course, by Hector McNeil, who by then had been elevated to the Cabinet as Secretary of State for Scotland.

Ian's reluctance to stand against his old colleague was only overcome by Hector's insistence that he 'come and fight the good fight'. For a second time he was urged to adopt the National Liberal label and thereby be assured of Tory support, and again he refused, telling them that while he would always 'oppose Socialism', he would not change his colours in the split Liberal Party. Most of the Tories accepted his decision, but J.S. Thomson, an enterprising and influential and well-liked local business man, did not. He stood as an 'Independent' advocating a coalition government under Winston Churchill; Ian McColl came second, but Hector McNeil won the election with a vote only slightly larger than the combined votes of the other candidates.

When Ian McColl returned from the campaign, Sandy Trotter told him that Lord Beaverbrook had remarked, 'That young man should determine whether his future lies in newspapers or in politics'. Ian decided to concentrate his talents on journalism, and the loss, I am sure, was Parliament's.

Labour was defeated in the General Election and Hector McNeil lost his Cabinet seat, but he continued as MP for Greenock until 1953 when, during a visit to New York, he collapsed suddenly and died.

The 1950s

The reporter's life was a world away from the disciplines of business, office or factory. There was a tacit understanding that a reporter in pursuit of a hot scoop would spend more freely than could perhaps be strictly justified. As long as the credulity of the accountant was not taxed too far, editor and management alike took a relatively tolerant view of inflated expense sheets.

On one occasion, Ben Allison submitted an account which included the item 'To lunch with the noted advocate R L Stevenson'. The sheet was duly passed by his news editor, Jack Coupar, initialled by me and then by the editor, Sandy Trotter, and thereafter passed by management.

Ben managed to secure a copy of this sheet, which he would exhibit for years afterwards as a triumphant example of one of the more esoteric art-forms in the reporter's portfolio.

Not so fortunate was a rival reporter from the south during the search in Tobermory Bay for the alleged 'treasure ship' of the Spanish Armada. He claimed the daily charter of a launch to take him to the scene of operations. A television news team was also covering the search. In one panoramic sweep of Tobermory Bay, the camera rested on a tiny rowing-boat whose oars were being plied by the distinctive figure of the enterprising reporter....

The ragamuffins

IN THE 1950S, EVENTS seemed to come marching in double-quick time.

A Lascar seaman named Mussa Ali was landed from his ship in the Clyde in the spring of 1950 and was admitted to Knightswood Hospital as 'an unusual case of chickenpox.' Mussa Ali was 39 years old, a humble and timid little man who constantly apologised for being a bother, and the nurses who were sorry for him kept reassuring him and slipping him the cigarettes he craved and could not afford. When the rash cleared up he was discharged. Four days later he was rushed to Robroyston fever hospital – he was carrying the dreaded germ which no microscope could detect. He had smallpox.

A massive screening operation began, to trace everyone who had had contact with him, and then to find everyone who had had contact with the original contacts. Twenty volunteer doctors and nurses and porters and maids were sealed with the patients inside Robroyston's isolation compound. Their only link with the outside world was a telephone. They wore second-hand (or third-hand) suits and dresses, torn stockings and down-at-heel shoes, because whatever they wore would eventually be burned. They called themselves 'The Ragamuffins'.

Everywhere in the outside world, people lived in fear of the invisible danger: who knew if the salesgirl in the shop was a carrier, or the stranger waiting beside you at the bus-stop, or even your neighbour? More than 300,000 people queued to be vaccinated.

Only Ben Allison could have secured Mussa Ali's passport picture, enabling us to front-page it as 'The Cause Of It All'. The timid little Lascar seaman survived; but seven others did not. Among the victims was Janet Fleming, a 29-year-old doctor. She died on 8 April, just one week before the emergency was officially declared over.

It was Ben Allison (of course!) who secured the only picture to be published of this heroine of the plague, too. He was on Saturday duty for the Sunday Express when he interviewed her family at their home in Hamilton, leaving the house just before it was sealed by the health authorities.

MacDonald Daly, the editor of the *Sunday Express* in Scotland, was delighted to learn of the exclusive picture, but was less entranced to discover where it had been obtained. He ordered Ben to send in his report by telephone, and to leave the picture at the office entrance in Albion Street. On no account was he to enter the building.

Sandy Trotter endorsed MacDonald Daly's cautious judgment. So Ben was left outside the *cordon sanitaire* and barred from Albion Street throughout the following week. He spent the time at the Press Club (where, he said, smallpox was not a notifiable disease), playing snooker with whoever was prepared to risk exposure, and communicating with the office only to ask for his expenses.

CHAPTER 12

The miracle of Knockshinnoch

OUR REPORTING STAFF NEVER totalled much more than a dozen (our population explosion came in the plenteous era of the 60s) but we rallied everyone we could muster when we heard what had happened at Knockshinnoch Castle Colliery, in Ayrshire, on the afternoon of 7 September, 1950.

Above the men working at No 5 Heading, storms whipped sweet Afton's waters into flood and rain fell relentlessly on the fields, soaking them like sponges until, in one of them, the ground sank and thousands of tons of moss and sludge poured down through a crater to the mine-shaft below. Eight men reached the surface. No one knew where the others were.

What followed was a miracle scripted by human endeavour. The pity is that it all had to be recorded within the cramped compass of our still paltry papers, at the fag-end of newsprint rationing.

Our squad was headed by Jack Coupar and Drew Rennie, whose job was to organise the news operation on the spot, set up an *ad hoc* News Desk operation, allocate tasks to the group and telephone to report important developments as well as at fixed times geared to copy deadlines for the different editions of the paper.

Among those who went with them were Mamie Baird and our chief photographer, Albert Barr, with two other photographers and a mobile 'telephoto unit' for sending back pictures by wire. They were joined at the scene by Jimmy Ballantyne, our staff man from Ayr.

Our first mobile News Desk was set up in a farmhouse near the colliery, and everyone ate and slept there as and when they could for the next three days. From the *Evening Citizen* they were later joined by Ian Forbes and photographer Bill Johnston.

Our squad arrived in the gloaming as scores of helpers were stopping up the crater with pit props and branches of trees and straw and whatever else lay to hand. No one could tell whether any besides the fortunate eight had survived. It was not until after 10 pm that we found out – the men had been mustered by their overseer, Andrew Houston, at the West Mine telephone station: 116 trapped men had answered his roll-call; 13 were missing.

From West Mine a tunnel ran into the Castle workings. It was blocked. Behind the trapped men was a wall of mud; in front of them was a wall of coal. They had no hope of escaping by themselves.

At 3 am, a message chattered out on our Creed machines from the Press Association. It said that one of mining's worst-ever calamities seemed inevitable. But then came a chink of light: officials poring over maps found a barrier of just 24 feet of coal separating the men from some abandoned workings in Bank 6.

That was the encouraging news. But to everyone's dismay, along the way to that barrier of coal was a 400-yard-long cloud of poisonous gas. Fans were set up on the perimeter of the cloud to try to disperse it. Our late editions that morning could tell only of the long wait to find out if that cloud could be dispersed.

At daylight, hope rose: the fans had cleared enough of the gas to enable a squad to reach the 24-foot-barrier, and to allow the men on both sides to start digging. Then at 11 am the pithead hooter sounded, to signal that a hole had been bored, allowing a squad of rescuers to go through wearing a hitherto untried type of breathing apparatus.

The 116 men who had subsisted for 34 hours on dirty and mouldy crusts and had slaked their thirst by moistening their lips with polluted water, had food and drink at last and – so they believed – deliverance.

But deliverance was not yet at hand. David Park, a Coal Board official, went in with a second squad to tell the trapped men that the gas was still too dense to allow them to risk leaving, and he elected to stay with them.

All through that Saturday of 9 September the amount of gas rose and fell and rose again, until at 11 am, during a sudden drop in the volume of gas, a squad went in with their untried respirators. They brought out on a stretcher a 19-year-old miner who was so ill and so desperately exhausted that he could not have lasted much longer.

After that – nothing, until six hours later the young boy's companions, fitted with the new respirators, one by one crawled through the narrow hole and came out in Indian file, stooping and stumbling through the gas to the 'fresh air base'. From there they went for half a mile along a route lit at intervals by volunteers who knew that one faulty lamp among them could cause disaster.

The rescue took seven long hours. At midnight Drew Rennie telephoned to say that the last of the 116 trapped men had reached the surface safely. He was the Coal Board official, David Park.

But there were 13 men still missing, and by nightfall on Monday, all hope for their survival had to be abandoned, and 13 families were left to mourn – 13 more homes at which to call, to offer sympathy, to be received as ever with dignity and understanding, to be given a photograph and a sentence or two to quote in a few lines of print as the only obituary the families would have of a lost one.

'Go in on tiptoe...' That was what Dave Smith had once taught me as the key to sympathetic journalism. But that wasn't always possible in the thick of things. The hundreds of relatives and friends and neighbours who waited at the pithead at Knockshinnoch could only watch, helpless to do anything else. In their frustration, one small group turned on the newspapermen who were among the crowd and the police had to intervene on their behalf. Even among the police on duty, patience grew thin, particularly towards the photographers.

'No matter how respectful and unobtrusive we tried to be, we seemed to them to be everywhere,' said Bill Johnston. 'And indeed we were. It was impossible not to sympathise with them, even though three of them threw me out of the canteen which the Salvation Army had set up. I landed at the foot of a flight of steps minus one Wellington boot and minus a new flash camera which, luckily, a Sally girl rescued for me later.'

Today, we still have this difficult problem to address, a problem which has been compounded by the ubiquitous presence of TV camera crews – and we have as yet not found the answer.

Two reporters from the old *Evening News*, Eric Sewell and Charlie Smith, contrived to be allowed to attach themselves to volunteers at Bank 6. They did not stay underground for long. Charlie Smith was soon choking, but they were down there long enough to appreciate what it was like, and for Eric Sewell to write an article which he entitled 'The Price of a Bag of Coal'.

What he wrote was unashamedly emotive. But then, there never had been an event in which we felt ourselves so emotionally involved – and that included even those back at the office who awaited every telephone call – nor one in which we felt so humbly aware of the terrible tragedies we were called upon so often to report.

CHAPTER 13

The Destiny Stone

SOON AFTER THE KNOCKSHINNOCH tragedy came a story which Scotland's newspapermen pursued with more curiosity than enthusiasm, because of what we feared would be its outcome – the search for the Stone of Destiny.

The Destiny Stone is just a 2½ hundredweight chunk of rock, a rectangular slab of sandstone. Just? Ah, but legend has it that it had been the pillar on which Jacob dreamed at Bethel, that it had been brought to Scotland by Scota (daughter of the Pharaoh from whom the Scots derived their name), and that not only could no one reign unless he or she had sat upon it to be crowned, but that so long as it remained in Scotland the land would stay in the possession of the Scots.

Whether or not King Edward 1 of England in 1296 accepted that it was a magic stone, he sought to ensure that no Scot should sit on it to become king, and he removed it from its resting place at Scone as a humiliation to the Scots; and no matter that it was claimed that the wily abbot of Dunstaffnage had palmed off on Edward an ordinary building stone, it had stayed at Westminster Abbey thereafter underneath the chair on which all monarchs sat to be crowned – that is, until Christmas Day, 1950.

The daring raid on Westminster Abbey has been well documented. It was carried out by three patriotic young Glasgow University students – Ian Hamilton (now a QC), Gavin Vernon and Alan Stewart – and Kay Mathieson, a teacher of domestic science.

When the whole story was eventually revealed, it proved the very stuff of adventure; at one stage of the raid Ian Hamilton and Kay Mathieson sat in a car outside the Abbey engaged in conversation with an inquisitive policeman, persuading him that they were romantic lovers, while all the time the Stone lay on the car's rear seat covered loosely by an overcoat.

The episode stirred deep and contrary emotions; among most Scots there was perverse pleasure at seeing the discomfiture of authority, but there was outraged condemnation by our own anglicised Establishment, and anger in high places in England.

The search conducted by Scotland Yard was frenetic; they even dragged the Serpentine. It was also incompetent; they ignored clues (during the raid, for instance, different officers had taken note of Ian Hamilton's driving licence, and of Gavin Vernon's name in a hired car receipt).

In Glasgow the search was the responsibility of Detective Chief Inspector Willie Kerr, head of the Special Branch in Scotland. Willie needed to find the raiders in order to find the Stone. Whether he and his fellow officers were anxious to turn them over to Scotland Yard and so for trial is another matter. We rather thought they did not. For our part, we and every other newspaper wanted to find them, too, so that they could tell their story.

Two years earlier, John MacCormick, our night duty lawyer of pre-war years, had launched the Scottish Covenant, calling for a Scottish Parliament to deal with Scottish affairs, and two million Scots had signed it. It was as obvious to us as it was to the Glasgow police that whether or not he and the Covenant vice-president, Councillor Bertie Gray, had any direct part in the exploit, they probably knew who did.

It was also obvious that if the raid had been carried out by Covenant supporters they must have been of the younger fraternity, for the leaders of the movement had always insisted on 'a reasonable constitutional approach' to their goal. So students were the most obvious targets, particularly those who had campaigned for John MacCormick when he won election as Rector of Glasgow University.

John MacCormick made himself readily available to all callers, whether reporters or police. He could not have had much time left to devote to his law work; I cannot remember how many times I trudged up to his office to see him with scraps of information or flights of fancy (as did countless others), to discuss various possibilities which we might print. If the police had paid attention to everything we and the other papers wrote, they must have been lost in a fog thicker than a London pea-souper.

Ian Hamilton himself has said that Tom Dawson of the *Daily Mail* could have blown his cover and printed the greatest exclusive of his career, but loyally kept silent; and he believed that others could have unearthed and printed evidence which would have exposed him and his comrades, but did not do so. I would not claim that we came as close as did Tom Dawson, but we were content to play John MacCormick's game and contribute to the fog. One of our staff was said afterwards to have stayed at one time in the same lodgings as one of the students; but if he did he certainly did not say so to me nor to anyone I know, and since he is now dead we shall never know.

The farcical search for the Stone went on for three months. The Yard sent a team to Scotland to interview suspects, but the three students on whom they concentrated their enquires countered every question. The game of bluff and counter-bluff could have lasted much longer if it had not become clear that King George was as upset as the Dean of Westminster alleged, and that he really seemed to believe that the loss of the Stone could presage the end of his royal house.

The war had ended just five years earlier, a war in which the king had shared with his subjects as best he could their hardships and dangers, and he was held in deep affection. Two petitions had been sent addressed to the king (the first, to our chagrin, was delivered to the *Daily Record!*), offering to return the Stone if it could be kept in Scotland for the future except for coronations at Westminster.

On the morning of 11 April the custodian of historic Arbroath Abbey found the Stone lying on the High Altar, draped in Scotland's national flag of St Andrew. We were tipped off by telephone, but while Mamie Baird was being driven to Arbroath at breakneck speed, the Stone was being rushed to Glasgow police headquarters, still wrapped in the flag, and reporters were invited to view it before it was taken south with what many saw as unseemly haste.

The Press conference was attended by the detectives from Scotland Yard who had led the unavailing search and who would take the Stone back to London. The first – and only – question was asked by Jimmy Donnelly of the *Evening Citizen*: 'Are you in touch with those who delivered the Stone?' It sent the detectives into a huddled discussion, at the end of which the reply was: 'We would prefer not to answer that question'.

The last newspaperman to see the Stone before it went back to Westminster Abbey was a 16-year-old copy-boy on the *Evening Citizen,* Stuart McCartney. After he had ended his day's duty he went to police

headquarters in Turnbull Street to go home with his father, Chief Inspector Bob McCartney, who was in charge of the city centre.

'Come and I'll show you a bit of history,' said his father, leading the boy along a corridor. At the end was the room occupied by Chief Superintendent Willie Ewing, the head of the CID.

'When the door of the room opened I saw the Stone lying on the floor,' Stuart was later to recall. 'It had brown paper on it, and I think it was on a pallet – I don't properly remember now. I got the impression that the squad just felt relieved that the Stone had been found. I was very young at the time and did not fully appreciate that I was looking at a part of Scotland's tradition. My father said, "You can give it a wee pat, if you like". So I did.'

The Stone of Destiny is carried away from Arbroath Abbey, to be hurried south to Westminster Abbey

The Stone which went to London came back across the Border 46 years later, to lie with the Honours of Scotland in Edinburgh Castle, on condition that it can be borrowed for any future coronation ceremony at Westminster. But psst! There have been so many suspected sleights of hand in this merry game that it would take a magician to know if whoever is crowned is sitting on the true and original Destiny Stone.

In the spring of that year, Sandy Trotter told me that I was to be seconded to London for a time, but he could not tell me why (or he had been enjoined not to say why); and, just as intriguingly, there was no explanation forthcoming when I arrived in London.

I met the Beaver then for the first, and only, time. I had no way of knowing whether being taken to see him was to be of significance for my future. On the way to his eyrie, I hoped he would not ask me about my political beliefs (for these were rather nebulous) or my religious beliefs. The bizarre thought occurred that if (stern Presbyterian that he was) he should ask if I knew my Catechism, the only thing I could remember was the first question and answer: 'What is the chief end of Man?' Answer: 'Man's chief end is to glorify God and to enjoy Him forever.'

Lord Beaverbrook did not ask me about the Catechism. He asked me very little, in fact, and whatever he did ask I don't now remember, so the interview must have made as little impression on me as it did on him. Perhaps he was too engrossed in the pile of newspapers propped on his lectern; or perhaps he surveyed this specimen and decided at a glance, as he had done with Hardie Stewart, that he did not like the look of me.

In the second week I was taken on to the London back bench. It was a frenetic time, for the submarine *Affray*, wildly off course, had dived in the English Channel and was missing with 75 men on board. It was feared that her air supplies would not last for long enough to save the crew unless she were found quickly (she was located two months afterwards, in 258 feet of water, with faulty breathing tubes). Several of us were passing possible Page One banner headlines to Christiansen's deputy, Ted (later Sir Edward) Pickering, when I was taken aside to talk to Chris in his room. He said he had to tell me that Charlie MacNicol (who had already had a major heart attack) had suffered another setback. I was sorry to hear it, and suddenly felt warmth for the grumpy old bear.

Chris went on: 'You will know, or you will have guessed' (I had done neither) 'why you are here. You may be offered a position with the *Sunday Express*. But although we hope that Mac will soon be better, we don't know how long he will be lost to us and I would like you to go back to Glasgow instead as Sandy Trotter's Managing Editor.'

Of course, I agreed. So I went back to dwell once more in the tents of the righteous.

The term 'Managing Editor' can mean fulfilling one of several roles.

I had supposed I would revert to the back bench, but Sandy Trotter had different ideas. I was to act, in effect, as his deputy during the day, while Ian McColl was in charge of the paper during the night.

I hope I was not too much of a nuisance in my daytime role to Jack Coupar, who took over the day News Desk from me. If I was, at least he never showed it.

Charlie MacNicol, who had been one of the 'midwives' at the birth of the paper in 1928, died the following year, in May 1952, and we helped to throng the church at his Requiem Mass. Chief Sub-editors are the sergeant majors of newspapers; the young hate their guts, and remember them with gratitude only when they have passed out on parade as men. Ask Charlie MacNicol's son, Ian MacNicol. Ian was one of the generation drilled by James MacCausland, for whom typography was a branch of magic of which he was acknowledged as Supreme Wizard – but who was also the most authoritarian of perfectionists known to young sub-editors.

CHAPTER 14

Is that all right? the Queen asked

THE MOST MEMORABLE ROYAL family picture to mark Princess Margaret's 21st birthday was not taken by any of the fashionable circle of royal photographers, but by our own Chief Photographer, Albert Barr.

Albert and his wife Emily were my closest companions for many years. Emily had a heart as big as a house, and her house was open to everyone and home to many strays. The cats were named the Major, (the first arrival), the Lieutenant and the Sergeant and so on, in descending order of rank.

If Albert was not born with a camera in his hand, he certainly grew up with one. His father Matthew was famed as Glasgow's pioneer press photographer. The pictures he took during a lifetime with the *Evening Citizen* would have formed an important part of Glasgow's pictorial history, including the infamous Oscar Slater trial, had they not been lost during the removal of the *Citizen* from St Vincent Place to Albion Street in 1940.

As soon as Albert was old enough he followed his father into the *Evening Citizen*. On his return from wartime service, in which he went on taking pictures on reconnaissance with the RAF, he and his *Citizen* colleagues were merged with our photographers on the *Express* to form a single unit, operating on rota for the two papers.

No one ever needed to exaggerate Albert Barr's exploits, such was the legend he became among us. News photographers, as distinct from the foxy paparazzi, were a distinctively remarkable breed, often more tenacious and more daring than their reporting colleagues; and of that breed I hold the corps of which Albert was commander and role model as the most remarkable of all.

The first major story he covered for us was when a US Superfortress plane crashed during snowstorm into a hill at the top of Succoth Glen in Argyll. For six frustrating days no recovery party could reach the plane and its 20 airmen. But it was known all 20 were dead, because Albert and his cameraman colleague, Bill Johnston, along with a doctor and a policeman, had already been there.

Albert was over six feet tall, and of impressive bulk. His younger companion, Bill Johnston, was just as tall, and just as fit as he had been when he was demobbed from the Guards. But when they set off up Succoth Glen, with their cameras strapped to their backs, both were wearing street shoes, lounge suits and light raincoats. They sank knee deep in the snow, and waded, often waist deep, through streams and marshes, battered by icy wind, slithering and falling until they reached the hill, which they then had to climb. When they reached the top, on their hands and knees, they found there only a black scar which once had been a plane, and the doctor in their group saying, 'No, there is really nothing we can do here.'

In August 1951, teams of reporters and photographers from every newspaper and pictorial magazine, including the élite of Fleet Street's cameramen, and invaders from the Continent, descended on Deeside for Princess Margaret's 21st birthday celebrations, and every morning and afternoon for a week they roamed the picnic areas on the moors around Balmoral, hoping to see the royal family and thereby pre-empt the official birthday picture which was expected to be issued to everyone on the day itself.

Albert Barr and Mamie Baird were our team. One of their rivals, from the *Daily Mirror*, went on a scout in an open touring car, standing up in it with massive binoculars to sweep the surrounding moors like some wartime Army commander. But neither he nor any other found any trace of the royal party.

On 20 August, with one day remaining, the search parties interrupted the hunt to take lunch as usual at the Royal Hotel in Ballater. Albert Barr resented the interlude. As everyone went into the lounge to take after-lunch coffee, he implored Mamie to forego the luxury and leave at once to resume the search. His impatience was rewarded just ten minutes after they left the hotel and moved off across the moors around Balmoral.

The royal party had set out from the Castle by car, but its members were leaving it at intervals to walk, and Albert and Mamie came across them as they were walking across a little bridge on a road near Loch Muick. The Queen was wearing a long tartan skirt and jacket, and for the walk had resorted to a Greta Garbo type of slouch hat and sling-back shoes. The two princesses also wore tartan skirts and jackets, and Princess Elizabeth had added a head scarf. The only one in the party who was not in tartan was the male equerry, who was wearing plus fours.

The *Express* car stopped abruptly. It is doubtful which of the groups was the more surprised. But whatever protocol may have demanded of such circumstances, Albert was in too much haste to ponder. He jumped out of the car and approached his illustrious quarry with camera poised.

All Albert was thinking about was the composition of his picture. But no one else was. Princess Margaret detached herself from the royal group to come and peer into the press car, exclaiming over all the camera equipment in it. Albert was in no mood for the normal courtesies: he wanted to get his picture and get away before any rivals appeared on the scene.

'He wasn't in the least bit embarrassed,' said Mamie, 'but I was, and rather apologetically I said something to the effect that we hoped they wouldn't mind if we took a picture to celebrate the birthday of the princess.'

The Queen could not have been more gracious. 'Of course not,' she said, and marshalled her straggling party immediately, bringing even the exuberant Margaret to order, and then marched them forward, with herself and the princess at the head, calling out, 'Is that alright?'

Albert was too busy to do anything but nod; he had not, in fact, waited for permission, gracious or otherwise. The picture which the Queen organised was a bonus – and what a bonus! Albert was now in a fever to see them depart the scene before any of the opposition turned up, and was intensely relieved when the royal party drove away.

Back at the hotel that evening Albert could scarcely restrain the temptation to proclaim his triumph. But he could at least drop hints about it, and as he stood them all a round of drinks at the bar he said, 'You've all had it!' He refused to be drawn further, however, and the other

World exclusive for Chief Photographer Albert Barr... Princess Elizabeth (on left) and Princess Margaret (on right next to her mother) point accusing fingers at Albert Barr and Mamie Baird. The man with his back to the camera is Peter Townsend... Not even the *Express* knew that at that time he and Princess Margaret were already embarked on their doomed love affair

photographers could only hope that he was fooling them. It was only when he knew the first editions had been printed that he told them it had been no joke.

Albert's bonus for the exclusive picture was £5 (Mamie was given the same amount), although it must have made a little fortune for our syndication department in London. The picture went all round the world, and many times over: the only man in the photograph, the one in the plus fours, was the equerry, the unhappily-married Group Captain Peter Townsend, whose headlong romance with Princess Margaret was to end in tears for them both.

In July 1953, as Princess Margaret was scheduled to leave with the Queen Mother on an African tour, it was announced at the last moment that Group Captain Townsend would not be accompanying them. Then, in October 1955, the princess announced she had decided not to marry him: 'Mindful of the Church's teaching that Christian marriage is indissoluble. and conscious of my duty to the Commonwealth. I have resolved to put this consideration above all other,' she said...

Mamie Baird went to Benbecula in the following spring and ended up being pictured on the pages of our rival papers.

Benbecula barely justifies its description as an island; it is squeezed so tightly between the Uists that you can almost spit across to North Uist at one end and to South Uist at the other. In the guide books it is noted as the place where Flora MacDonald sheltered the fugitive Bonnie Prince Charlie from his pursuers, but that is a very old story and Benbecula had never registered at all in the Richter scale of newspapers attention until in May 1952, at a place we had never heard of, 43-year-old Mrs Catherine Campbell gave birth to girl triplets in a cottage which had neither electricity nor running hot water.

The tiny township of Eochar, where Dr George MacKinnon delivered little Mary Catherine, Theresa Maria and Christine Anne, was not even listed in any gazetteer, nor located on any map when we looked for it, but it was readily accessible. Or it might have been, had there been an air service on that Sunday to the little Benbecula airport which served the two Uists.

The first plane was scheduled to leave on Monday morning, and everyone was booked on to it – everyone except us, that is. We phoned Mamie Baird and warned her to be ready to join our chartered Rapide plane at dawn, together with photographer Bill Sykes and a telephoto operator. When they landed at Benbecula airport and went in a hired car to the cottage, they found Dr MacKinnon tending the mother and babies, and everyone (including the husband, crofter Angus Campbell) in a state of great excitement – none more so than the couple's seven other children, four of whom were by his previous marriage.

The doctor said the babies should go to hospital in Glasgow, but no air ambulance had been arranged. Mamie said later, 'I asked him, half-jokingly, why he needed an air ambulance – there was plenty of room in our plane.' 'The very thing!' he replied.

'I didn't know as much about babies then as I do now,' said Mamie, 'but I realised that we were assuming a great responsibility, and I said the mother would probably need to come too. The doctor agreed. This left the pilot very worried. He would need oxygen, he said, in case he had to fly at high altitude at any time during the journey. So the doctor telephoned the cottage hospital, and two large cylinders arrived, in the charge of an imposingly large nursing nun who said she would be flying with us. The local priest arrived, too.'

Mamie Baird holding two of the Benbecula triplets as she flew them home
from hospital to their island home

The priest was the late, much-loved, Father John Morrison. 'He was greatly amused when he saw that the rug which the district nurse was carrying to wrap the Campbell babies in was in the MacDonald tartan,' said Mamie. 'He took the mother, the babies and the nurse in his car, and I joined them – there was no way I was going to be separated from them. Bill Sykes, the wire man, the pilot and the nun came in the hired car. All the way to the airport, Father Morrison was singing 'The Campbells are coming'.

'During the flight the pilot radioed to Renfrew airport to request an ambulance to meet us. I knew that the freelance reporter who covered the airport would alert all the other papers, but I was not going to let them have any part of my exclusive. So I asked the nurse, 'Do you mind if I carry the babies off the plane?' and she agreed. We landed at Renfrew after a 40-minute flight and the plane taxied up to the waiting ambulance.

'When I stepped off the plane with the babies in my arms there was a great burst of flashlights from the assembled photographers. The only one who didn't take a picture was Bill Sykes. He had been taking photographs at the cottage and all the way over. Maybe he had run out of flashbulbs.

'I had a great story to write about how I brought the babies to hospital in Glasgow, but there was consternation when it was realised that we didn't have a picture at the airport. The other papers were not in the least put out: in both the *Record* and the *Daily Mail* I was pictured as 'the 42-year-old mother of the triplets' arriving with them at the airport after her harrowing journey from the islands!'

CHAPTER 15

Never on a Sunday

IT WAS ALREADY LATE summer when John Cobb, holder of the world land-speed record, came north to Loch Ness with his jet-propelled boat *Crusader* in a bid to become the fastest man on water. And perhaps it was too late in the year.

He set up base with his 30-man team at the hamlet of Drumnadrochit on the inlet of Urquhart Bay. His 30-year-old wife Nicky came with him. Reporter Bill Allison and photographer Bill Johnston booked into the local hotel two days before Cobb's arrival, expecting to stay for a few days. The few days lasted five weeks, and they came to know him well during that time.

John Cobb was 52 years old, 'A big man, over six feet tall, with a surprisingly quiet voice. So diffident,' said Bill Johnston – 'the sort you'd never expect to see hurtling over the water at breakneck speed; he looked like someone who ought to be sitting in a little punt with a fly-rod in his hand, trying to catch trout. He never once turned away the crowds of people who wanted to see *Crusader*, and even to sit in it. The young Princes Richard and Michael of Gloucester clambered all over it to their hearts' content.'

Crusader went into the water on tests several times during those five weeks, but never on a Sunday, although on at least two Sundays the weather could have allowed the record bid. The racing driver told Malcolm (later Sir Malcolm) McCulloch, the then chief constable of Glasgow, who had arrived on holiday, 'I promised to respect the Scottish Sabbath day of rest.'

On Sunday, 28 September, 1952, Loch Ness was calm, and he decided that if it remained so he would make his attempt the following day. On Monday it was still calm. At daybreak he took *Crusader* onto the loch and waited for a radio report of wind and surface conditions over the measured mile. Before he left the jetty he thought he detected a ripple on the water; but at noon he nevertheless began his run.

While his wife Nicky watched from the shore with binoculars, he took his speedboat thundering up the north run at an average of 206 miles an hour, touching 240 at one point. Bill Johnston kept his camera focused on the boat, and continued to do so as it slackened speed to turn and begin the second run which was needed to make the record attempt official.

John Cobb... he made a promise

Bill Allison saw three sudden V-shaped ripples before the bow dipped. *Crusader* vanished amid a cloud of spray. When the cloud cleared there were just a few pathetic scraps of wreckage where the boat had been, and John Cobb lay half-submerged in the water fifty yards away.

Bill Allison was in the boat which reached him first and pulled him on board. As they sought to revive him he mumbled a few words. But when he was landed back at the jetty it was obvious that nothing could be done for him.

Both the reporter and the photographer ever afterwards wondered whether, had John Cobb been other than a most sensitive man, he would have chosen one of those calm Sabbath days rather than the one he did when he drove to his death. Experts later theorised that those V shaped ripples had set up a resonance on the hull which caused the wreck.

'Whatever the cause, I believe he made the attempt just because he could not bring himself to wait any longer. He was driven by frustration,' said Bill Johnston.

We had other pictures as reserve for Bill's. Among the crowd watching from a bluff above the loch was the son of Lord Provost Wotherspoon of Inverness. Sandy Trotter never had any compunction about using his friendships as occasion warranted in the service of his paper. So when the Lord Provost, who was his colleague on the Tourist Board, telephoned to say that his son had filmed the scene, he gave him '3 1/2 hours at the most' to drive in his Rolls Royce to Glasgow to meet the first edition deadline with the film – and the Lord Provost arrived with time to spare.

Actually, his journey proved not to have been necessary, for Bill had captured on camera every second of that fateful run. But it was very nice of the Lord Provost, and we were very grateful to him.

CHAPTER 16

The Princess Victoria disaster

For most people who are old enough to remember, 1953 was Coronation Year – a time to wave flags and to be joyful. But it began with disaster.

On the morning of Saturday, the last day of January, photographer Bill Johnston came on duty for the *Sunday Express*, expecting to be sent to a football match. But the early radio bulletin had reported that a hurricane had hit the north of Scotland, and he and reporter Ian Forbes were detailed to fly north to record what damage had been done. They returned to Albion Street from the airport to say that the pilot had declared – quite rightly – that the weather was too dangerous for flying.

Brendan Kemmet, the *Sunday Express* news editor, was disappointed. But he was determined not to give up: it seemed that there was a ship in distress in the Irish Sea, and surely the pilot could reach THERE with them?

The ship was the Stranraer to Larne car ferry *Princess Victoria*, carrying a crew of 49 and 127 passengers. Her first SOS was sent by radio operator David Broadfoot two hours after she left Stranraer harbour and headed up to the top of Loch Ryan, and thence into the Irish Sea.

David Broadfoot's radio telephone was linked to the shore, but not to other ships. His message to Portpatrick radio station said the ship was hove to at the mouth of the loch and that she 'was not under command'. In fact, when she left the shelter of the loch and turned towards the Irish coast the following sea had burst open her stern doors and buckled them; the sea had flooded into her car deck and could not be stemmed; her cargo had shifted, and the flood had poured through a fireproof door into the first class lounge and cabin accommodation. She was listing heavily to starboard. Lifejackets had been issued to the passengers and crew.

During the next four hours, no help reached her. Portpatrick lifeboat pounded a helter-skelter way to the north while (such was the confusion in messages relayed between ship and shore station and thence to the coastguards who guided the lifeboat) the *Princess Victoria* was being swept far to the south. The destroyer Contest, which the Navy sent out from Rothesay Bay, could not find her either at this time.

'The pilot of our plane said the weather was still atrocious,' said Bill Johnston, 'but if we were really determined to go we could hop into his

96

old Rapide biplane – so off we went. All we knew at this time was that the *Princess Victoria* was somewhere in the Irish Sea, and that's a awful lot of sea.'

In fact the *Princess Victoria* was somewhere off Belfast Lough by then. A last SOS from David Broadfoot placed her there, and said that she was 'on her beam end'. By then the passengers were hauling themselves on lifelines up to the port side, and David Broadfoot, in the radio room, must have known that he had foregone his last chance of life.

When the order was given to abandon ship, only six lifeboats could be used; life-rafts were slipped, and men women and children jumped into the freezing cold sea.

A lifeboat with the only survivors from the Princess Victoria shelters in the lee of the rescuing ship Pass of Drumochter

'Our pilot had been right,' said Bill. 'The weather really was atrocious. It was the most terrifying time of my life. For a very long time we could see nothing.'

But one of four ships which left the shelter of the Lough in answer to the SOS had found wreckage a few miles eastward of little Mew island. It was now 4.45 pm, in gathering dark.

'We were on the verge of giving up,' said Bill, 'when we saw smoke and we headed straight towards it. We circled around a small coastal tanker; it was the Pass of Drumochter. Two lifeboats were sheltering in her lee and there were people in the water. I kept urging the pilot to fly lower. The spray from the sea was covering us, and he kept shrugging off my pleas. Suddenly I became aware that he was having difficulty getting his old Rapide up again. We were low on fuel by then, and the darkness was closing in, so we flew on to Ireland. The pilot then told us he had had to fight a dangerous strong down-draught, and that if we had gone any lower he would have had to ditch. Truly, ignorance is bliss.'

Bill and Ian Forbes went on to Dunaghadee to await the survivors coming ashore. The occupants of only one of the lifeboats sheltering in the lee of the *Drumochter* were saved by the Dunaghadee lifeboat. A man Bill had photographed clinging to a raft or a large piece of wood was never seen again. There were 29 people on board the surviving lifeboat, and 13 others were picked up – just 42 out of a complement of 176 souls. Captain James Ferguson went down with his ship.

Few news events in those days were able to force football entirely off the front pages of Saturday sports editions. The *Princess Victoria* disaster did. It was the most appalling of all the sea tragedies which happened around our Scottish coasts – and heaven knows there have been all too many of those over the years.

CHAPTER 17

Not just the Coronation

CORONATION YEAR WAS WHEN Mamie Baird fell foul of the Army, and when she fell in love, and also when (unintentionally) she upstaged the Queen. She was sent to St Mary's Episcopal Cathedral in Glasgow to report the wedding rehearsal of the marriage of Mary Connell, youngest daughter of Glasgow businessman Charles Connell, to the Hon David Montgomery, son and heir of the Viscount Montgomery of Alamein, unaware that in the London editions much fun had been made of the wedding preparations. These had been planned with such military precision by Monty's staff that our irreverent colleagues in the south had labelled it 'Operation Confetti'.

When Mamie introduced herself she was met with a tirade from Monty's officer in charge of proceedings. Her equivalent of 'Please Sir, it wasn't me' went unheeded. No plea of mitigation was entertained. Had she been in uniform the sentence of the court martial would have been that she be drummed out of the service. Mamie fled, and back at the office she hid in the ladies' toilets to weep. 'No one had ever spoken to me like that before,' she said.

Her self-respect was restored to some extent when Arthur Christiansen sought to lure her to Fleet Street. Although Chris may have needed little persuasion to send the invitation, it had been prompted by Eve Perrick, one of Chris's two foremost women columnists (the other being Anne Edwards). The most acerbic of women writers are often warm-hearted in private, and Eve Perrick was one such; she had never forgotten the help Mamie had given her in fashioning her column from Deeside during the Princess Margaret birthday celebrations.

But not all Chris's inducements, nor his blandishments, would induce Mamie to stay on after a three-month stint in London. She said her heart was back in Scotland. Specifically, it was in the possession of a handsome young man, bearded as a Viking of old, named Magnus Magnusson.

Magnus, an Icelander by birth and the son of Iceland's consul-general in Scotland, was brought up in Edinburgh, and was dux of the Academy there before going on to Oxford on a scholarship. He was later to become a household name as the question-master of BBC's long-running *Mastermind* quiz programme.

In the early 1950s, to help finance his stay at Oxford, he had begun his journalistic career as 'Mr Handyman' of the *Edinburgh Evening Dispatch*. If ever there had been a reversal of roles in his TV quiz programme, his chosen subjects would have included not only archaeology and Norse mythology, about which he has written several books and programmed countless documentaries, but might also have embraced upholstery and joinery. His knowledge of these practical subjects was culled from researching various do-it-yourself volumes in the local library while at home on vacation from Oxford; it was then distilled in a weekly column he sent from the university to the paper's office in Edinburgh.

The Chief Sub-editor of the *Dispatch* was the most faithful follower of his column, until he re-wired his house in accordance with Magnus's instructions. At the last moment, before switching on, he thought it prudent to call in some independent advice. 'It was just as well he did,' said Magnus, 'otherwise he could have reduced his house to cinders.' That was the end of 'Mr Handyman'.

Magnus had no shorthand when he joined us, but he could at least use a typewriter. This was due to practice derived from typing out a translation of a three-act play in Icelandic which he was going to produce with his College drama group, and then making fifteen copies of it on his father's old Imperial machine, 'because I'd never heard of carbon paper then.'

The newly-fledged Oxford graduate joined us as a freelance, one of the team reporting the Edinburgh International Festival. And that was when he first met Mamie Baird.

At the time the Edinburgh staff were also trying to find Isabel, teenage daughter of the Bolivian tin-mining magnate Señor Antenor Patino. She had eloped with a young man-about-town named James Goldsmith, son of Major Frank Goldsmith, director of the Savoy Hotel. They had planned to marry at Gretna Green, without realising that marriage in Scotland still required a three-week residential qualification.

The distraught millionaire was also trying to find his daughter. The only people who were not searching, in fact, were reporters from the Mirror group who were helping the couple to keep clear of Señor Patino's wrathful pursuit. The millionaire had gone to ground in a bedroom of the Caledonian Hotel in Edinburgh, from which he kept in touch by telephone with his posse of hired detectives, and since we did not have a clue about the couple's whereabouts we were keeping watch on the father's movements.

Albert Barr, our chief photographer, alleged that two of those who took turns of duty on watch in the Caledonian Hotel spent more time finding quiet corners of the hotel to sweet-talk together than they did keeping watch. Mamie and Magnus said that it would not have mattered how vigilant they had been – when the elopers finally appeared in public, it was in the company of the *Mirror* reporters, who had acted as witnesses at their wedding ceremony at the registry office in Kelso.

The romance of the runaway couple ended in tragedy. Isabel Patino died giving birth to a daughter. The bereaved young husband then immersed himself wholly in business, so much so that his unreconciled parents-in-law sued for custody of the child on the ground that he was too busy to care for her. But Jimmy Goldsmith won custody of the infant.

By the time of his own death, 42 years later, he had married twice more, had acquired seven other children and was renowned as Sir James Goldsmith, tycoon and politician. He had amassed a fortune estimated at £1.6 billion. As founder and leader of the Referendum Party opposed to a federal Europe, he spent £20m of his own money to fund its campaign in the 1997 General Election. He himself stood as a candidate, despite the fact that he was terminally ill by then.

The Coronation of Queen Elizabeth coincided with the conquest of Everest, which led to the famous Express headline 'All This And Everest Too!' If we went a bit over the top on the day, it was forgivable. But it impinges less on my recollection than the post-coronation royal visit to Rutherglen.

Rutherglen is a part of Glasgow which has never belonged to Glasgow – at least, the 25,000 or so who live in it have never acknowledged the relationship, any more than the burghers of Leith have ever admitted belonging to Edinburgh.

On the day the new Queen Elizabeth came among us we were convinced that Rutherglen belonged to Mamie Baird. 'Well,' she said afterwards, 'it's the oldest royal burgh in Scotland, it's where I was born and brought up and my father had been a town councillor, and brother Archie was a noted footballer with Aberdeen.'

Mamie was also a regular singer in the local operatic society. So when she was chosen by the Palace officials to represent all the accredited press group, what followed during the Queen's visit to Rutherglen on 21 June should not have surprised us. As the royal car entered at the top of the town, the children who lined the route cheered rapturously and waved their little flags. They cheered again when the rest of the entourage appeared.

Mamie was in the third car of the entourage. Suddenly she heard cries of 'Oh, it's Mamie Baird!'

'I began to feel a bit silly,' she said, 'sitting there all dressed up with my straw bonnet and white gloves and just staring at them all, so I waved back. The word must have passed along the route, into Overton Drive and Stonelaw Road. All along the way I heard it over and over: 'It IS Mamie Baird! That's her in the black dress and white hat.'

'We came into the Main Street. At the town hall, the Provost and his fellow dignitaries were waiting, and he came forward to greet the Queen. As she stepped out of her car I slipped out of mine, so as not to miss anything. There are tenements all around the town hall, and overlooking it. Then from one of the windows above I heard a voice which I recognised as belonging to an old neighbour: 'It is SO Mamie Baird. I know. I used to wipe her wee nose on my pinny at the back door'.'

The report of the royal visit was not of the usual kind, for we told her to tell it like it was, and we headlined it as 'The Day the Queen Came to My Town'. Her old English master, Mr Cowper, would have approved.

Mamie said afterwards that it was the most enjoyable royal event of her career – 'and I think the Queen enjoyed herself, too. She was so relaxed during the 'wee tea' in the Town Hall that she actually took her lipstick out of her handbag at the table and freshened up her make-up in front of everybody.'

When Mamie and Magnus were married in the following year, many sightseers turned up to see the bride arrive at Wardlawhill Church in Rutherglen and to bid the young couple happiness as they left. No doubt that old neighbour with the pinny was among them.

Of course it would have been unthinkable that happenings in the year would not have included Albert Barr.

When the Earl of Dalkeith married lovely young model Jane McNeil, Albert set off to take pictures at Bowhill House, but he never reached the earl's ancestral home to record the wedding celebrations. He landed instead in Edinburgh Royal Infirmary. Drew Rennie, his reporting companion, was lucky, escaping almost unhurt as their car skidded and crashed near Shotts. After he was patched up he went to see Albert, who lay uncharacteristically quietly in a ward bed.

'Look in the inside pocket of my jacket,' said Albert.

What Drew found was a spool of exposed film. Albert had been thrown out of the car when it overturned. As he lay on the roadway awaiting the arrival of an ambulance he had been taking pictures of the crash scene. He had only stopped when he lost consciousness.

1955... Sandy Trotter had been editor for 21 years... he was given a celebration anniversary lunch at Glasgow's Central Hotel

The youngest copy boy was chosen to hand over one of the presentations, and Jack Campbell (on extreme left of picture) proposed the toast and presented another. Arthur Christiansen, who came to add his congratulations, is on the far right. He seemed wan and stressed, but no one suspected that within a year he would, be seriously ill.

The anniversary editor was also presented with a souvenir spoof paper entitled *The Sandy Express* in which Alhambra Theatre manager Bert Lumsden was called upon to give him the key of the First House.

His happiness was compounded during this period of his editorship – the football team which had been his favourite since boyhood won the League Cup and in the following season the Scottish Cup.

On the morning after the Cup Final game everyone – except one diehard who could not, or would not, disown his allegiance, attended news conference wearing enormously fashioned rosettes in every colour except the maroon of Heart of Midlothian F.C.

CHAPTER 18

Codename Snowdrop

THE GREAT BLIZZARD OF January 1955 closed 70 main roads, and even clogged the hands of Big Ben; but it visited nowhere with more malevolence than the hinterlands of Caithness.

Fifty-eight passengers were trapped in trains when the storm struck in the middle of January. In isolated crofts and hamlets, families stared at impending starvation, huddled inside walls which creaked and groaned against the weight of snowdrifts, and watched in dread lest the snow encroached even higher over the rooftops and engulfed their homes altogether. No one could reach them. Roads no longer existed.

The Navy's Fleet Air Arm and the RAF mounted a huge relief operation code-named Snowdrop. When the Fleet Air Arm landed their planes at Wick to set up base there, Drew Rennie and Bob McWilliams and photographer Albert Barr went in with them, to be joined by our local correspondent John Donaldson and local photographer Ian McDonald.

Our team's intention was to fan out from the old fishing town to try to reach some of the beleaguered homes. But outside Wick was a white wilderness. Every attempt to venture more than a mile had to be abandoned, and at first they could only glean what was happening over whichever telephone lines were still operational.

The leader of the rescue operation was Commander Parker – 'a real-life film-star figure complete with white scarf,' as Drew Rennie described him. He could well have seen our team as an encumbrance. Instead, he used them as allies, taking whatever intelligence they could gather from their telephone searches. In return he allowed them to attend briefings when his pilots came back to base from their flying sorties. His men were tirelessly taking their helicopters, often defying blinding snowstorms, to drop food and other needs wherever the marooned families had marked out on the snow their messages for help.

When the blizzard had lasted three days and showed no signs of abating, the Navy sent its aircraft carrier Glory to help. She anchored in bleak Loch Eriboll, on the remote north-west corner of the coast, and ran a cable to the telephone line on shore to link up with the Snowdrop base at Wick. Glory was there as Commander Parker's fuel depot; she carried so much helicopter fuel on her flight deck that her officers called her a floating bomb, and all smoking on board was forbidden.

The day after she arrived there was a lull in the weather. But the meteorologists were forecasting even worse to come, and a national disaster was feared if all those calls for help, dotted everywhere on the white-out landscape, could not be answered quickly. On that day of respite 12 Sea Hawks went out on patrol to look for more signals, and seven Navy helicopters made no fewer than 34 sorties to drop supplies, and the RAF made eleven flights from Kinloss.

During the respite, too, a Whirlwind, the Navy's largest and most modern helicopter, took off on a mercy mission which would cover more than 300 miles. In the West Coast hamlet of Culkein, ten miles from Lochinver, 11-year-old Donald Matheson was desperately ill with pneumonia, and in the village of Knockan, perched high in the hills east of Ullapool, 76-year-old Miss Mary Macleod was ill with a seizure. A smaller helicopter had been beaten back on the previous day.

Photographer Albert Barr joined the Whirlwind crew, courtesy of Commander Parker; perhaps the fact that Albert had flown over the Burma front as a wartime reconnaissance photographer influenced the Commander's decision to grant permission.

The Whirlwind flew to the Glory in Loch Eriboll to take on fuel and then, guided in by a bonfire, landed in the main street of Lochinver, where Dr Robert Ferguson was waiting to board. The good doctor had struggled all the previous day to reach his boy patient, and was haggard with fatigue.

First the Whirlwind flew to help the elderly patient at Knockan. 'The villagers had had no contact with anyone for nine days,' said Albert. 'They all turned out to conduct us the three quarters of a mile to the cottage where Miss Mary Macleod lay. We had no stretcher, but we took an iron bedstead from a nearby hut, and carried her on it to the chopper, lurching alarmingly as we stumbled and slipped. When we landed again in Lochinver's main street we carried her, still on the iron bedstead, to the door of the local hospital.

'Then we flew to Culkein to fetch the sick boy. He was only semiconscious when we got there, but his mother insisted on making tea for us all. Before she left she patted her son's head and said to us, 'God keep you safe'. We left the doctor at Lochinver and flew on with the boy to Wick. We were lucky. Next day the blizzard was back as bad as ever.'

The only one in our team to reach a beleaguered village on foot, unaided by the Navy, was Magnus Magnusson. Magnus was a late reinforcement for the team. He decided to try to reach the village of Braemore, about 20 miles south of Wick, in the shadow of 800-ft-high Achinavish Hill. The ten families there had appealed for help – they were 'down to our last potatoes.'

When he arrived in Wick he found a skipper of a fishing smack, George Sinclair of the *Speedwell*, who agreed to take him and photographer Ian McDonald down the coast as far as the little tidal harbour of Dunbeath. They landed there – or rather, they ran aground there – in the dark and lay stranded until they refloated on the incoming tide and squeezed into the harbour to make rendezvous there with George Gunn, the brother of one of the Braemore villagers, who had volunteered to guide them to the village.

Magnus saw no point in hanging around and waiting for daylight – after all, another newspaper team might be trying the same ploy somewhere else. So off they set in the glimmering darkness. It was 8 pm. For five hours they ploughed their way towards the village, following the line of half-buried telegraph poles. At one point Magnus nearly stumbled against the wires themselves, fifteen feet above where the road should have been. They skirted past places where their guide knew there were tarns and bogs, pulling one another out when they sank to the waist in snow, and often having to call a halt through sheer exhaustion.

They arrived at 1 am. All the villagers got up to welcome them, astonished that anyone should have been so foolhardy as to attempt such a trek. Magnus' arrival was doubly welcome, because as well as sweets for the children he had lugged a bottle of whisky and some tobacco all the way in his rucksack – although he said afterwards that he had been sorely tempted to jettison it, to lighten the load on the nightmare journey.

Magnus and Ian stayed in the home of Bill and Josephine Gunn, who told how the villagers had spent their marooned days, trying desperately to keep their sheep alive and sharing out their dwindling supplies. The local schoolteacher, Mrs Reid, had got the children meticulously noting every item of food they had been sent on occasional air-drops, to ensure that they could pay for everything when the emergency was over.

Next morning Magnus found a phone box which was still, surprisingly, in operation, and phoned in his story to Glasgow. Jack Coupar, the News Editor, reacted promptly and arranged a helicopter to drop supplies of bread, milk, butter and potatoes, and some hay for the sheep, and bring the pictures of the expedition back to Wick.

'What about Ian and me?' said Magnus.

'Sorry,' he was told, 'I'm afraid you'll just have to get back out of there the best way you can, old son.'

'That's News Editors for you,' said Magnus.

They were lucky: whether by design or good fortune, the helicopter Jack Coupar organised was able to uplift not only the precious negatives but the intrepid pair as well. Rival news photographers who heard on the grapevine that a helicopter was coming in from the stranded hamlet with two people on board were waiting at the airport to take pictures of the arrival in Wick, and were mortified to discover the identity of the passengers.

The relief of Braemore... Magnus Magnusson (on right) with William Gunn, whose brother George guided Magnus in the dark through the blizzard to reach the beleaguered village

The picture was taken by John (Ian) McDonald, Magnus' photographer companion on the arduous trek

Magnus earned his first by-line for his front-page Braemore story. And there was to be a pleasing grace-note to the yarn, more than 40 years later. When Magnus was the subject of Michael Aspel's *This Is Your Life* programme in the autumn of 1997, one of the surprise guests who was flown down for the occasion was none other than photographer Ian McDonald from Wick. It was the first time they had met since they had made their epic trek through the snow to Braemore.

After the Snowdrop story which saw his name in lights for the first time, Magnus figured in a succession of roles with the *Scottish Daily Express*, presenting his 'Festival Diary' and his 'Edinburgh Diary', and as 'Donald Sage' in the *Sunday Express*, besides turning out a stream of feature articles on every subject under the sun.

Then in December, 1955, both he and Mamie Baird were relegated to a subsidiary role as we introduced to the reading public their 3-month-old daughter Sally, in a picture four columns wide under a banner headline which blazoned the news of 'Mamie's Baby'.

CHAPTER 19

The 'Top Twenty' killer

THE DO'S AND DON'TS IN the *Express* style-book included a list of forbidden clichés which Arthur Christiansen, our ever-watchful style-master in London, had mischievously headlined as 'Avoid These Like the Plague'. One of them was 'Fear stalked the streets....' But the day came when the phrase did not seem such a cliché after all.

Fennsbank Avenue in High Burnside, near Rutherglen in Glasgow, paralleled the avenue in which I lived with my wife and schoolgirl daughter. The visitor who called at the home of the Watt family at No. 5 Fennsbank Avenue at around midnight on Sunday, 16 September, 1956, carried a gun. When he left the house, 17-year-old Vivienne Watt was dying and her mother, Mrs Marion Watt, and her aunt, Mrs Margaret Brown, were both dead.

We did not know who the gunman was, although we were to get to know him all too well later. We headlined him as 'The Top Twenty Killer', because of what Deanne Valente told the police.

Deanne was Vivienne Watt's friend and next-door neighbour. The two girls had spent the evening in Vivienne's bedroom, listening to the radio. From 11 pm it had been tuned to Radio Luxembourg's Top Twenty song hits. At 11.50 pm Deanne went home.

From her own bedroom she could still hear Vivienne's radio. Doris Day was singing *Che Sera Sera*. At midnight the programme ended. Deanne heard no shots. Nor did a night watchman at a building site nearby. In those ten minutes before midnight, so the police surmised, the radio must have masked the sound of murder.

A home-help who called at the house in the morning went inside with the help of the postman. Together they found Vivienne in her bedroom, alive but beyond aid, and the two older women in their beds in another room. They had all been shot in the head.

In common with our neighbours in High Burnside we bolted and barred the doors and windows of our homes. The local ironmonger rapidly ran out of stocks. We went to sleep at nights with heavy sticks or golf clubs by the bed. Pet dogs hitherto confined to kitchens were given the run of the house, and those of us who had never thought of taking such precautions now found a sudden urge to fit alarms. Children were kept indoors after dark, and no one, least of all teenagers, went out in the evenings unaccompanied. Fear stalked the streets...

Vivienne's father, William Watt, a master baker, was summoned back from Lochgilphead, where he had gone on a weekend fishing trip, taking with him the family dog, a black Labrador called Queenie.

A week after the murders, Jack Coupar brought him into my office at Albion Street. William Watt was a big, burly man who bore his weight like a heavy burden upon him rather than with the assurance of the police officer he had once been. He said that the police were hounding him, and that he needed help. He swore that he had known nothing of the tragedy at his home before he was told of it after breakfast at the Lochgilphead hotel. But the police did not believe him, and were pursuing him with relentless questions. It was making other people suspect him, too.

I told him that any statement we printed could not call into question the activities of the police, and that whatever was published would not stop the police from carrying out their duty to inquire into all the circumstances of the case. I also said that if he protested his innocence in print, this might only give publicity to a suspicion which many until then might have had no reason to harbour. If he wanted to say anything, he should simply appeal to the public for help in finding the person who had shot his family; he agreed, and we printed his story.

The police continued to disbelieve him. They found bloodstains on the sheets of his bed (he said he had been paring a corn on his foot). They timed the journey from Lochgilphead to Burnside, across the Renfrew ferry, and they learned from a ferryman that a car had been driven across at 3 am. The ferryman wrongly identified the make of car, but he said that the driver had a black dog with him. William Watt was arrested on Thursday, 27 September, and charged with the three murders.

While the accused father was locked up in remand in Barlinnie prison, I had a telephone call from his lawyer, Lawrence (Lawrie) Dowdall, who was the best-known criminal lawyer in Scotland at the time. He said that his client had asked if I would go to meet him in the jail.

If the prison officers assumed that I was one of the great lawyer's assistants, I did not feel any obligation to identify myself as a newspaperman.

William Watt had been in prison for a month or more, and I suppose he felt in need of a friend. When he asked if he could count on my assistance I said he could, although I could not see how I could help; and when he asked me if I still believed in his innocence, I said Yes, I did indeed.

Apart from instinct, I had good reason to say Yes, because Lawrie Dowdall, too, believed in his innocence. Peter Manuel, a prisoner in Barlinnie who had been convicted of a break-in a few days after Watt's arrest, had told Lawrie Dowdall that he KNEW that Watt had not committed the crimes. Moreover, after an unnamed prisoner had spoken about the murders to Detective Superintendent James Hendry and to the Glasgow Procurator Fiscal, Robert McDonald, a note had been slipped under the door of William Watt's cell in C Block. It said, simply, 'The man who talked about the Burnside murders is called Manuel'.

Peter Manuel was a psychopath, an arrogant braggart desperate to be recognised among his criminal peers for more than just his comparatively petty record. Lawrie Dowdall might therefore have dismissed his claims as idle boasts fuelled by a diligent reading of newspaper reports, had Manuel not let slip some details about the killings which were known only to the police. Dowdall was convinced that Peter Manuel did indeed know the killer – and he was equally convinced that the killer was Manuel himself.

On the afternoon of 3 December, Lawrie Dowdall telephoned me and advised me to be at the gates of Barlinnie prison at 5 pm sharp – William Watt was being released from jail. I took Drew Rennie and Alastair Wilson and chief photographer Albert Barr, and off we went to Barlinnie. Meantime, Jack Coupar was arranging for a decoy car to stand outside the prison after the release, to throw any other newspapermen off the scent. He assigned stocky little Jimmy Henderson to go with it. Jimmy demurred: his wife was expecting to give birth at any moment, and he wanted to be with her in hospital.

Jack Coupar had been in the Tank Corps in the desert during the war and liked to think of himself as a brusque, John Wayne type of character, an uncompromising disciplinarian. 'You'll go or you're fired', he barked.

'In that case I'm fired,' said Jimmy Henderson, and walked out of the office. (To no one's surprise, when Jimmy came into the office next morning expecting to draw his wages, there was no mention of the sack. Instead, Jack Coupar kept face by telling him severely, 'You're on Sheriff Court duty all week.')

Alastair Cameron had been sent to Barlinnie in Jimmy's place, and spent two idle hours outside the prison, as did a few rival reporters in their cars who were hoping to catch someone who was already miles away by then.

William Watt had walked through the prison doors promptly at 5 pm, and we bundled him into our car. He was excited and voluble, and didn't care where he was going as long as it was far enough from his recent domicile.

'How far' was to Drew's home territory in Fife, at Ladybank, where his good friend Graham Bell owned the Royal Hotel. 'Hello, Scoop,' said Graham as we arrived – it had been Drew's mocking nickname as a junior reporter in Fife.

There was no time by then to provide Glasgow with a full story. I telephoned a report telling of the sudden release, quoted William Watt's immediate reactions, and ended with the promise that the released man would be telling his own full story exclusively in the *Scottish Daily Express*, beginning next day.

Drew Rennie and Alistair Wilson then sat with him for several hours preparing the story which would run over several days. They didn't tell him, of course, that they had already prepared a very extensive dossier on him which would have been published as a very different story if he had ever gone to trial and been found guilty. Newspapermen have to be realists, too.

It was midnight before they called a halt to the interview. It had been a disconcerting experience at times. Freed from the shadow of the scaffold, Bill Watt was in turn elated and dejected. He would burst into tears without warning.

By the end of the evening we were all on first-name terms: he called us Jack and Drew and Alistair, and we called him Bill. We went out for a bed-time stroll, in the belief that none of our rivals knew where we were. As we walked along a quiet road, Watt asked me to walk ahead with him. He seemed desperate for further reassurance. 'You DO believe I'm innocent, don't you? he asked. 'Yes,' I replied, 'You know I do.' He didn't say any more, but gripped my arm fiercely.

Graham Bell could provide only two bedrooms. That posed a rather delicate problem. Who was going to share a room with William Watt? I suppose it must have given him added assurance of my belief in his innocence when I elected to share one of the rooms with him, while my three colleagues (to their secret relief, I suspect) shared the other.

In the morning we were surprised to find a posse of newspapermen gathered in the station square outside the hotel. Our hideaway had been betrayed by the fact that we had used the telefoto machine at Kirkcaldy repeater station to wire pictures to accompany our story for the Express.

The hotel stood on a corner facing the railway station. A large back door led from the yard into the street. Drew Rennie felt secure in the protection of his friend Graham Bell and thought we ought to stay put, but when we telephoned Glasgow, Sandy Trotter overruled him, and said we had to find another sanctuary.

The escape plan we concocted involved the use of our two cars and of a small enclosed van lent for the occasion by Graham Bell. One of the cars was to be a decoy, carrying a hooded figure in the back seat with a shrouded heap beside him; we hoped that the opposition would take the hooded figure to be their quarry, with one or other of us crouched beside him in the back. Since I had to return to Glasgow, I was to be the hooded figure.

This car was to leave the station yard and make a dash for the Kinross road which led to Glasgow. Then the van carrying William Watt, driven by John Nicoletti, was to slip out and make for a side road which led to the main Perth road. The other car, driven by John Chalmers, was to be the back-up getaway car, and once the van had shaken off any pursuit its occupants were to transfer to this second car.

In the event, everything went wrong. The opposition had made a compact to split their forces and share the spoils. One group followed the decoy car, and quickly detected the ruse. When the van emerged, the main opposition group gave chase at once, and John Chalmers in the back-up getaway car found himself trailing their cars and a long way behind the van.

There followed a hair-raising chase along the quiet country roads worthy of any film scenario. For mile after mile John Chalmers tried to overtake the rival cars one by one, veering wildly over grass verges and occasionally banging into them. Eventually he managed to interpose himself between the van and its pursuers. He slewed his car across the narrow road, effectively blocking it, and forcing them to halt.

Meanwhile the van, with William Watt, Albert Barr and Drew Rennie crouched in the back, was bucketing along at 70 miles an hour as before, rocking alarmingly from side to side. Suddenly they became aware of a gurgling, spurting noise, and realised that they were sitting on a can of petrol without a cap. They stuffed the opening with rags, and hurtled on. It was not until they reached the outskirts of Perth that they felt clear.

They went on to Drew Rennie's home in Dundee, but Drew's mother became alarmed, so they left for new quarters and spent the night in the home of Jack Forsyth, our Dundee circulation representative, before heading up into the glens of Angus. There they passed an uneasy week holed up in the Glenisla Hotel, which was owned by another of Drew's friends, Bill Ferrier, before returning to Glasgow when the Watt exclusive had run its triumphant course.

The drama surrounding Bill Watt was to continue. But for the time being I was not to be involved, for more personal matters intervened.

CHAPTER 20

The Nameless Ones

ANY WOMAN WHO CAN charm a newspaperman to believe he should give up his all for not so much as a wee cuddle is well worthy of a mention in our despatches.

Until Miss Sheena Govan brought her small band of followers to Oban to preach their mission, we had never heard of her. Few had. We called them The Nameless Ones because we couldn't establish any other name for the sect. From each of her members she required that they cease to live as husband and wife, father and mother, son or daughter. Her followers saw her as the New Messiah.

Our correspondent in Oban alerted us to the fact that in the cottage the little community had rented there was a struggle going on for the heart and mind of a young mother, and Drew Rennie, Magnus Magnusson and Ronnie Burns were despatched to the west Highland seaport and holiday town to record the drama which was about to unfold.

Mrs Sylvia Astell had come with her husband, and their 21-month- old infant Christine, to decide if she should join the sect, as her husband Fred wanted her to do. He had himself joined three months earlier, giving up an engineering job and his home in Shipley, Yorkshire.

Mrs Astell's distraught mother followed the couple to Oban, protesting that her 27-year-old daughter was not acting of her own free will. Four days after arriving at the cottage, the tug of war over her loyalties had not been resolved, and Mrs Astell and her baby left with Sheena Govan to stay for further meditation at a hillside farmhouse on the western peninsula of Mull.

When husband Fred arrived in the evening he was told that his wife did not want to see him until next day. At 8 am he prayed on a hill behind the farm, before calling at the house. After being admitted, he spent two hours talking to his wife, and then announced that everyone in the farmhouse was happy. 'My wife is staunch,' he told us. 'She will not waver, no matter what her mother says.'

Sylvia Astell, in fact, had already written to her mother, who was waiting in Oban, to say she would not see her, and ended her letter: 'My love for Fred is still as strong as ever, but my love for God is greater.'

Interviewed at the farmhouse, she underlined that decision: 'The day before I left Shipley I told friends that I would not go to Fred; but when he came and explained everything to me and told me how wonderful Miss Govan was, I felt I must go to join him. I have found true happiness now. I must forsake all, as my husband has done, to serve God. My mother will never make me change my mind. I have found Miss Govan a wonderful teacher. She is a wonderful person, and I have really found God through her.'

The bizarre tale then took an even more curious twist – husband Fred was ordered out of the farmhouse. Had he begun to recant his vows? He returned at midnight, saying he wanted to take his wife and baby daughter away. When he was turned away he called up to the room where he thought he saw the silhouette of his wife at the window, and when his pleas went unheard he engaged the farmer's family in an angry exchange which ended only with the arrival of a police car.

Sheena Govan, leader of 'The Nameless Ones'

At 2 am Sheena Govan left the farm and motored thirty miles to Grass Point, at the other end of the island where a launch awaited her. She left Sylvia Astell with a message: 'Before you can become a disciple you must see your mother and speak to her with your heart.'

The tormented husband followed his high priestess's car, but as she boarded the launch she told him, 'No, you must not come with me. We must all work this out alone.' He went back to the farm, in time to see his wife being driven away with the child, and he reached Grass Point too late to speak to her before the departure of the launch which was to take her across the Sound of Mull to Oban, and to her mother, waiting at Ganavan Sands with a car. When we asked him why he was still following his wife he said, 'Although I no longer regard her as my wife I want to welcome her into the fold.'

The three main characters in this tortuous drama were now all on the mainland, but each of the three principals had by now been 'appropriated' by rival newspapers: Sheena Govan was travelling in the *Express* car 'whithersoever God intended'; her disciple Fred Astell was in Oban under the wing of the *Daily Record*, searching for clues to the whereabouts of his wife; and Sylvia Astell was in Glasgow with her mother, superintended by the *Daily Mail*. If it had not been so potentially serious, it would have been ludicrous – all these newspaper cars haring round the Highlands trying to dodge each other or find each other.

Eventually a deal was struck between the *Express* and the *Record*, and Fred Astell and Sheena Govan met up again to 'plan our way forward' (so they said). A five-minute phone-call at midnight to Sylvia Astell's hotel room in Glasgow persuaded her to leave the child with its grandmother and come to a tripartite rendezvous in a hotel at Inverbeg on the shores of Loch Lomond. All three then repaired back to Mull, to the far western end at Kintra, to pray together and to receive Sylvia into the Nameless Ones.

Did Sheena Govan break up the Astell family? 'It is unjust to say that,' she said. 'It is not necessary for a husband to leave his wife. A man and wife can do our work together.'

Probably no one will ever fathom the compelling quality of this enigmatic woman whom her devotees said had 'eyes which glowed like fire.' When we probed her background there was no early hint of direct divine inspiration. She was the younger daughter of John George Govan, who founded the Faith Mission in Edinburgh in 1886. But her movement had no connection with her father's. The Faith Mission, now known the world over, which trains pilgrims to go out in pairs all over the country, has a declared 'conservative evangelical' doctrine, and when it learned of her group it sent letters to all its members asking them to inform everyone that she had never worked for the Faith Mission: 'we entirely dissociate ourselves from her and her movement and all that it stands for.'

Her father had died when she was 15 years old. When the war began she joined ENSA to entertain the Services on various fronts. Then, in 1948, she married Peter Caddy, a squadron leader in the RAF. Seven years later they divorced at her request and she reverted to her maiden name of Sheena Clare Govan.

Peter Caddy then gave up his commission to join her movement as, he said, 'one of her earliest converts. I think I came to know, very soon after we married, that she was emerging into someone great.' It was Peter Caddy who had introduced Fred Astell to the movement.

For a brief spell 'The Nameless Ones' became known to hundreds of thousands of newspaper readers, because wherever Sheena Govan went she was accompanied by reporters from many newspapers. The press gang never knew where or when they might eat by day or where they might spend the night.

'She kept getting messages from God,' said Magnus Magnusson. 'She would say, 'We are going to Fort William,' and then half an hour later say 'God says we are not to go to Fort William.' The messages always came at the most inconvenient times. So it was arranged that Ronnie Burns should start getting messages from God, too, and after that we had meals at rather more reasonable hours.'

Ronnie Burns, who had been a noted Olympic swimmer for Scotland, was so trusted by Sheena that we unashamedly traded on this to seize the initiative from rival newspapers. And if Bob Russell of the Daily Mail ever wondered why his very name was anathema to Sheena Govan, we could have told him: she did not like his long moustaches, and our mob had suggested that he was no doubt a disciple of the devil.

Not all the newspapermen in her entourage were as case-hardened as ours, however. Two young reporters, who shall be nameless, fell under her spell, and might have left home and family had not their colleagues set upon them. One of them had to be tied down – literally – while his colleagues counselled him for hours on end to brainwash him back to his senses.

Sheena Govan has been dead for some years now. Her ex-husband, Peter Caddy, went on to establish a community at Findhorn on the Moray Firth. He died in 1993.

As soon as the travelling press circus lost interest and came back to base, the Nameless Ones faded into obscurity. We can find no trace of them today – not even on the Internet.

CHAPTER 21

Tears for a nice wee paper

THE PUNDITS IN OUR trade had long known the answer to the question of whether three evening newspapers could survive in a city the size of Glasgow. What they had not been able to predict was which of them would be the first to die.

The answer came on 17 January, 1957. The funeral was at Kemsley House; the body was that of the *Evening News*. Many fellow journalists joined the mourners, not only because any loss is a loss to us all, but because it had always been a jolly good wee paper.

The question then became whether two evening papers could live in Glasgow – and, if not, whether the *Evening Times* or the *Evening Citizen* would survive. The impartial would have voted for the Times. It had always dominated the market in the city itself and within a radius of sixty miles around. At its peak it had sold more than 300,000 copies per day. Both papers were primarily Glasgow and West of Scotland publications.

However, since the *Citizen* had arrived in Albion Street as a full member of the *Express* stable, John Harvey, the group circulation manager, had vigorously promoted the *Citizen*, not only in Glasgow and its environs but also in Edinburgh, Fife, Dumfries and the Borders. He set up *Citizen* offices in 16 major or minor towns with sizeable populations, from which he thrust into the outlying areas. Here were not only spoils to boost the fortunes of the *Daily Express* and the *Sunday Express*: this was the soft under-belly of the *Evening Times*, and by the 1950s the *Citizen* had gnawed into much of that soft under-belly, although there was still much flesh left to gnaw.

We at the *Express* were already flushed with success. In 1951 our sales topped 600,000 copies a day. But the journalist does not willingly adhere to a group; he lives for his own paper – and so we had given little more than a passing thought to the *Citizen*. It just happened to be in the same house.

Journalists are also isolationists even within their own paper. While they see their primary function as providing the reader with news, whatever the cost, a group general manager (with whom the journalist seldom comes into contact) looks after the physical and financial complex, directing other bosses who run the circulation, advertising, publicity, accounts and production departments, and HIS (or HER) primary function is to give the journalists (however grudgingly) the means to let them fulfil their ambitions.

Our group general manager since 1940 was A.H. (Sandy) Bruce. Between our two Sandys, Bruce and Trotter, there was a mutual respect and understanding and close friendship, and Sandy Trotter knew the truth of this better than we did. At a morning news conference where we were congratulating ourselves for hitting that magic 600,000 mark, Sandy Trotter read the Lesson:

'Yes, yes,' he said. 'You may well congratulate yourselves. But just remember that you are only one side of the coin. It's one thing to seek the news and write about it and present it in a worthwhile paper; that's the exciting bit. But it has to be sold; that part is a hard slog.' He was right.

The hard slog is the lot of the circulation manager's foot soldiers, the corps of representatives familiarly known as The Reps. Their task is to ensure that wherever the paper is sold there are enough copies of it available, and to see that even more are sold through publicity and good salesmanship.

Sandy Bruce himself had been their overlord before the war. Afterwards, when the *Citizen* and the *Sunday Express* had been taken on board, each title had its own circulation manager, reporting to John Harvey.

Selling the *Citizen* called for a strategy different from that used for the other titles, because an evening paper has a shorter shelf-life. It was therefore distributed directly from Albion Street or, in the country areas, directly by the reps, who ran their own offices and kept their own accounts. But in the main branches the rep not only undertook distribution of the *Citizen* but oversaw the distribution of the other titles through the wholesaler; he was also responsible for extraneous titles like the *Rupert Annuals* and the *Junior Express*. He thus found himself with three taskmasters in addition to the overlord. These reps knew no lines of demarcation, nor were they to do so until a later reorganisation of the force.

Ronnie Fowler, who had started as a 15-year-old messenger-boy in the Ayr office in 1940 and risen to the upper echelons of management before he retired, was a rep for eight years. During his time as North Ayrshire rep he loaded a hired jeep every night with copies of the *Citizen* and took it out of Kilmarnock ('with no heater, even in the coldest weather') to Hurlford, Mauchline, Sorn, Catrine, Old and New Cumnock, Loganswell, Kirkconnel and Sanquhar, whence he would send his hired vendors to deliver to people in their homes. 'We never had a recognised day off,' he remembered. 'The only compensation was the excitement of it.'

Among the main branch reps were half a dozen battle-hardened survivors of the 1930s who had graduated from the corps of 'doorknockers' in the free-gifts war of the time – extroverts every one, in an odd way epitomising the dramatic product they sold.

One of the most colourful among those veterans of the thirties was 'Winkie' Littlejohn. He wore a Crombie coat and a pork-pie hat. The dark looks and stocky stature would remind us now of the fabulous Brazilian football star Diego Maradona. He may never have known 'The Hand of God', as Maradona did when he scored that controversial goal against England in the World Cup, but Winkie believed that his own hands were endowed with superhuman power. Let him find a newsagent prepared to pit his strength for a wager and he would arm-wrestle with him; the prize would be an addition to the client's supply of papers and a promise to give preferential display to *Express* copies on the counter inside the shop and to its contents posters outside it. No one kept a tally, but it was generally held that 'Winkie' Littlejohn scored more goals than he conceded.

Another was 'Malky' Handyside. Everyone in the retail trade knew him. He made sure of that. On occasion he would wear spats over his shoes and carry a silver-topped cane. In summer he favoured a straw boater hat and tussore silk jacket. He was a frustrated vaudeville actor; on the slightest pretext he would launch into a Frankie Vaughan routine. When he decided that his vendors were deserving, he would dispense half crowns with careless abandon.

All the reps had a daily 'personal supply' of newspapers which they could use to 'top up' at main points of sale, and it was not unusual to be called on at 4 am to stencil on to these copies some item of late news.

With the *Citizen* came 'The Bush', a miniature, albeit cumbersome, printing press. It was used primarily to promote evening paper sales among the racing and football fraternity.

There were no licensed betting shops at the time. Although the first television broadcast took place in Scotland in 1952, for many years thereafter there were few owners of TV sets, and punters depended on evening newspapers to supply them constantly with results.

Special supplies of the *Citizen* were printed for despatch to branches. The *Citizen* was a broadsheet then (as was the *Scottish Daily Express* itself – it did not go tabloid until January 1977). Each page was eight columns wide. The end column of Page One of the *Citizen* was left blank to accommodate 'Stop Press' news or, in newspaper parlance, 'Fudge'. On Saturdays the bottom halves of columns one and eight were left clear to print football results as well.

On arrival at the branches a typed stencil was wrapped round either one or both drums of the Bush and adjusted to rotate on to the position of the blank columns of the paper. Copies were then fed into the machine at the rate of one quire (two dozen copies) at a time.

David Aitken, who was Mr *Citizen* in Falkirk area, remembers that on one Saturday he spent the entire afternoon 'bushing in' race results, and the half-time football scores, and then found that he had been using unsold copies of the previous day's paper. Since no one complained, it has to be assumed he could have printed the results on sheets of plain paper for all the difference it would have made to the punters.

At times – usually crucial times – a vendor might not appear, and David Aitken had to scour the lodging houses to find a replacement. Vendors were paid the same percentage as newsagents, but exclusive *Citizen* vendors were given special terms, and one or two who vanished did so with the entire takings.

In the districts these were only occasional difficulties, but in Glasgow itself disappearances of casuals were an everyday hazard. As many as 100 or even 200 sandwich-board bearers might be recruited for publicity at football grounds. They were transported to the venue and paid £1 if they stayed the course; but however vigilantly they were supervised, sandwich-boards could be found abandoned and their bearers tracked down to a local pub. That would never have happened in Eddie McKenna's day. No city vendor would have dared to abscond, with Eddie McKenna to face.

Eddie was no longer in charge of the street vending operation, which had become too large to handle along with his other operations. It was now part of Ronnie Fowler's remit.

From the time Eddie began, with that paltry return for his agreement to drive papers to Oban, Eddie had made a goodly amount of money. You might have said that money stuck to him. I once watched him take in money and I said to him, 'Eddie, you counted every note up to the last one, and then you stopped counting. I was wondering why?'

'Oh,' he replied, 'You never know, there could have been another stuck to the last one.'

Eddie bought property cheaply during the war and held it to sell in the post-war market. He then set up a small garage around the corner from No. 195, in College Street, where he built up a fleet of cars of varying reliability, with drivers of similarly varying reliability, to take reporters to news events at frightening speeds. In an emergency, however, he would take papers himself to a vending site, turning up in his personal Rolls Royce, fedora hat tilted back on his head, a fat cigar in the corner of his mouth.

He burned his fingers only once, to my knowledge, when he imported cars from Czechoslovakia. The Government insisted on duty being paid before sale and, since he could not raise the finance to meet this impost, many of the cars lay rusting at Leith docks while his capital dribbled away. But none of us would ever have begrudged Eddie McKenna whatever good fortune came his cavalier way.

The *Citizen's* assault on the *Times's* hold on Glasgow included the exploitation of every event which could provide an excuse to produce a 'slip' souvenir edition. A personality in the 'pop' scene or the theatre had only to show his or her face in town. Even the religious crusade by the

American evangelist Billy Graham was milked – tastefully, of course, as befitted the occasion. The normally raucous vendors with their cries of 'Read All About It' were replaced by recruits from church youth clubs to woo the thousands who queued nightly at the city's Kelvin Hall and went to Ibrox Park and Hampden at final Rallies in numbers which equalled the ground record for attendances at football games.

The *Times'* soft under-belly eventually extended to the fringes of the city stronghold, because the City Fathers, who knew what was best for the under-privileged, had decanted hundreds of thousands of them to the outskirts of the city to give them better houses in which to live, but at the same time had unwittingly given them a poorer quality of life in which to enjoy them.

Harry Finch, who eventually became our director of publicity and promotions, arrived then, bringing with him the concept of a 'House-wives' Club' for the harassed wives and mothers of the housing schemes, coupling this idea with direct delivery of the *Citizen* to people's homes. The operation was integrated into the Street Sales department. Everyone who joined the Housewives' Club was given a diary and free entry to shows staged exclusively for them by the multi-gifted Archie McCulloch.

In his early teens, Archie McCulloch reported football games for the local weekly *Govan Press*, augmenting his income by contributing to larger papers results of minor games, some of which were by clubs of his own invention. He went on to report for the larger papers real games played by real teams, and might have made his name entirely in journalism had he not met the late Hughie Green.

He was supposed to be Hughie Green's Gang Show publicity manager, but he could not resist involving himself in stage production and direction and became as much hooked on show business as on newspapers. On the way he acquired as his wife the singer Cathie Wood, 'a delightful little bit of the scenery', as he put it; as 'Kathy Kay' she became The Fireside Girl, a star of Billy Cotton's Band and of radio and TV.

During the war Archie had charge of entertaining the Armed Forces throughout Scotland. After it, no one could have told (not even he) whether at any given time he was acting as feature writer, columnist, radio commentator or theatre impresario.

It was while he was a feature writer and entertainment columnist for the *Citizen* that he ran into a real life drama. He was on the way to Motherwell with photographer Jack Hill when they came across a gunman who had held up a post office in Tollcross and was being chased by several men. Jack Hill pointed his camera at him from the window of the car, and the gunman pointed his gun back at them. As Archie and Jack clambered out of the car, the robber seized a passing woman shopper and held her as a shield. For several minutes they played cat and

A Glasgow housewife hostage with a gun at her back

mouse, the gunman behind his hostage, with Jack and Archie only a few feet away, until the arrival of two police officers. The police were unarmed, of course, but they kept edging forward, and the robber's nerve finally cracked and he gave himself up; but all the time his finger had been on the trigger of his gun, Jack Hill's finger had been on the shutter of his camera.

The pair never got to Motherwell. They took their exclusive story and pictures straight back to Albion Street, and Walker Sinclair, the editor of the *Citizen*, printed a special edition.

Archie and his troupe of housing-scheme entertainers not only contributed greatly to the sales of the *Citizen*, but brought a deal of brightness into an otherwise grey existence in those cultural deserts of Glasgow.

In 1957, when the *Evening News* folded and the survivors rifled the corpse, the *Times* took most of the spoils, and the circulation gap widened to 60,000.

It could have seemed a less than propitious time to drop the pilot, but Walker Sinclair was transferred to the *Express* and I was appointed editor of the *Citizen* in his place – to the disapproval, I learned later, of John Gordon, who apparently said that the appointee should have been a younger person. I was 44 years old then, while John Gordon himself was 67! He was reputed to travel in his company-owned Rolls Royce to collect his old age pension, and then instruct his chauffeur to stop at a fashionable tobacconist so that he could spend it on Havana cigars.

Three years earlier, it had been suggested to him that he himself should give way to someone younger, and he did so – albeit reluctantly – in favour of Lord Beaverbrook's proposed successor, John Junor, but he was given the title of Editor-in-Chief. To soften the blow, the Beaver suggested that he could perhaps write a column, and John Gordon's trenchant 'Comment' column on current affairs had now given him renewed acclaim; he was to continue to write it as long as his health permitted. By that time its following was so great that John Junor had to continue it, first as 'JJ' and then under his own name. 'JJ' imparted to the genre an extra caustic flavour and a number of quotable phrases like 'Pass the sickbag, Alice'; he also gave national fame to the little Fife town of Auchtermuchty – a place with which he himself was only acquainted as a place through which he passed on his way to play golf in the Royal and Ancient's Spring and Autumn meetings at St Andrews.

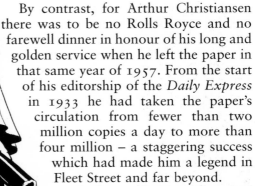

In John Gordon's final farewell to the company the old Rolls Royce was replaced by a Rolls of his own, a gift from Sir Max Aitken – and who would deny that the Grand Old Man deserved it?

By contrast, for Arthur Christiansen there was to be no Rolls Royce and no farewell dinner in honour of his long and golden service when he left the paper in that same year of 1957. From the start of his editorship of the *Daily Express* in 1933 he had taken the paper's circulation from fewer than two million copies a day to more than four million – a staggering success which had made him a legend in Fleet Street and far beyond.

Perhaps the acclaim had been too much for Lord Beaverbrook to stomach, although he had always recognised the vital part Christian-sen had played in the paper's runaway success. At all events, Chris had suffered a heart attack

John Gordon by Giles

in the previous autumn, during the time of the Suez crisis; Ted Pickering had acted as editor during his illness, but we all expected (as Chris himself did) that normal service would be resumed after convalescence. But it was not to be. When he returned to the office to pick up the reins among his old staff he was shocked to find he had no right to be there.

It is said that when he went to see Lord Beaverbrook about it, his lordship escorted him to the lift and said, 'Well, goodbye Chris. Sorry to see you going down.'

It was a cruelly abrupt and humiliating end to the career of the greatest editor the *Daily Express* ever had.

CHAPTER 22

Living with poor relations

THE CITIZEN STAFF MIGHT well have shared John Gordon's disappointment over the choice of a new editor, albeit for different reasons. Walker Sinclair, who was still several years away from retirement age, had steered a steady course through difficult waters and he was deservedly respected. Moreover, his successor was coming from the other side of the house (literally, because although the third floor was shared, the staffs of the *Express* and the *Citizen* occupied opposite ends of it, and their salaries and rewards and lifestyles contrasted considerably).

Willie Steen, the Deputy Editor, had been a *Citizen* man throughout his career, apart from a period as a Reuters war correspondent; Jimmy Brough, the News Editor, had been there since he left school, and the rest of the staff were equally dedicated.

Close alliance with the circulation department in Walker Sinclair's time, mainly involving souvenir editions and slip pages for the House-wives' Club shows, had already helped to eat into the *Times's* lead, and we would obviously continue that policy. But Willie and I also decided that the *Citizen* would keep as closely as possible to the Christiansen mould without damaging its perceived image.

It was difficult at first to adjust from what had been the relatively free-spending environment of a national morning newspaper to the meagre fare on which an evening newspaper had to exist. I had obviously come to live with my poorer relations. Stuart McCartney, the one-time office boy who had patted the Stone of Destiny in 1951, said to me many years later, 'Everyone on the *Express* saw us as the Cinderella paper.'

Well, they would, wouldn't they? I had felt exactly the same.

Lord Beaverbrook told the Royal Commission on the Press that he ran his newspapers for propaganda, and that to do so he needed a steady circulation figure and a healthy balance sheet. But, he added, that sheet should not run to excessive profit. His son, Sir Max Aitken, was on his way back from Albion Street to the airport to catch the plane to London one day, when he divulged to John Paterson (later our group general manager and finally our chairman) that the group was heading that year towards a large profit. He added gloomily, 'My father will NOT be pleased.'

So, that year, a huge spending programme was ordered. It was spent on sales promotions. That was how any surplus was normally spent. At other times the reps knew only stringent economy, so that they came to refer to the years as 'hunger or bust'.

The strategy as it applied to the *Citizen* was that since the paper which sold most copies and at the same time made the most profit would win the war with the *Times*, aggressive selling had to be accompanied by a firm clamp on 'constant' or 'continuing' overall costs. The strategy also called for close collaboration with my opposite number in management, who had arrived from London. Unhappily, he did not share the same beliefs as the two Sandys; rather, he considered editorial matters to be as much within his province as managerial matters, and there were several skir-mishes before David Aitken arrived as his deputy and then succeeded him. Between David Aitken and Ronnie Fowler, who became the *Citizen* circulation manager, and myself, there was then all the rapport the two Sandys could have asked for.

There was no budgetary control as such, but a close watch was kept on those 'overall continuing costs' by Tom Blackburn and his watchdogs. The most important item of these was staff costs. In all my time as editor I can recall having recruited only one person who could not have been justified as a 'one-for-one' replacement in the strength of the regiment. That exception was Cliff Hanley.

After reading Cliff Hanley's *Dancing in the Streets*, that joyous portrayal of earthy Glasgow tenement life, I wanted to serialise it in the *Citizen*. The late Sam McKinlay, who was then the Editor of the *Evening Times*, had forestalled us, however, so we took the author instead.

Cliff began with a series of articles entitled 'Glasgow A to Z', and we soon began to wonder if we would ever get beyond C, because he found so many things to pronounce upon, such as the atom bomb and capital punishment and capitalism and sundry other subjects with which the *Citizen* was not always in sympathy.

In a totalitarian society he would have been awarded the Alexei Stakhanov Medal for production. In between writing an article a day and hiking with Barbara Moore on her charity walk from Land's End to John O' Groats, he wrote film scripts and plays, and collaborated in the composition of that alternative national anthem, *Scotland the Brave*. When he left to write even more books we missed him sorely.

One of those I recruited to the *Citizen* as a 'one-for-one' replacement was my old reporting colleague, Bill Johnston. He had left the *Express* to pursue a private venture; when that proved unprofitable, the *Express* would have willingly taken him back, but he chose to join the *Citizen* instead. Tom Blackburn could not have guessed that I reckoned Bill had more value than any three replacements – I reckoned he was a 'three-for-one' replacement!

Another important 'continuing costs' item was wages. Stuart McCartney was now 21 years old. He could not secure a mortgage to buy a house because his weekly wage was 15 shillings (75p) short of the

Building Society's requirement, so he asked Jimmy Brough for another £1 a week. Although I do not recall the circumstances, I do not doubt my part in this: Stuart told me many years later that Jimmy Brough had returned to say that he had consulted me and that, regrettably, any increase for him would distort the wage structure. So Stuart McCartney went to the *Daily Mail* for the means to secure his mortgage, and was lost to Albion Street for several years.

However, so long as we accepted that there was no family treasure chest to provide finery, and we remembered our proper station in life and entertained no lofty ambitions to expand either in numbers or in wage bill, it was soon evident that we were not going to be inhibited in our programme to take Cinderella to the ball.

We had a staff which included people of talent, able to play in any position, and no prima donnas among them – in soccer parlance, 'playing only for the jersey'. We had enough money to buy serials and short stories and cartoons; we had access to the London *Evening Standard* features such as Sam White's 'Letter from Paris', and articles which included those sent by Jean Campbell as she roamed the world's capitals (since she was the Beaver's grand-daughter one would have ignored these at one's peril). We could also recruit, by the back door as it were, taking freelances on board for specified purposes and periods of time to write articles when our own numbers could not cope.

The first time we really opened the purse strings was to finance an expedition abroad for Malcolm Munro. As many people were leaving the Clyde at that time as had left in the 1930s. Malcolm went to Canada as emigrant number 1556 so that he could tell at first hand what the hundreds of would-be emigrants in the queue could expect to find.

Pat Haughan, a welder in a Govan shipyard, saved for more than a year to scrape together the £250 which would take him and his wife Rita and three children to a supposedly better future in the New World, and Malcolm became one of the family by proxy.

In the interests of his story he was given an expense allowance so restricted that even the most prudent manager would have approved. He took a job in a Toronto steelworks, but it was never clear whether he did this in the interests of story or to augment his parsimonious allowance.

We also sent Duncan McNicol (and thereby unearthed another young talent) to Germany to investigate whether the citizens of Lunneberg were justified in accusing the Highland Light Infantry of nine days of rioting terror in concert with the Welsh Regiment. Of his own volition the young reporter went on to Hamburg to observe shipyard practices there. He was sufficiently impressed by German efficiency to write a series of articles setting out lessons which could be applied in the yards of the Clyde.

The *Citizen* had a more middle-class character than its rival *Times*.

On Saturdays it paraded its respectability with a full page in its early editions devoted to church notices and church affairs, edited by a very nice old retired minister, the Reverend Duncan Campbell. In its later editions it printed a sports edition and began to shout as stridently as any football fan.

We decided that if we were to reach more of that mass male readership we would have to shout louder, so we gave a cloth cap to Malcolm Munro. Malcolm was number ten in a family of twelve reared in the tenements of Maryhill where they believed in Partick Thistle miracles, and he knew the idiom. He used to say that when he was born, 'Nurse Kelly told my father 'Congratulations... I think it's a baby'.'

The baby became a very big boy indeed; so we called him 'Big Malky' and 'The Heavyweight Champion of the Fans'. We gave him most of an inside page of the sports edition, and allowed him free rein to write about senior football, within the limits of decency, as a counterweight to the authoritative and much respected contributions of the Sports Editor, George Aitken. We also gave him his own readers' letters space, and we advertised his presence with posters at every game he reported, until he became a kenspeckle figure wherever he went. He was eventually lured away to the *Daily Mail*, alas.

Our sports edition was printed on green paper; the *Times* was printed on pink. A disturbing feature of this colour contrast was a suspicion that while the green colour was accepted by the followers of Celtic and by neutrals, this perhaps militated against its sale among 'true blue' Rangers supporters.

During a conference with our colleagues in Circulation, we discussed if it would be better to print the sports edition on neutral white paper. In the middle of the discussion I thought of Jimmy McCluskey from my schooldays in Govan. Jimmy had been the centre forward of the Car-michael Street Rovers, which had been formed by dint of a collection from parents who could ill afford to contribute (and from shopkeepers who probably felt they could ill afford not to). I had been deputed to buy a strip for the team with the collection. The only strip I could find at that price was a second-hand reject in green and white hoops.

Three members of the team refused to play in it. Jimmy McCluskey said that if we did not play in it he would not play at all. Someone suggested we dye the jerseys, and Jimmy said he would not play if they were dyed blue. So Mother soaked them with a red dye in the back-green washhouse. The first time we played in them it rained heavily and the team came home like a tribe of little Indian braves.

At 195 Albion Street we finally decided to ask our suppliers to give the *Citizen* a less pronounced shade of green paper. If Jimmy McCluskey ever bought the *Green Citizen* it is doubtful whether he would have noticed the difference; it certainly had no noticeable effect on sales, one way or the other.

I poached now and then from Big Brother Express such notables as Robins Millar to write, and Jean Baird the fashion artist to produce sketches; so long as what I asked them to do did not conflict with whatever Sandy Trotter might require of them at the time, he turned a blind eye.

I even kidnapped Mamie Baird – and her baby – without protest. 'Kidnapped' is probably too strong a word; let's just say that I borrowed mother and child. So the baby became 'Poggles', and Mamie wrote articles headlined 'Every Monday, Regular as Wash Day – Life With Poggles'. 'Poggles' is now, of course, television's assured and lovely Sally Magnusson.

We spirited Tom Allan over to the *Citizen* as well. The Reverend Tom Allan was the most noted preacher of his day. In the RAF during the war he had been a voice on the radio, taking his message to the Services, and after the war he became the voice of the evangelical Tell Scotland movement. It was Tom Allan who brought Billy Graham to Scotland. He was warm and generous of heart, and greatly beloved of the young.

I wanted him to write for us, particularly in the 'Church Page', but he had already bound himself to the *Times*. When I went to see him at his charge at St George's Tron I knew he would say No, that he could not desert the *Times*. But I did not care if he wrote for Sam McKinlay so long as he wrote for us as well. I suggested to him that both papers might provide a vehicle for his message, and he undertook to consult with Sam. Sam may have thought us devious (although in truth that was not the case) but, bless him, he showed the same Christian charity as Sandy Trotter and said he would not object.

I had not only great respect for Sam McKinlay, but a great liking too. We were friendly adversaries. Sam was a former British Walker Cup player; somehow he was managing not only to edit his paper but also to write for golfers weekly in the *Times'* stable companion, *The Bulletin*, and fortnightly in its other companion, the *Glasgow Herald*. I was thankful that he was doing it for them and not training his musket in our direction. After *The Bulletin* ceased publication in July 1960, Sam continued to write about golf for the *Glasgow Herald* as well as editing the *Evening Times* until he retired in 1980. Dr Sam McKinlay (he had been given an honorary LLD by Glasgow University) died in January, 1998, at the age of 90.

When, eventually, Tom Allan thought he could not do justice to his obligations to both papers he stayed on with the *Citizen*. I was very happy he did so, not only for the sake of the *Citizen*, but for my own sake too, because I became very close to him in the years which followed, until his untimely death at the age of 48 in 1965.

In the autumn of 1957, my first year with the *Citizen*, my little

Cheekyface fell ill on holiday and we brought her back from France in an air ambulance. The doctor in charge at the hospital run by kindly nuns at Lannion in Brittany could only say that 'Madame me presente un tableau bizarre'. It was left to an uncompromising (and rather unfeeling) surgeon in Glasgow to pronounce a doomful opinion unencumbered by Gallic finesse.

Many people went in extremity to see the Reverend J Cameron Peddie, as I did then. Cameron Peddie was the author of *Miracle of Healing*, which I had serialised in the paper. Even before that he was famed in Glasgow as the one who had done more than any other to wean the city's gangs from violence. When what was described as 'The Battle of Crown Street' was waged on the doorstep of his church in the Gorbals he reconciled the enemies and formed the first of what became a total of 30 non-denominational clubs.

He had been 73 years old and was about to retire from his church when one day, he said, he found meaning in the words of Christ to his disciples in the Garden of Gethsemane: 'Could you not watch with me one hour?' He began to pray and to meditate for an hour every day before midnight. At the end of five years in which no sign had come to him, he found he could heal the sick by touch and by prayer.

I recall now that there never was a Church of Scotland minister who more resembled Pope John Paul II, but I do not recall what this saintly old man said to me in his vestry – if, indeed, I heard his words; I know only that when he laid his hands on my head I felt a stillness such as I had never known before. He gave me a copy of a prayer to be said nightly at the same time as he would be at his devotions, and for some months afterwards it happily appeared that that blunt Glasgow surgeon could have been grossly mistaken.

Many things, understandably, became less important to me at that time, and I had almost forgotten about William Watt and the continuing search for the man who had killed his family.

CHAPTER 23

To trap murderer Manual

DURING THE LAST TIME we had talked to Bill Watt he had said, 'What little of my life is left will be spent finding that brute.' In his mind, the brute could be none other than Peter Manuel, the man who while in Barlinnie prison had said he knew who the murderer was. He could not confront Manuel, who was still serving his sentence for breaking into a colliery, but he began to frequent Manuel's world, finding out from other criminals what they knew of him and of his habits.

Manuel, however, in his twisted mind had enjoyed the police chase and William Watt was part of the great game. As soon as Manuel came out of prison in November 1957 he called Lawrie Dowdall and asked him to arrange a meeting. Bill Watt went to the meeting alone. Lawrie Dowdall called it a foolhardy act. When Bill Watt later told Drew Rennie what had happened at the meeting, we thought it foolhardy too, and he himself conceded that probably it had been.

Bill Watt had gone to the meeting believing that Manuel wanted money, and in the hope that he might trap Manuel into making admissions. Manuel, on the other hand, only went there to tease and torment him. They sat in a corner booth of a lounge bar in Renfield Street, facing each other. Manuel handed him a folded copy of that night's edition of the *Evening Citizen*. In the empty Stop Press column he had written, 'I don't trust the two at the next table. Act as though you know me,'

Bill Watt brushed the paper aside. 'If it's money you're after, you're wasting your time,' he said. 'And if I get the slightest indication that you had anything to do with what happened at Burnside I'll tear you limb from limb.'

Manuel sat up erect. 'People don't do that to Peter Manuel,' he said with icy calm. He then put a photograph on the table. 'That's your daughter, isn't it?' he said. The picture Bill Watt looked at was not of Vivienne. Only later did he remember having seen a likeness in a photograph in a newspaper. It was a picture of Anne Kneilands, the young girl found strangled at the beginning of the year near the 5th tee of East Kilbride golf course.

Manuel tore the picture into shreds and then suggested they go 'somewhere we can talk privately'. 'Somewhere private' was a pub in Crown Street. There, as proof that he knew the murderer, Manuel provided a description of the house in Fennsbank Avenue, even more detailed than the one he had given at his meeting with Lawrence Dowdall in Barlinnie. As a climax he said, 'I know who killed your family – it was Charlie Tallis'.

In the fanciful tale he then wove, he claimed that Charlie Tallis, a petty criminal acquaintance, had committed the crime in error. Tallis, he said, together with a man he named as Martin Harte and a woman named Mrs Bowes, had gone to Fennsbank Avenue to rob a safe known to be in the home of the Valentes, but had broken into another house by mistake. They found it empty, but hid there until midnight listening to Vivienne Watt and Deanne Valente playing the radio in the next house until the programme ended. Then they broke into what they believed to be the Valente home, where in panic they shot the people in it.

Tallis, he said, had given him the gun and asked him to get rid of it, and he had thrown it into the River Clyde. His tale ended with a boast: 'After I spoke to Hendry and McDonald in Barlinnie I took the noose from your neck and hung it between your head and mine.'

Serial Killer Peter Manuel.
'No one will take my picture'
he said... But Ronnie Burgess did

By then Bill Watt felt he needed a witness to what Manuel was telling him, and he called his brother John to join them in a pub in Bridgeton. They went on from there to John's house, where John's wife Sarah gave them a meal. During it, Manuel said, 'I'm going to help Mr Watt. I know who did the murders' – and he repeated the tale of Tallis and his companions.

But he could not be trapped into any significant admission. Instead, at one stage he mocked, 'By the way, who did you pay to do it?' John Watt seized his brother's arms to stop him leaping on his tormentor, and Manuel said it was as well he had stopped, 'because if you had laid a hand on me I would have crucified you'.

Next day John said, 'I'm sure if you had hit him we would not have been alive now, and Sarah would not be alive, either. He didn't blink an eyelid. I'm sure he had a gun.'

Bill Watt drove his adversary home at 7 am and arranged to meet again – this time with Lawrence Dowdall present. At that meeting Manuel repeated to the lawyer his fantasies, but he made one blunder which was to lead to his undoing: he also volunteered the information that before the Burnside murders Tallis, Harte and Mrs Bowes had broken into a house in Bothwell. There Tallis had thrown Mrs Bowes on to a bed in a quarrel and his gun had gone off. The shot had missed Mrs Bowes, said Manuel, but it had embedded itself in the mattress – 'and if you find that bullet you will prove Mr Watt's innocence.'

That statement later did help to prove Bill Watt's innocence, but it was also to tighten the noose around Manuel's neck. In the following month Henry Platt, the owner of a house in Bothwell, brought to the police a bullet his wife had found in a mattress in his home, which had been burgled on 15 September 1956, a few days before the Watt family killings. The bullet was proved to be from the gun which had killed the Watts.

Two weeks after that last meeting between Manuel and Bill Watt and his lawyer, Isabelle Cooke was reported missing from her home in Mount Vernon, feared dead; and then on 6 January 1958 Peter Smart, his wife Doris and their 11-year-old son Michael were found shot dead in their ransacked home in Bothwell.

As the evidence against Manuel was piling up, and the trap was about to close, he began to know fear for the first time. Whereas he had exulted in the belief he could lead the police a merry dance, he became nervous about the fact that they did not confront him, and he brooded over not knowing why they did not do so, and of not knowing what they were doing. The attention of newspapermen, which he had craved, also became an irritation because they were concentrating on probing into his life without coming to him.

Every newspaperman in Glasgow was now convinced that Manuel would be arrested and stand trial, and they gathered every available scrap of information about his background. Most reporters chose a pub in Bellshill as a base from which to gather their information. (If one wished to throw the opposition off a scent, the strategy was to tell a 'secret lead' to a barmaid named Nellie. When she was teased about her inability to keep a secret she said, 'It isn't me who can't keep a secret. It's the people I talk to.')

A worried Manuel came to Albion Street in late December asking to see Drew Rennie. They talked together in the Dunrobin bar around the corner from the office for more than two hours. But while Manuel derived no hint of what Drew knew about the police inquiries, the reporter also gathered nothing from Manuel except the familiar tirade of wild allegations of harassment of himself and of the involvement of Mr Watt and others, and boasts of how in his time he had consistently foiled Lanarkshire police – even claiming to have fooled Scotland Yard and the FBI during the disappearance of the traitors Philby and MacLean.

Chief Detective Superintendent Alex Brown of Glasgow CID finally swooped on Manuel's home, where he found stolen articles linked to the crimes, and Manuel realised that his father could be charged with the thefts. During a dramatic meeting at which his parents were present he broke down. When his mother urged him to 'tell us the truth, son', he confessed to killing the Watt family, and the Smarts, and Anne Kneilands. He then took the police to a ploughed field and told them where to dig, and they found the half-naked body of Isabelle Cooke.

At the *Citizen*, Jimmy Donnelly had gathered all the background we needed and it was already set up in print and ready to publish. Not only the Manuel background was in print. We had even prepared a front page to publish at the end of his trial. It was dominated by a photograph of Manuel (which we believed was exclusive to us) spread across seven of the page's eight columns. It was a face so evil that it seemed to leer out of the page. Above it we put a one-word streamer head line: GUILTY! It never occurred to us that there could be an acquittal. The end column (the Stop Press column) was left blank.

The page was moulded and casts were made of it for the presses. We also set a few lines of linotype giving the news (in anticipation) that he had been found guilty by the jury in the High Court; these were inserted into the Stop Press 'fudge' boxes which would be clamped onto the machines in the column space left empty in the casts.

During all this time my abiding and overriding thoughts had really been elsewhere, with my stricken little Cheekyface. One dull April morning I had to put away the card of hope which the Rev Cameron Peddie had given to me: God had had too many prayers, and it seemed that He could not possibly answer them all.

The loss of little Cheekyface that morning created a black hole from which I did not emerge until, three years later, I met Margaret, a lovely young dark-haired girl who was really a white witch, and she wove a love spell which has lasted throughout our married life to the present day.

Peter Manuel went to trial on 12 May 1958. It was known that in the week after he left Barlinnie prison he had gone to Newcastle and there shot – for some unknown reason – a taxi-driver. Since he could not be charged with this in a Scots court, a detective from Newcastle waited in the court corridor with an arrest warrant.

Manuel pleaded not guilty to all the murder charges, alleging that Mr Smart had killed his own family and then taken his own life, and he cited alibis in every case except that of the Watt murders. For that charge he reserved his hatred of William Watt, against whom he laid a special charge of impeachment. He told the court that he had been framed by the police, and that he had confessed only to protect his family from police threats.

The man on whom he vented his spleen came to the court in a wheelchair. Bill Watt and reporter Philip Mackie had been together in a car when it crashed and both had been injured, Bill Watt seriously enough to warrant a stay in hospital before being pronounced fit enough to go to court to give evidence.

Manuel dredged up all the evidence which had confused the police in the initial arrest, but in so doing merely discredited it further. But his vendetta did not end there. On the fourth day of the trial he dismissed his distinguished counsel, Harold Leslie (later Lord Birsay), took over his own defence and recalled Mr Watt to the witness box, at one point openly accusing him of killing his own family.

'You are a liar!' Bill Watt roared.

The trial ended on the 16th day. The jury found Peter Manuel guilty of all the murders except that of Anne Kneilands, because his confession to it lacked the corroborative evidence required by Scots law.

Lord Cameron sentenced him to death.

The moment the jury returned its verdict we took a phone call from the court building and pressed the button which started our presses. We flooded the city and all around it with copies which, with their never-before-seen picture of Manuel, screamed for attention, and we did not stop the presses until the *Scottish Daily Express* demanded them as of right for their own first edition.

It was some time afterwards that I discovered that the picture of Manuel had not been an exclusive after all. Its ownership was shared with the *Daily Mail*. Ronnie Burgess, who joined the *Express* in October 1957, and was with us thereafter for 35 years, told me: 'I was on the *Scottish Daily Mail* at the time of the Anne Kneilands murder, in company with their reporter Eric Moncur. At the police conference we were asked if we would help to keep the event in the public eye. No matter how trivial the information might be, the police needed people to come forward with anything they might have seen.

'We heard about a worker who was complaining that a pair of wellington boots and a pick-axe shaft had been stolen from a hut. The CID and the uniformed police were conducting a door to door inquiry in the area. I agreed with the *Express* photographer Ronnie Taylor that while he covered the door-to-door inquiry I would go with Eric Moncur and the *Express* reporter Ronnie Burns. We found the hut. Inside was a chap named Peter Manuel, who gave the reporters all the details of the alleged theft. As he was talking at length I could not help but notice his black piercing eyes. Not a nice fellow, this one, I thought.

'I asked if I could take a picture of him. He said, 'No way is anyone taking my picture'. When I asked him to hold up a pair of wellington boots like the ones which had been stolen, he said, 'Do you think I'm soft in the head? If I hold them up you'll photograph me with them'. But he did in fact agree to hold them out of the door, with him hiding behind it and with only his hand showing. Since it was getting dark, I used a flash for the picture and this attracted the attention of a uniformed policeman who was standing nearby.

He came over to ask what was happening and decided he had better have a word with Peter Manuel. The policeman knocked on the door, only to be told by Manuel to 'f—- off'. The policeman then identified himself as Sergeant Burns of the Rutherglen police, and at this Manuel opened the door, smiling and explaining that he thought it was the photographer who had knocked.

'I grabbed the opportunity to get his picture. Manuel then went berserk, shouting and swearing and threatening 'I'll get you for that, you bastard!' The sergeant told him to cool it. He offered to accompany me down the road and did so, with me feeling those piercing eyes following me every step of the way.

'Next day the front desk receptionist at the *Daily Mail* office told me that a scruffy looking chap had been in asking for a photographer of my description. She told me he had pulled back his jacket and pointed to what she took to be a gun, and said to her, 'When next you see him, tell him I have a message for him'. But she was quick-witted enough to tell him that although I had been working in Glasgow, I had gone back to Manchester because that was where I was based. And with that the man went away.

'Little did I know who Peter Manuel was when I sent the picture along to Ronnie Taylor and got one in return about the door-to-door inquiry. It was some time after I joined the *Express* that chief photographer Albert Barr took me aside and said, 'How about that for a picture, then, chum? And it's exclusive.'

'I agreed that it was a good picture, but said that I had taken it while I was working for the *Daily Mail*. 'No, no,' said Albert, so I told him about the shared picture agreement.

'I remember when I was sitting on the press benches during the Manuel trial I was always waiting for him to turn round and look at me with that smile, and for him to mouth that he would still get me. So I was pretty happy when Lord Cameron sentenced him.'

What happened to the picture at the *Mail*?

'They mislaid the negative, and there was a frantic search,' said Ronnie Burgess. 'Fortunately for them, every negative at the *Mail* was contact-printed and sent to the office of the town in which the picture was taken. This was to enable anyone who wanted to buy a copy of any picture printed in the paper to see what it would look like. So they eventually found a copy. It measured four by five inches.'

Many years later I met Bill Watt again. He was living in a little town far from the past he could not forget. Manuel's crime and his vendetta had cast a long shadow.

There are some who in the face of truth prefer the lie and to think ill. The persecution of this innocent man, whom Manuel robbed of his family and then pursued with falsehoods, continued even after the murderer had paid his due penalty.

'The boycott of my bakery still went on,' he told me, 'and my business declined so far that I had to give up. What kept me from despair was finding Lorna.'

Lorna was Lorna Craig. He met her a few weeks before Manuel's trial when he called at his brother's flat and his brother introduced her as a neighbour.

'It was Lorna who most sustained me during the trial when I had to confront that evil man again, and it was she who sustained me after it, too,' he said. 'We've been married now for more than 20 years. We moved out of Glasgow to live in Edinburgh at first, but that was not far enough so we came here. We have a little garden but I can't do any work to look after it because I still suffer from the effects of the car crash I was in. But we are both very happy.'

CHAPTER 24

Bishops in the Kirk

LORD BEAVERBROOK, BORN INTO and nurtured in the Presbyterian doctrine, was (or so it was always said) tolerant of other people's religious beliefs – so long as they did not interfere with his own. Stern and sure as he was in the faith of his fathers, he was less certain of the steadfastness of others in the Kirk. Lest any frail vessels in the tribe might come to hanker after false gods, he had adjured his editor in Scotland ever to keep on his desk a copy of the Westminster Confession of Faith, and to see to it that no one tampered with it.

Some misguided divines tried in 1959 to do just that, presenting a report for the General Assembly of the Church of Scotland proposing the introduction of bishops in presbytery.

None of us ever saw that copy of the Westminster Confession of Faith on Sandy Trotter's desk. One has to suppose that he kept it in a drawer, but in any case he needed no summons to arms from the great defender. He knew instantly what his duty demanded. He called into council Ian McColl, who was the session clerk of Sandyford Church in Glasgow, and the Reverend Duncan Campbell, 'Churchman' of the *Citizen*, to help him plan a campaign.

As what became known as the Bishops Report was debated in presbyteries up and down the land, all our readers, whether they belonged to the established church or not, or if they even went to church at all, were told in leader columns and articles day by day exactly how and why the authors of the report had so grievously erred.

Presbytery after presbytery threw out the report. The most outright rejection and the most damning indictment of it came from Glasgow, which then published a 31-page pamphlet entitled *Glasgow Speaks*. It went to every one of the fathers and lay brethren who met in the General Assembly in May, and they rejected the report overwhelmingly.

The Beaver telephoned: 'You have your headline, he said. 'Jehovah has triumphed, the people are free'.

A week later he telephoned (prompted, it is suspected, by Lord Rosebery, Sandy's friend and leader in the Scottish Tourist Board), and said to Sandy: 'They are saying a most terrible thing about you...' (Pause) 'I thought you were a Presbyterian?'

Said Sandy: 'I am.'

'Now I am told,' Lord Beaverbrook went on, 'Now I am told that you were a choir boy in the Episcopal Cathedral in Edinburgh.'

'Yes sir,' said the former choir boy, whose voice had long since broken. 'But I was young and I needed the money.'

A few months later Sandy Trotter was appointed chairman of the company in Scotland and moved into an office on the top floor. One could see this elevation as meet reward for his labours – had he not taken the sales to over 600,000 copies? – and as giving him blessed relief from the relentless pressures of editorship. One could see it also as further enhancing his stature in public life. He had made countless friends, from porters to peers. Incredibly, he had found time to devote himself to the Scottish Tourist Board, and to helping Borstal boys and other causes. Just two years earlier he had fronted an anti-tuberculosis campaign which persuaded 75 per cent of Glasgow's population above the age of 15 to queue to be X-rayed, and as many to do so in Edinburgh.

But I could not think he accepted the translation to higher office without regret – that he would not miss the raw excitement which he had known for so long on the floor below.

A young man called Roger Wood was sent up from Manchester to take his place. He was a most capable journalist and was much liked by many. But the link with my old chief was broken and I missed him. However great were Roger's accomplishments I kept thinking that more money and resources were now being put at Roger's disposal than had ever been made available to Sandy.

The change had an effect on my attitude to our companion paper. Although the *Evening Times* was constantly in our sights, it was rather against Big Brother that we truly measured ourselves. It was, one has to suppose, akin to sibling rivalry. Big Brother operated in a larger battle scene, but when the news happened in our more restricted circulation area it was Big Brother we hoped to equal or surpass. Not that that happened very often. But the change of editor made our relationship seem more distant.

The news which broke soon afterwards, however, was too appalling to be seen in terms of rivalry.

CHAPTER 25

Hell Street, C.3.

THE FIRST THOUGHT WHICH came to people's minds was of 'Dixon's Blazes'. But the old ironworks were gone and in any case the famous constant glow they cast above the city had never been so lurid as the red monster which raged over the Glasgow night sky on 30 March 1960. It destroyed 19 lives, and those included men who were our next-door neighbours in the Salvage Corps, some of whom often shared a pint and a gossip with us in 'Tom's Bar'.

The monster began with a few puffs of black smoke out of the windows of a whisky bond warehouse in Cheapside Street, off the waterfront, but the brigades soon arrived in force, for a whisky fire is potentially more dangerous than any other. First among the newspapermen to arrive were reporter Stan Stewart and photographer Ian Elder. They had been there for about ten minutes when they felt a tremor beneath their feet.

'I suppose it was instinct which made me move back about thirty feet,' said Ian. 'The rumble increased to a roar, and we saw the whole building bulge outwards, like in a slow motion film, and then as we ran for our lives it erupted outwards and upwards in flames.'

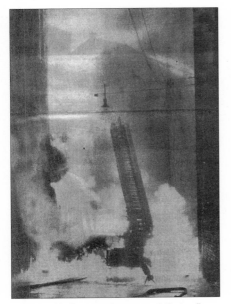

Cheapside Street... the moment that a fire engine disappeared in flames
30 March, 1960

When the two turned back to look, two turntables had disappeared in a cloud of fire, and with them a fireman who had been perched atop one of them. The fire engine which had been near them was gone, too. There was only an ugly pile of shattered stone and timber which glowed red like coals alight. The crew who had manned it were buried underneath.

A brave young policeman ran to the blazing pyre, tore away burning rubble with his bare hands, and dragged out two of the firemen. Another two tenders were engulfed as other parts of the building fell. Stan Stewart thought his companion had been lost; but he found the photographer crouched behind a surviving tender, taking pictures.

Bill Johnston was coming out of a cinema when he saw the glare, and he knew he would be needed long before his duty with the *Citizen* was due to begin next day. He hurried home to find the telephone ringing and to be told, 'There's a helluva fire at the waterfront.' He reached Cheapside Street at midnight. The fire was still raging. Every now and then, as whisky vats exploded, bursts of flame rose ever higher, over the roofs of tenements, sending families fleeing into the streets to safe distance.

In the midst of it all, said Bill, a kind woman appeared with a pot of tea and three cups – 'This for more than four hundred firemen! But the Salvation Army turned up with urns of hot tea. The good old Sally Army are always there when they're needed.'

Jimmy Donnelly remembers seeing Firemaster Henry Chadwick standing beside the twisted wreckage at midnight, and at first light of day seeing him still standing there, looking at the hideous scene in dazed disbelief. The firemaster was to say later that 'not all the water in the River Clyde could have helped us put it out'; but, said Jimmy, 'we did not ask him many questions because every time someone spoke to him he could not answer without crying.'

The owner of a little shop at the top of Cheapside Street put an empty sweetie jar in the window with a label saying 'For the widows'. It was quickly crammed with silver and notes, and emptied and re-filled again many times that day; when the whole of Glasgow was asked to give, an official fund reached £186,000.

The front page of next morning's *Express* carried the picture Ian Elder took as he turned to see one of the turntables swamped in flame. We filled the front page of the *Citizen* with another of his pictures and we headlined it:

HELL STREET, C.3.

It seemed the only way to describe the most horrible disaster in the peace-time fire service.

Nine months later, Ian Elder was at Princes Dock waiting with firemen who answered a radio call from the captain of the German vessel Pagasund, coming up river with a cargo of matches, newsprint and wooden bobbins for thread. Under her battened hatches the cargo was ablaze. Ian Elder began to take pictures of the squad of firemen as they donned breathing apparatus and strapped on torches. When the first hatch was opened a few wisps of smoke emerged.

'I thought to myself that this was probably not going to merit being in the paper,' said Ian. 'Nonetheless, I ran to the waiting office car and gave my pictures to the driver so that he could get them to the office in

All that was left... a funeral pyre for a brave crew

time for the Citizen's first edition. When I got back I heard a shout of 'Get help, quick!' and I saw a fireman being pulled out on to the deck, unconscious. I leapt on to the ship just as a second fireman was brought up. I had no idea that the fumes from that cargo could have been so lethal.'

In the six minutes he had been away, one fireman after another had fallen to the deadly gas, and as each one fell a companion had gone down into the hold until as many as twelve had unhesitatingly risked their lives.

'The deck looked like a wartime casualty clearing station,' said Ian Elder. 'When the driver returned to take my new pictures back to Albion Street he brought a message from the News Desk asking me to telephone in. Could I, I was asked, identify the men in the picture I had taken as they prepared to go into the hold – one of the officers had died in hospital. He was Company Officer Douglas Mearns, the officer in charge of the river fireboat, who had been the first to go into the hold. It was a chilling thought that just ten minutes before he died I had taken his picture – a terrible reminder of Cheapside.'

The 1960s

Last night of the Glasgow trams... 1962

More than 250,000 people stood for hours on the streets of Glasgow in the rain on the night of 4 September 1962, for one reason only – nostalgia.

They were there to say goodbye to the city's trams.

It had been a long love affair (ninety years, to be precise) and for most of that time 'the caurs' had been their only form of transport – jangling juggernauts in which the 'clippies' (conductresses) who took the fares became renowned for their repartee.

Ninety years was too far for most of the people that night to cast back upon, but many could remember that in pre-war days, depending on where you lived, you recognised the tram which would take you home by its colour-band – blue or red or green or yellow or white. The most you had to pay was tuppence-ha'penny, and for that anyone so minded could travel up to 22 miles (from the Renfrew Ferry to Milngavie).

The last service to be abandoned was the one from Auchenshuggle (and there's a name to conjure with – it is alleged that it was INVENTED as a terminus by the first city transport manager, James Dalrymple).

From Auchenshuggle on that September night a whole cavalcade of history set out, led by a team of white horses pulling Glasgow's very first tram to trundle along the seven-mile route to the city.

All along the route, police tried in vain to stop people putting pennies on the tramlines to be buckled as souvenirs. And all along the seven miles the 250,000 cheered.

The only time they forbore was when a Number 64 bus bearing the legend AUCHENSHUGGLE on its destination board passed through the Gallowgate in the opposite direction. They booed until it was out of sight.

CHAPTER 26

Trouble in paradise

ROGER WOOD'S 18 MONTH SPELL with us in Glasgow was never dull. Roger had style. The new editor of the *Scottish Daily Express* spent prodigally, delighting in cocking a snook at management. His habit on return from supper after the first edition was to re-enter among his toilers with a shouted greeting of 'Hello there, genius!' (and to observe mischievously who among them was the first to look up in recognition), and then to cry with arms upraised : 'Editorial is KING!'

He cared not tuppence for the London hierarchy. His bravura extended to making himself unavailable to receive Lord Beaverbrook's repeated telephone calls, sometimes ignoring them for days on end.

To give him his due (which I did only grudgingly because of my long attachment to his predecessor), Roger imparted new impetus and brought new blood to mix with our own aristocracy. He appropriated more space from whichever feature pages retained undue London influence, including the leader page, so that he could give more room to the trenchant and controversial Charles Graham, his chief leader writer, and to the pawky features writer, Willie Hunter.

His news staff did their best to live up to his claim that the editorial staff were royalty. One of their last triumphs during his time was the exclusive story of the alleged murder on 'God's Island'.

'God's Island' is Gigha, a flat and rocky islet six miles long and two miles broad, a couple of miles away by ferry from the mainland peninsula of Kintyre. It was probably some holidaymaker who coined the term, enchanted to find the island so unspoiled. Lieut. Colonel C.L. Horlick, the owner of the business which made the famous bedtime drink, had bought it after the war and stipulated that it should remain unchanged forever.

The island had only 150 people living on it. It had no need of police – two volunteer special constables sufficed. But the paradisal peace was shattered when ferryman Alan Flanders was shot dead in the ferry house.

Alan Flanders had lived in the house with the island girl whom he married after leaving the Royal Navy. The marriage had not been idyllic. When detectives arrived from the mainland his 30-year-old wife Christine told them that on the day of his death she had feared he was about to kill her. She had picked up the shotgun he had put down at his side when he lay down on a settee, and the gun had gone off accidentally.

The story of the ferryman's death was a major exclusive for the

Scottish Daily Express only because Drew Rennie managed to get Campbeltown Airport to open on a Sunday.

Philip Mackie had planned to spend a holiday on Gigha that year, as he had often done before, and he had many friends there. One of them telephoned to tell him what had happened. He and a photographer could reach the island on the Sunday ferry and return by it before nightfall (but only just), but a 100-mile long journey thereafter precluded getting pictures back to Glasgow in time for the edition. Drew Rennie, who was in charge of the News Desk that day, hired a plane and spent the next hour or more persuading the Campbeltown Airport to allow it to land and to stay open for it to take off again.

Philip Mackie and the photographer scrambled out of the plane and drove to Tayinloan to board the ferry. All that Philip could do was to collect a snapshot of the dead man from his friend, and give it to the photographer, who took a few hurried pictures of the scene and caught the last ferry back to Tayinloan on the mainland and thence to Glasgow by plane from Campbeltown.

Philip stayed on to telephone the story. The police had not believed Christine Flanders, but most of the islanders did. They included Colonel Horlick's wife, who had remained a friend of the accused woman throughout her arrest and subsequent trial at Glasgow High Court.

Christine Flanders was acquitted of the charge of murder, and went back to the island in September in the company of the colonel's wife, who shielded her from the curious and permitted no newspaperman to interview her except one who would do so on behalf of them all. She chose as their representative Philip Mackie. She also permitted one photograph, on condition that her charge would thereafter be left alone.

Roger's studied avoidance of Lord Beaverbrook's calls could not have damaged his career too much, because when Lord Beaverbrook recalled his maverick editor in 1961 he appointed him Bob Edwards' deputy in London. Ian McColl was then left in charge of the paper in Glasgow.

Roger's departure coincided with that of Magnus Magnusson's – he joined the *Scotsman* as assistant editor and from there went on to make a career on television with the BBC.

CHAPTER 27

12,000 reasons

SANDY TROTTER AND I MET from time to time after his elevation to the chairmanship, but there was no occasion to seek his counsel; nor did I do so when we decided to print a series of articles in the *Citizen* by Tom Allan in the May of 1961. The Reverend Tom had become a good friend and a valuable contributor even beyond the confines of the 'Church Page'. He had gone to Moscow to investigate how authentic was the new freedom of worship accorded in Russia and her satellite states, and he had visited Rome and attended an audience with the Pope to describe the Eternal City through Presbyterian eyes.

One day Tom and I spoke about the religious intolerance which prevailed in the West of Scotland. He said he thought that too many people lived in a kind of ghetto within the walls of their own belief, and I suggested to him that he talk to people of different persuasions and explain their faiths to others.

I called the series 'Faith to Faith'. Tom chose to interview five people – a Jew, a Catholic, an Anglican, an agnostic and a spiritualist. The Jew was Dr J.K. Cosgrove, Scotland's leading rabbi; the Anglican was Dr Mervyn Stockwood, the outspoken Bishop of Southwark; the Catholic was the well-known writer Colm Brogan; the agnostic was the MP and TV personality John Freeman; and the spiritualist was Dr John Winning, the medical practitioner who was vice president of the National Union of Spiritualists. No other faiths were represented – there was not such a diversity of faiths in Glasgow in those days.

It was the presence of the Anglican which caused Sandy Trotter disquiet. It had been less than two years since he had been called upon by Lord Beaverbrook to campaign against Bishops in the Kirk, and with hindsight I suppose it would have been courteous to have spoken to him about the series in advance rather than have to be summoned to do so.

I argued that Tom Allan was known as a committed minister of the Church of Scotland, that the series was not concerned with the structure of the churches but only with people's faiths, and that I did not think that Lord Beaverbrook, nor anyone else, would be likely to take exception to its contents. Sandy Trotter said that when he had asked to see me it was not with any intention of interfering, but that he hoped I had taken all factors into account; and he added, in his paternal way, that it was wise policy to avoid any discussion of the differences of religions.

I did not tell Tom Allan about the conversation. As it happened, our Anglican prelate never referred to his role as a bishop. However, after the two-week series had ended, Tom and I had to accept the fact that we did not appear to have done very much to advance the cause of religious tolerance and understanding.

The series could not have escaped the attention of Lord Beaverbrook – we knew that he had a little research group which filleted the public prints every day to feed him with the choicest cuts. Nonetheless, there seemed no reason for unease; nor was there any when I was summoned in September to see Sir Max Aitken in London.

On September 16 a barrier had collapsed towards the end of an Old Firm game between Rangers and Celtic at Ibrox Park in Glasgow; two people had been killed and 44 injured. My absence from the office that Saturday (I had gone into the country for the afternoon) had been cause for disapproval in some quarters – particularly since the office had not been able to reach me by telephone. But that was certainly not a hanging offence; it was generally accepted that evening newspaper editors were not required to be present throughout the Saturday football edition times (although the ever-vigilant Tom Blackburn was known to believe that no one ever needed a holiday, nor even a day off).

Max had always been a kind friend to me. He said, 'I'm sorry, but my father has decided he would like to make some changes...' He ended by saying, 'We wouldn't like to lose you,' and he proposed that I return to the *Scottish Daily Express* as Managing Editor. Tom Blackburn and Sandy Bruce (who was by now his deputy) took me to lunch that day and they both urged me not to resign. In truth, it had not occurred to me to resign: I could not contemplate any home other than 195 Albion Street.

Peter Baker, another of Lord Beaverbrook's favoured young men, was appointed editor of the *Citizen* in my place. Several of my friends suggested that I had blotted my copybook with the 'Faith to Faith' series. I could not accept that. Nor could I believe that my absence from the office at 5 pm on the afternoon of the Ibrox story on 16 September had anything to do with it. The fact was that Lord Beaverbrook had 12,000 other reasons to dismiss me. The circulation gap between the *Citizen* and the *Times* had narrowed from over 60,000 to 12,000, but I think that Lord Beaverbrook had grown weary of waiting for it to close; at the same time he had wanted to blood one of the young eaglets who waited in the nest in London.

I returned to Albion Street and said goodbye to my Citizen colleagues with real sadness; I had loved every minute I had been among them.

The role of Managing Editor is whatever is decided it should be at

We called this happy Citizen picture 'High Noon... Christmas Day in the Gorbals... and it won for 21 year old photographer Stewart Fair an award as one of the top twenty *Encyclopaedia Britannica* Pictures of the Year, in 1960

any time. It can be a prominent one, only a little less than that of the editor; it can be directed towards instigating the news gathering process or translating it into print; or it can be more directed towards management itself. My former role as a news instigator had now been otherwise filled; even my old office was occupied. My niche was to be in management. Yet it never occurred to me to wonder if Tom Blackburn and Sandy Bruce had been right in their advice to me. I was only made one offer from another newspaper and I made no response, for I could not cut the umbilical cord.

CHAPTER 28

A black eye for Big Brother

WHEN THE LITTLE CITIZEN gave the Big Brother *Scottish Daily Express* a black eye it happened (ironically for me) a few weeks after I had departed. Fittingly, it was delivered by Jim Brown, whose elder brother Ian Brown was already a *Scottish Daily Express* executive (and later, when we left Albion Street, would become its editor).

Jim was a talented and tenacious young man who had joined the *Citizen* from the *Ayrshire Post* during my regime. In July 1961 a taxi-driver named John Morton Walkinshaw was found dead in his cab in a street in the Castlemilk estate in Glasgow; the passenger who had hired him had left him with a bullet in his brain. The police arrested Walter Scott Ellis, a notorious gun-carrying criminal, and charged him with the murder.

Jim Brown was at the High Court in Glasgow on the day in October when the trial ended. Several of the newspapermen who waited did so with expectations, for (as it subsequently became obvious) Ellis had been lavish with promises of exclusive interviews in the event of being acquitted. Some who waited were taxi-drivers who thought lynching a fate too good for the killer of their comrade, while others were henchmen of the accused who were determined to protect him. There was the usual crowd of onlookers who were there for no reason other than curiosity, and the usual numbers of police to see that there would be no disturbance. But disturbance there certainly was.

The jury returned a majority verdict of Not Proven – a verdict only available to Scottish courts. There followed a mini riot, which later became the subject of a Press Commission inquiry.

Ellis emerged from the court buildings and immediately became lost in a mêlée: various reporters were clutching and shouting at him, outraged taxi-drivers were howling at him, and his supporters were roaring with delight. When he could be seen at all in the scrum he was shouting for help, ironically not to his fellow mobsters but to the police.

The police were powerless. So were his henchmen, although one of them at least was doing his best. This was 'Banjo', whose nickname was not bestowed because he was a musician: he had a broken leg in plaster, and a crutch which he wielded to good effect. As the struggling mob reached the pavement it was Jim Brown who had his arms locked round the head of the prize. He bundled Ellis into the *Citizen* car, or what he thought to be the *Citizen* car. It belonged to the *Daily Record*. His own car was standing immediately behind. He manhandled the helpless hostage out of the *Record* car into his own and was driven off at speed to a hideaway on Loch Lomondside. He was away and beyond reach before anyone realised whose car it was which contained the now-hysterical Walter Scott Ellis.

At first the *Mail* thought that the *Express* had taken Ellis away, and the *Express* thought that the *Mail* had him, or the *Record*. When the three rivals consulted they concluded that Ellis must have left with his own gang, and took comfort by thinking that at least they had not been scooped.

But you cannot share a home with anyone and expect strict privacy – certainly not if there is a common telephone exchange. On the first occasion on which Jim Brown telephoned his editor from Loch Lomond, Peter Baker asked him where he was. Jim said he could not tell him; nor did he tell him when Peter Baker asked him again during his next call. On the third occasion Peter Baker insisted: 'You cannot withhold information from your editor.' Young Jim Brown replied, 'I know you wouldn't tell anyone yourself, but I warn you that if I say over this telephone where I am, it will not be long before others know, too.'

Peter Baker ignored the warning. Within hours a posse of *Express* reporters arrived at the hotel where Jim Brown and Ellis were holed up.

Ellis was by now becoming an embarrassment, anyway. He was demanding money. Money? From the *Citizen*? Jim Brown handed over his prize to Big Brother. There was not much of Ellis' story left to tell.

Brother Ian would never tell me precisely how the *Express* had learned what Jim had told his editor; nor would Jim. They joked with one another about it... all's fair, after all, in love and newspaper war. But they both agreed that an editor should know when not to ask a reporter what he feels he has good reason not to divulge.

Jim Brown eventually went into newspaper management. In 1995, with the backing of the huge American finance company KKR, he headed a £205 million management buy-out of Reed Regional Newspapers, and at the insistence of KKR he became chairman and chief executive.

It was a far cry from the Citizen of 1961.

CHAPTER 29

Truce with the enemy

ON THE DAY IN OCTOBER 1961 when Lord Beaverbrook slipped away from the Central Hotel to take Lady Dunn to Torphichen churchyard to declare their marriage-by-custom, he had been in good humour during lunch with us. He was pleased to find at his right hand Ian McColl, his old ally in the Bishops in the Kirk struggle. But when Ian abstained from the drink which was in plentiful supply, the Beaver expressed astonishment. 'You don't drink whisky? You don't like whisky? Tell me, do you pass on your teetotal views to your readers?'

Ian replied that if anyone wished to drink himself into the grave that was his prerogative, but he would not follow him, whereupon his lordship said for all to hear that 'Ian McColl is indeed unique among my editors!'

(Later, when Ian went to London to become editor of the *Daily Express*, he would take champagne, but that was only because it was apparently obligatory for Fleet Street editors. He would also take wine on social occasions, but in all the time I have known him he has never touched spirits.)

Lord Beaverbrook did not share Ian's dislike of whisky. We had procured for him his favourite rare blend, which he poured into his glass by his own hand in generous measures. He also professed his astonishment that he had found a member of the Aitken family working for the paper in Glasgow, and he chided David Aitken for not having declared himself. David was the Beaver's great-grand-nephew: his grandfather David and the Beaver's father were brothers, and both had been born at the family's Silvermine Farm in Torphichen (there really HAD been a silver mine there once). But when David was brought into the company, Lord Beaverbrook ordered that he should make his way without divulging the family connection, and David started in Glasgow as a junior circulation clerk. Those of his friends who knew of the Beaver's decree of silence found the public acknowledgement rather belated – but perhaps His Lordship had now considered that 'the boy had done well' by then.

David Aitken himself was delighted, all the more so when, a few days later, Tom Blackburn summoned him to London, where he found himself managing the *Sunday Express*. But it transpired that Lord Beaverbrook had other plans for him. Peter Baker was said to have told Lord Beaverbrook when he was appointed editor of the *Citizen* that he would close the circulation gap with the *Times* within a year, or even earlier. He was not given time to fulfil the promise; instead, he was recalled to London to join Bob Edwards, taking up position immediately behind Roger Wood in the line of succession.

The fight between the *Citizen* and the *Times* had gone more than ten rounds by now. Both antagonists were exhausted, locked in a clinch from which neither could break for fear of falling down. Both papers were operating at a loss. The *Citizen* had an annual deficit of between £50,000 and £70,000, and Lord Beaverbrook decided that the fight was too costly.

David Aitken

He asked David Aitken to identify areas in which economies could be effected. But when it was proved that it would be impossible to make these savings without giving advantage to the *Times*, he decided to seek an accommodation, and David Aitken was sent to parley a truce with the enemy.

The proposal he carried for Lord Beaverbrook had a simple logic. Both sides accepted that only one evening newspaper was viable in the market and neither was willing to concede to the other. But cut-throat competition was pointless in the meantime; they should therefore both seek to economise and to cut their losses on the way towards a single paper, under whichever flag it would come to live. The approach was well received, and a series of talks began to identify the areas in which they could make savings in unison.

In the course of these talks the *Citizen* found that it had a new editor. Bob Edwards, the editor of the *Daily Express* in London, came to Glasgow to lunch with us in February 1962. Towards the end of lunch he took a telephone call from London asking him to see Max Aitken on the following day. Bob said he guessed he was going to be sacked, and he was right; Roger Wood was installed in his place.

Bob Edwards attributed his fall from grace to jealousy by Max Aitken, 'who just could not bear that Lord Beaverbrook was more fond of me than of his own son'. Thus did the gods of classical antiquity play with the fates of men. Bob's fall from grace did not last long, however: Lord Beaverbrook wanted him restored. During one meeting between them the prodigal suggested that the editorship of the *Citizen* was vacant and that he was willing to go there for the meantime.

Peter Baker had not been replaced officially, but Willie Steen had been acting as editor and everyone expected him to be confirmed in the post. Instead, Bob Edwards came north. He afterwards referred to this period as his 'exile in the Gorky of Fleet Street' – a phrase which, however obscure, had the ring of martyrdom about it. It is little wonder that he found his exile irksome, and that he could make scant impact on the paper – the key to the cashbox was tightly in management hands.

By the autumn of 1962 the rapprochement between the *Citizen* and the *Times* was going on apace. Each had given up branch offices in favour of the other, integrating the staffs. The numbers of editions had been cut. Plans had been drawn up to integrate transport fleets and to teach hitherto exclusive vendors to shout for '*Times* AND the *Cit-i-zen*!' It was even proposed to ban football writers from going to matches abroad unless mutually sanctioned, and to abandon the distinctive green and pink newsprint of the Saturday sports editions (why had I ever worried about Jimmy McCluskey?), even though this would have saved less than £20 a week.

The talks were now joined by the papers' principals, Sir Hugh Fraser and Sir Max Aitken, and the meetings moved down to Harrods. The negotiators could not be said at any time to have conducted a cloak-and-dagger operation. They were known to be meeting, and the results of their meetings were plain for all to see. But the trade unions were distinctly unhappy with what they saw.

CHAPTER 30

A bishop defies his Church

THERE WERE NO SHACKLES on the *Scottish Daily Express* as there were on the *Citizen*, and even if there had been it is doubtful if Ian McColl would have felt inhibited. You might have hesitated to match him in a ring with anyone above welterweight, but he was a doughty two-fisted fighter for all that. He delighted in wordy battle, toughened as he was in the debating chamber and the political arena. He was forthrightly honest, disconcertingly so for some people. Although not a Bible-thumper, he was well-versed in the scriptures, able to trade chapter and verse with anyone – even with Lord Beaverbrook if need be.

Ian McColl was indeed unique among his lordship's editors, not just by reason of his abstinence but also by the rapport which formed between them during the last years of Lord Beaverbrook's life. The Beaver found it good to talk to him. He would telephone on Sundays : 'Ah, Ian, you've been to the kirk?' (he took that for granted). 'Tell me, did the minister preach the True Word?' He would then expect to be told what were the Bible readings and the content of the sermon. He also wanted to know what was going on in Ian's parish. At times he could be mischievous: 'Why was the Moderator wearing a ring? Wasn't that an Episcopalian practice?' 'Isn't it the case that the Secretary of State for Scotland, Michael Noble, is not a true-born Scot and so has no right to be wearing the kilt as he does?' (The Secretary of State had every right to do so, in fact.)

But Beaverbrook also wanted to talk about all matters of import in Ian's province, and he was not averse to infiltrating his own views thereon, although they were always carefully phrased, such as 'I'm not conversant with the situation – I simply give you the idea', or 'Don't be influenced in the least by this suggestion – just think about it on its merits and come to a decision according to the interests of the paper.'

In his first year of office as editor of the *Scottish Daily Express*, Ian thus found he could count on staunch support for whatever policy he perceived as being helpful to Scotland, irrespective of whether or not it coincided with national policy devised in London. While the London paper was proclaiming Lord Beeching as the saviour of the railways, Ian McColl inveighed against the cuts which were biting so deeply and woundingly into Scotland's rural lifelines; and if in the end the axe still fell on the Border routes, the crusade he waged helped to save the lines in the far north.

Another thing which Lord Beaverbrook's Presbyterian editor did that year was to give shelter to a bishop in trouble, and one feels that the Beaver would have applauded even if the bishop had been an Anglican.

An anonymous caller telephoned our Aberdeen office and said that there had been so much gossip about the Roman Catholic Bishop of Aberdeen's housekeeper that the perceived scandal had reached Rome and that he had been ordered to dismiss her. The Right Reverend Francis Walsh was defying the Church's order. Philip Mackie went to see the bishop, who at once conceded not only that the information was correct but that he wanted to have the truth made known and thereby to have his housekeeper protected from further gossip. She had done no harm, he said; he had refused to dismiss her because he considered the order to be unjust. He then called the housekeeper into the room and introduced her.

Ian McColl at his desk on the 'back bench'

Mrs Christine MacKenzie had been the wife of a Church of Scotland minister. She had agreed to a divorce on grounds of desertion, rather than cling to an unhappy marriage, and had gone to live in an abbey guesthouse in Elgin where she became a convert to Catholicism. Bishop Walsh had confirmed her in the faith.

'I told him that I needed to be sure he really wanted the story to be published,' said Philip. 'He said he was quite sure. I then told him that I was concerned that the story should be precisely as he would like to see it in print, and advised him to talk to his closest friends in the church. I kept Ian McColl fully informed, of course, and Ian encouraged me to do everything as I saw fit and to tell him when it could be published.

'I returned next day with reporter George Hunter and a photographer, who took pictures, and I promised the bishop that I would let him see what I wrote. This was the first and only time in my career I agreed to such a condition, but I don't regret it. When I went back the bishop approved the story for publication. But I still advised him to read it at leisure, and then telephone me when he had done so.

'Our cub reporter at the time was Ron Neil (who was later to become Head of BBC Television Production in London). Ron was given the story and pictures to take to Glasgow and he handed the package over personally to Ian McColl, who kept it in a safe place in his office to await my call to check that the bishop had his given final approval.'

Ian McColl and two of his reporters had been privy to the bishop's trouble for two weeks and had kept mum. Even so, Ian McColl telephoned the bishop to confirm his approval, but also to warn him that upon publication he could expect to be pursued by all the media. Bishop Walsh said he still wanted the report to be published.

'We developed a follow-up story under the editor's guidance which brought the bishop much sympathy and support, and the Church authorities were grateful, too,' said Philip. 'Nevertheless the Church did not relent, and the bishop resigned. He went away to live quietly (and with little money) in a cottage in Ireland, and his housekeeper went to look after him. He kept expecting the Church to admit that the order had been wrong, but it never did.'

Before leaving to catch the plane to Ireland, Bishop Walsh rested at Philip's house in Bishopbriggs in Glasgow, and there he met for the first time Ian McColl, the editor in whom he had confided his dilemma.

'The bishop said he wanted to bless my house and my family,' said Philip. 'I am not of his faith but I was happy and moved to have his blessing. Shortly before he died I was told he was ill and went to see him at his home in Ireland. I took with me a pipe and some of his favourite tobacco which he had been able to get only in Glasgow. When we said goodbye in the garden he wept, and so did I. He was one of the most understanding men I have ever known.'

The first rival newspaper to call on the bishop was the Aberdeen *Press and Journal*. It simply printed the *Express* version verbatim. Ian McColl telephoned its editor and told him that while it was not unusual to paraphrase, it was not acceptable to print another newspaper's report in full. 'I can only say to you,' he was told, 'that the bishop told us he would not talk to us, but that everything in the *Express* report was true, and we had his authority to repeat it so long as we printed it word for word.'

Philip Mackie later joined the staff at Buckingham Palace, and was attached to Prince Charles' entourage; he continued as an unofficial adviser after he retired. He said, 'When I see how some tabloids now feed on indiscretions and scandals, real or supposed, I am glad that we acted so very differently that time.'

CHAPTER 31

Big names make news

IAN MCCOLL BROUGHT TO HIS editorship of the *Scottish Daily Express* a rare capacity to motivate others. Probably the only rich vein he left unmined was 'The Glasshouse', the partitioned-off room in which a corps of fast copy-takers typed up the telephoned reports of correspondents and staff on on-out-of-town assignments. The denizens of The Glasshouse were rather more engaged with the theatre and radio and television than in the Entertainments pages of newspapers (in which there was already an overabundance of writers). Their interests were literary rather than journalistic – and what a vast repository of talent it was!

Thus, when times in the Glasshouse were quiet, John Law and Bill Craig would engage in banter which informed scripts for Stanley Baxter and others on TV. John Law became a Light Entertainment executive at the BBC in London, responsible for programmes such as the Morecambe and Wise show, while Bill Craig translated to the small screen the Lewis Grassic Gibbon classic, Sunset Song. Tommy McGee wrote the definitive biography of Betty Grable, and Frank Allison became such an authority on Frank Sinatra that people from all over the world used to telephone him to verify details. Carl MacDougall became an award-winning novelist, and Tom McGrath became a highly successful playwright.

Some of those whom Ian McColl motivated had not even been aware of their potential – but not Drew Rennie. All that Drew ever needed was a loose rein. Ian McColl gave him that, appointing him Assistant Editor in charge of features. He also put at his disposal a corps of his most able writers and sub-editors. The writers included Charles Graham and Willie Hunter, along with Brian Meek and Neville Garden.

The only time the Editor felt he had to pull in the reins was when Drew asked one of his sub-editors who had a stammer if he could write about the difficulties of his fellow-sufferers. Though the suggestion was put with diffidence, its apparent insensitivity horrified Ian McColl. The sub-editor was Jack Webster, who insisted that it was what he wanted to do, and so Jack Webster transferred to the writing staff and became a noted columnist in his time. He also cured his impediment by his own efforts, became much in demand as a public speaker and was voted a Speaker of the Year.

Drew Rennie had a wide remit; and since he recognised no frontiers in his interpretation of the brief, inevitably he trampled on a few toes. He was no stranger to that. The first toes he trampled on had belonged to our companion *Sunday Express*. During his reporting days on the *Express* he had been sent to the Open Golf Championship at Carnoustie, assigned to find a front page news story.

The *Sunday Express* had already signed the favourite, the great Ben Hogan, on exclusive contract to tell his story of the event. Some time before coming to the championship, Ben Hogan and his wife had been in a car crash which had nearly killed them both, and Valerie was still suffering from her injuries. Drew and his companion, photographer Ian Elder, came to know her well.

There were 36 holes to play on the Saturday and Valerie was anxious. She suddenly said, 'I just hope Ben will be okay. He's been up all night with what looks like 'flu.' That quote provided Drew with his front page story – and it was exclusive. It also infuriated the *Sunday Express* Editor, MacDonald Daly, and his Sports Editor, the celebrated golf writer Harry Andrew.

'Ben Hogan's articles gave the Sunday Express a lot of additional prestige,' Drew said. 'But it also gave me an insight into the value of signing up big names.' (Sorry, Drew, but Arthur Christiansen had already determined that – one of his constant reminders was that 'Names Make News').

At St Andrews, 1964... Jack Nicklaus, Open Golf Champion, with Drew Rennie on left of picture and sports writer Brian Meek on the right

The first 'big name' Drew signed up was Arnold Palmer, at the 1960 Centenary Open Championship. Palmer came second to Ken Nagel. The following year he signed up Arnold Palmer again, and this time Palmer won. Thereafter Drew acquired a reputation for forecasting the championship winner and securing him in advance to write for the paper.

His most notable capture was the Argentinian-born football coach Helenio Herrera.

In 1963, Scotland's football fortunes were at a low ebb. Even the mighty Glasgow Rangers, a dominant force for so many years, had been thrashed 6-0 by Real Madrid at La Ciudad Deportiva (City of Sport) in the first round of the European Cup.

Helenio Herrera was at that time the manager of Inter Milan. He had invented a system of attacking in force out of massive defence. It became enshrined in Italian soccer as 'catenaccio' ('the bolt'). Although he was acknowledged on the international scene as being the great innovator of his day, his name meant little to people in Scotland – except to Drew Rennie.

Drew sent writer George Reid to Milan to ask Herrera if he would accept, at our expense, a number of football managers and their trainers as his guests for a week at Inter's training camp and show them his methods. Herrera agreed.

The invitation was canvassed among all the leading Scottish clubs. Only two accepted – Jock Stein, then manager of Dunfermline Athletic, and Willie Waddell, then with Kilmarnock, who were to become League Champions in the following season.

George Reid and photographer Peter MacVean went with Jock Stein and Willie Waddell to Milan. We called the enterprise 'Challenge to Scots Soccer'.

Herrera held nothing back. He was to have cause to regret it, but that was to be four years later....

Meantime, in 1965, Rangers were drawn against Inter Milan in the European Cup. The Scottish team lost the first leg in Milan by 3-0. The home leg was scheduled for March 3. Drew Rennie sent Jack Webster to see Herrera and to persuade him to put his name to a series of exclusive articles which Jack would ghost-write for him,

Herrera came to Glasgow three days before the tie. Accompanied by Jack Webster and Drew Rennie, he went to Ibrox Stadium 'to measure it inch by inch', and predicted confidently that his team would win. It didn't – but his massive defence held Rangers to a single goal, and gave Inter Milan victory, on aggregate, by 3-1.

Two years later, in 1967, Jock Stein, who by then had become manager of Celtic, took his team to Lisbon to the Final of the European Champions' Cup. Their opponents were Inter Milan; in the contest between pupil and master, Jock Stein's Celtic won a famous victory by 2-1. It was a pity that Helenio Herrera, so gracious when he had imparted his knowledge to the tyros from Scotland in 1963, should have refused to join all the others in the post-match banquet.

And who can say whether Rangers would have won the European Cupwinners' Cup, as they did under Willie Waddell's charge in 1972, had their manager not gone to see Herrera in Milan all those years before?

It was because of the Herrera episode that the most remarkable of all sports reporters came into our orbit. Jim Rodger described himself as 'a wee miner from Shotts'. The wee miner became the confidant and adviser of a legion of football players and managers whose careers and fortunes he advanced without ever seeking reward; he gave help, too, to anyone who asked.

When Drew Rennie and Jack Webster met Herrera in London on his way to Glasgow in February 1965, they were irritated and puzzled to find the little round figure of Jim Rodger constantly close at hand. 'He seemed to know every move we made,' said Drew. 'We made up our minds we just had to have him on our side.'

Jim was not disposed to be on our side, however. He disliked the *Express*, believing it to be unsympathetic to the miners, but after much persuasion he agreed to meet Ian McColl 'for a friendly talk only.' He came warily, bringing his miner's lamp as symbol and talisman. But when in the 'friendly talk' he spoke of family links with the Salvation Army in Aberdeen, Ian McColl referred to that city's noted evangelistic minister, the Rev William Still.

Jim Rodger, self styled as 'a wee miner from Shotts', is seen here with the then Prime Minister, James Callaghan, one of the many celebrities whom he brought as speaker guests to Newspaper Press Fund lunches

'Is Bill Still a friend of yours?' said Jim Rodger. 'Then I'm your man.' When he left with his miner's lamp he had not even asked what his salary would be.

Jim Rodger not only knew evangelistic ministers. We came to learn that he knew Cabinet ministers, too, and could count as a friend many of the great of the land. When he assumed the secretaryship of our newspaper charity in Glasgow and the West of Scotland he brought all these friends in as a lure to give prestige to our fund-raising events, so that whereas by our own puny efforts we had left him with a deficit of £3 17s 6d, every year thereafter our committee sent more money to the national Newspaper Press Fund than did any other in the country.

Drew Rennie's next famous capture was Muhammad Ali, who had won the world heavyweight boxing champion-ship as Cassius Clay but had changed his name after joining the Black Muslim sect in 1964. When he came to Glasgow in August 1965 to take part in an exhibition promotion at Paisley Ice Rink no one was quite sure what to call him – but what he called himself was forthright enough: 'The Greatest'. His other name was 'The Louisville Lip', conferred by reason of his gift of repartee and his flights of fanciful phrases such as 'I float like a butterfly and sting like a bee'.

He agreed to put his name to a series of articles. Jack Webster, who was to ghost-write them, accompanied him everywhere during his stay among us. Ali even took the chair at our morning editorial conference, lording over everything, and from the editor's chair he went to sit in the Bard's chair at Burns Cottage in Alloway. There he said ('as a fellow

19 August 1965... Muhammad Ali in the editor's chair

Left to right, Jack Webster; Tommy Allan (deputy sports editor); Albert Barr, (chief photographer); Bill Young (deputy pictures editor); Angelo Dundee (Ali's manager); Ian McColl; Drew Rennie; James MacCauland (chief sub editor); Jack Campbell and Alan Fielding (deputy features editor)

poet') that he could not understand how HE had not heard of this great poet, Robert Burns, and was inspired to start versifying himself. 'I wish I had had my tape recorder with me,' said Jack.

We all loved him. So did the crowds of fans who followed him everywhere. One admirer was a young black woman who turned up at the entrance to the McDonald Hotel at Eastwood Toll in Glasgow when Ali was having lunch there, and claimed to be a friend. The manager did not believe her, and told her to leave. Ali saw the two engaged in dispute, and had her brought to his table. Her name was Jan Scotland – yes, Scotland; and she really had been one of his childhood playmates in their home town of Louisville in Kentucky.

The matron at Glasgow Western Infirmary, where Jan was a junior nurse, had not believed her, either. So Ali and all his entourage went with her to the Infirmary, and he toured the wards, talking to all Jan's patients and fellow-nurses and signing autographs – some on plaster-casts.

'When I met him much later, when he was showing the symptoms of Parkinson's syndrome, and only a shadow of what he had been,' said Jack, 'I could have wept for him.'

Stuart McCartney came back to Albion Street at this time. The *Citizen* might not afford another addition to the staff, but the *Express* could. He had acquired a nickname – 'The Bullet' – which was said to have been bestowed on him as a cub reporter with the *Citizen*, although I was not aware of it at the time; but everyone knew him as 'The Bullet' by the time he came back, and to this day his grandchildren are said to refer to 'Papa Bullet'. He had acquired a reputation among crime reporters as being able to shake hands with more detectives than anyone, and to have as intimate a knowledge of the underworld as of Bishopbriggs, where he lived.

His first assignment on his return to the *Express* had no connection with crime. It was to watch and report on a humdrum demolition at Braidwood, near Carluke. The demolition was so effective that it blocked the main Glasgow to London rail line. He telephoned in to the office in high excitement. 'Hey, this is a lot bigger than we expected,' and he proceeded to outline the story. His hearer said, 'Thank you very much, Stuart,' and he recognised the voice of his old chief at the *Daily Mail's* Glasgow office, whose number he had called by habit. He never gave anything away to the opposition after that. He did not even give them any quarter.

Among the many he knew in the underworld was Patrick Connolly Meehan, burglar and safeblower. Indeed, he knew him well – his father had arrested Paddy Meehan so many times that he had a wry sympathy for him, because, he said, 'he wasn't very good at his work. He always got caught.' Paddy escaped from Nottingham prison during a cricket match, and it seemed to the police that he then 'just vanished'. Someone in MI5 telephoned Stuart and arranged to meet him in a Glasgow hotel.

'What I am about to tell you cannot be checked and cannot come back to me,' he said, and handed Stuart a postcard. It was addressed to Meehan's wife; it came from East Germany. Paddy was later to allege that he was taken by the KGB to Moscow and asked to provide information which would help to spring from jail the Soviet spy George Blake. (He also alleged that he told MI5 about this. Whether he did so or not, Blake escaped from prison three years later).

'The Bullet' went to see Meehan's wife Betty at her home in Alexandra Parade in Glasgow. She denied having had any communication from her husband. But Stuart wrote the story and we published it. We were to hear more in later years of Patrick Meehan.

Lord Beaverbrook became ill in the summer of 1963, and into 1964. Just one month after he and Lady Beaverbrook had gone to Epsom register office and there renewed their vows, he needed her constant care. His illness, however, did not divert his attention from his papers.

He recalled Bob Edwards from exile with the *Citizen* in Glasgow (thus giving to Willie Steen the post which had rightfully been his). He also kept himself closely informed about the talks between the *Citizen* and the *Evening Times.*

Both parties were agreed that their economies had reached the stage at which they could go on to form a joint holding company to manage both papers. This was still the intention. But Sir Hugh Fraser meantime indicated that he was prepared to pay £750,000 to buy out the *Citizen,* and to throw in a three-year printing contract.

The offer did not enthuse Lord Beaverbrook. Nor did Lord Thomson of Fleet's intervention in the game. The Scots-Canadian millionaire ('just call me Roy') offered to match Sir Hugh's £750,000, but to couple with it a printing contract for any period between five to twenty years. He also said he would take on everyone on the *Citizen* payroll.

Tom Blackburn advised his chief to reject the offer. One of his objections was that Lord Thomson had baulked at taking responsibility for anyone other than future pensioners; the other objection was the presence of a stranger's organisation operating within Beaverbrook's own plant. Despite the rebuff, Lord Thomson gave a lavish dinner party in honour of Lord Beaverbrook's 85th birthday on 21 May, 1964. The old warrior struggled from his sickbed to attend and to speak. Eleven days later he died, in his wife's arms.

Since, unlike other newspaper owners, he had scorned investment in television or other fields, he left his son, Sir Max Aitken (who renounced his father's title) with his papers but with no other income to buttress them in a struggle against declining profits, rising costs, ageing plant and over-staffing in all areas.

Max had just begun a close examination of the way forward for his papers when this was interrupted by a call from his *Evening Citizen* territory, where some of the natives were becoming restless: Lord Thomson had opened up another front, seeking to buy the Outram company (owners of the *Evening Times*) outright. That in itself was enough to worry the unions; coupled with their knowledge of the plan to link the *Times* and the *Citizen* in a joint holding company, they were thoroughly alarmed.

The Scottish TUC sought assurance from Sir Hugh Fraser that it was not intended to merge the evening papers. The two baronets, together with Tom Blackburn and Outram's chief executive Alan Stephen, met a delegation in Sir Hugh's Glasgow office on 17 December. After the meeting a statement – to which the union delegates were party – confirmed that a joint company was being formed 'with the object of maintaining publication of both titles.' However, the unions continued to suspect that the carers intended one of their patients to die, and to the unions it mattered not a whit whether death was to come by sudden blow or by a thousand cuts.

By 1964 the *Express* in Scotland was so far ahead in the readership race as to be almost out of sight of the nearest other runner. No doubt we were insufferably arrogant, for we could also manifest our superiority in the numbers we could send to almost every news happening. But the opposition must have been surprised in May of that year when no less a personage than our chairman turned up when typhoid broke out in Aberdeen, city of pristine granite and unblemished beaches.

Sandy Trotter went there at the urgent request of his colleagues on the Scottish Tourist Board to try to stem a feared decline in visitor numbers to Aberdeen at the start of the holiday season. Adam Borthwick, who was our Chief Reporter in the north east, said that there was near-panic in the city. 'People were even shunning use of the public telephones for fear of infection,' he said.

Sandy Trotter called a press conference at once. He brought with him the Lord Provost and the Chief Medical Officer to promise daily discussion, and to seek help to present the facts in perspective and to allay exaggerated fears. The outbreak was traced to imported corned beef, ultimately said to have been tainted by effluent at its factory in Buenos Aires; but although 300 people were stricken by the illness, public attention was focused throughout on how the well the city was coping with the emergency. The fact that damage was not done to Aberdeen's squeaky clean image has to be attributed to the authorities and to the newspapers and, ultimately, to the behaviour of the citizens themselves. But if there are credits to be apportioned, it has to be said that our chairman Sandy certainly did his bit.

Sandy Trotter continued as our chairman until he retired in 1970. When he died five years later, in October 1975, his daughter Patsy, better known as Pat Sandys, the actress and now a noted television producer, arranged a memorial service with the help of her husband, Philip Bond, and her brother Michael; one can only hope that the ghost of the Beaver heard the Presbyterians among us as we joined in prayer and sang hymns in St Mary's Episcopal Cathedral for the cathedral's one-time choir boy.

CHAPTER 32

To right any wrong....

SIR MAX AITKEN LEFT Bob Edwards in uncomfortable occupancy of the editor's chair of the *Daily Express* in London for one year. He then replaced him with Derek Marks, our respected political correspondent. Derek Marks brought great weight to his new office; but in the so-called Swinging Sixties, in the face of rapid changes in newspaper readership choice and the growing challenge from television, he was not an inspired choice.

The contrast between the London and the Scottish editions became ever more apparent. Derek Marks was absorbed in the political scene; his critics said he was obsessed by it. In Glasgow Christiansen's dictum was not forgotten – that it was PEOPLE who made politics interesting. In the Roxburgh, Selkirk and Peebles by-election of 1965 the odds were stacked against the young Liberal candidate, David Steel. Ian McColl decided to throw all the weight of his newspaper behind the candidate whom he called The Boy David. The 'boy' won, and became the youngest MP in Britain.

Under Ian McColl's editorship, the Sixties were our most successful years; the crucial reason was that while we continued to present the news more absorbingly than others, it was done in tandem with a policy of trenchant campaign on public issues. Our battling welterweight editor did not have to go looking for a fight – he found plenty to hand.

Terence Rattigan's play, *The Winslow Boy* (later filmed), was based on the Archer-Shee case of 1908, in which a 13-year-old cadet, dismissed by the Admiralty on a charge of stealing a five-shilling (25p) postal order, was proven innocent only after a two-year fight through Parliament. OUR 'Winslow Boy '66' was Tom Marr, a minister's son studying law at Glasgow University.

In his first year there, while he was secretary of the Students' Representative Council, a woman secretary employed by the Council was alleged to have been subjected to a campaign of harassment and persecution. Tom Marr reported the occurrences to both the police and the university authorities. But when the police decided that it was a matter for the university authorities to deal with themselves, Tom Marr was among ten students arraigned before a disciplinary inquiry.

The inquiry sat in private, questioned the ten, and allowed them neither legal representation nor the right to call witnesses on their behalf.

In July 1965 the Principal and Deans Committee, empowered as a court by the Senate, sentenced one student to be banned for life, five to be banned for a year, and four to be reprimanded. One of the five was Tom Marr. He was accused on four counts, one of which was that he might have used his position more than he had done to stop the campaign – this despite the fact that it was he who had taken the matter to the police and to the authorities in the first place.

The university had maintained strict silence until then, and everything might have ended there, to the satisfaction of the university hierarchy, had it not been that the five students who had been banned for a year appealed.

There had been no appeal against the Senate's discipline in living memory. Now a special appeals committee had to be formed, consisting of distinguished men with no previous connection with the affair. For the first time the students were allowed legal representation and to lead evidence and to cross- examine witnesses.

The Senate court, with the Principal presiding, accepted all the appeals inquiry findings. But although Tom Marr appeared to have been cleared by the appeals inquiry of all charges, the Court did not accept his innocence. It said that it had taken a 'more serious view than the special committee had done of the secretary's responsibilities', and in place of suspension it imposed a reprimand.

The end to the secret trials brought the affair into our province. The Reverend Andrew Herron, who had advised the family as a close friend, was also a friend of Ian McColl's. Ian assigned Jack Webster to write an investigation, and we printed it on 10 January 1966 as 'The Winslow Boy '66'. The student who had been banned for life had already been named but we did not identify any of Tom Marr's companions in the appeals in case it might jeopardise their careers.

Tam Dalyell MP read the story of the 'Winslow Boy '66' and raised the affair in Parliament. He called it 'a squalid fix'. On 8 February 1966 the Senate surrendered, saying in a statement that while it 'rejected allegations of pressure by any senior members of the university on any person or body' concerned with the case, it now accepted the appeals committee's view that the charge against the secretary had not been established and it therefore rescinded the reprimand.

Tom Marr said, 'I have been completely vindicated, but it is due to a number of people, particularly Mr Tam Dalyell and the *Daily Express*, that justice has been done.' Andrew Herron, after labelling the statement 'a grudging acquittal', said that if the MP and the *Express* had not aroused public opinion, 'the whole thing would have been buried after appeal.'

In that year Ian McColl found a second plot to impose bishops on the Kirk by the back door – and foiled it with all the familiarly damning words as if the Old Man were still around. He exposed it just as a conference on church unity was due to begin in private at Holland House in Edinburgh, attended by 120 delegates from the Church of Scotland, the Episcopal Church of Scotland, the Church of England, and the Presbyterian Church of England.

Our report was instantly denied. But Ian McColl had proof, contained in what became known as the 'Grey Document'. It had been put into his hands by an alarmed professor of divinity of considerable eminence. The 'Grey Document' proposed a 'Binding Covenant', committing the Kirk to unite with the Episcopal Church of Scotland under bishops by Easter of 1980. By its terms, existing Church of Scotland ministers were to be recognised until their deaths, but all new ministers would be ordained only in the presence of a bishop.

The conference broke up in disorder with its objects unfulfilled. When the General Assembly of the Church of Scotland met in May, the Binding Covenant was shelved. A move to discontinue talks with the Anglicans was defeated, but only narrowly. But in November the *Express* revealed that the Kirk committee charged with continuing the talks was loaded with pro-bishop adherents, and after a full debate in which the *Express* was frequently quoted, the Commission of the General Assembly took the unprecedented step of dismissing the committee and of calling for a new list of names. The furious attacks on the paper by several prelates at Anglican convocations thereafter would have delighted the Beaver as much as they did his church-elder editor.

We then went to the help of Mrs Barbara Kinnaird, victim of a council's heartlessness. Stirling Council's children's committee officer had swooped on her home in Cumbernauld without warning, and taken away the 5-year-old orphan James whom she had nurtured since baby-hood. Barbara Kinnaird was left crying in the street.

The council would give no reason for its action. So the *Express* constantly asked 'Why?' For five months the council kept silent, leaving Barbara and her husband William the subjects of innuendo and malicious gossip. At one stage the council offered to tell us in confidence why they had taken the child, but only if we agreed not to tell the foster parents; Ian McColl rejected the offer. When the council eventually decided to issue a statement, it was only to confirm that James would not be returned to the Kinnaird home.

The book was closed. Barbara Kinnaird reconciled herself to the loss of the child she had loved and wrote a moving letter of thanks to the *Express*, and we were left only with the consolation that it was unlikely that such an exhibition of insensitivity would ever be allowed to recur.

In the midst of another campaign, this time calling for the reform of the prosecution system in which so many deals diluted justice, a question which had been posed often but had remained hypothetical required a real-life definitive answer: 'Could an acquitted murderer confess his guilt and still escape his deserts thereafter?'

Frederick Joseph Cairns thought he could. While he was in Barlinnie Prison serving an 18-month sentence for housebreaking, he committed the first murder to occur in a jail in Scotland when he stabbed to death a fellow prisoner, Alexander Malcolmson, in 'A' Hall. At his trial on 26 February 1966 the jury brought in our uniquely Scots verdict of Not Proven, and he was acquitted. He went back to prison to serve the remainder of his 18-month sentence, and when he was released, two of our reporters, Stuart McCartney and David Scott, met him. He told them that Yes, he HAD killed Malcolmson.

They brought Cairns to my room at Albion Street. Cairns believed, rightly, that he could not be tried twice for the same offence. So did we, but we thought, just in case, that we should warn him that he was risking trouble with the law, although what that trouble might be we had no way of knowing. He still agreed to make a full confession to the crime, and the two reporters, together with photographer Tommy Fitzpatrick, took him to a hotel at Killearn and taped what he said.

Ian McColl decided to publish the confession and find out what might ensue. 'But then Detective Inspector Bob McFarlane came to see David and Tommy and me,' said Stuart, 'and he told us that we were to be precognosced' (that is to say, swearing statements in advance of trial) 'because Cairns had been arrested and was to be charged with perjury to defeat the ends of justice. So the three of us were headed for the High Court, and it wasn't to be on the press benches but in the witness box.'

The question whether Cairns could properly be charged had to be referred to a bench of three judges. They said he could. Frederick Cairns appeared on indictment in January 1967 and was allowed bail. But once again he defeated the ends of justice. On 19 May 1967 he was rushed to Glasgow Royal Infirmary with a stomach ailment. Three days later he died.

In the meantime Drew Rennie, with his wide remit, was continuing to cast his net in pursuit of Christiansen's advice that 'Names Make News'. Few were escaping him: after Herrera and Muhammad Ali there were Pele, and boxing champion Sugar Ray Robinson, and motor racing champion Jim Clark.

Drew's intuition had been a wonder to his golfing friends. 'Champagne Tony' Lema had been such an outsider in the 1964 Open Championship that no one would have given tuppence for his chances – apart from Drew Rennie. Perhaps Drew carried a crystal ball in his suitcase. For instance, he watched the golf scores being posted by the 16-year-old son of a Bathgate train driver, and when the boy turned professional he engaged him to write for the Express every week. His name was Bernard Gallacher, who was destined to become the European Ryder Cup team captain.

Our rivals believed that the big names cost us a fortune. Not so; Drew Rennie negotiated the deals himself, 'and I paid only peanuts,' he said. 'I kept copies of the receipts. See?' – and he produced one of them. It was signed by Cassius Clay, acknowledging £375 ($1,000) as payment for four exclusive articles. In the year Bernard Gallacher wrote for us he was paid thirty shillings (£1.30) a week.

The galaxy of entertainment celebrities we projected in series included Max Bygraves, Shirley Bassey, and (surprisingly) Marlene Dietrich – surprisingly, because Marlene Dietrich NEVER gave newspaper interviews. But she did for the *Express*. She had been engaged to appear at Glasgow's Alhambra Theatre. Given her dislike of newspapers, Drew reckoned that the prospects of an interview were pretty forlorn, but he gave the task of approaching her to Bill Grant who was known to be one of her devotees. Bill found her daughter in London. He never revealed what he said to the daughter, but it was rumoured, justly or not, that he gave her the impression that his very livelihood depended upon interviewing her mother.

Drew Rennie was surprised by a telephone call. 'Mr Rennie, this is Marlene Dietrich calling from Gothenburg. Please tell your Mr Grant that if he comes to the theatre here on Monday next week I shall spare him a few minutes for an interview.' Drew wondered if it might be a hoax. 'Where should he meet you?' he asked. The voice said abruptly, 'In my dressing room before the start of the show', and with that the phone line went dead.

He was still suspicious, but after a call to Gothenburg had verified that she was indeed appearing in a theatre there, Bill Grant went to Sweden. The star who shunned reporters later said she was 'overjoyed' with the two articles Bill wrote, and when she came to Glasgow she insisted that Bill come to see her again.

We went back into the campaign fray in 1968, to unleash a furious public outcry over the shabby treatment meted out to Colonel Colin Mitchell of the Argylls, hero of Aden. 'Mad Mitch', as he came to be known, had marched his men at dead of night, with pipes skirling 'Campbeltown Loch', into the no-go Aden Crater, to recapture it from Arab terrorists; but unforgivably he had done it in defiance of Government policy and without sanction of either his brigade commander or of the general in charge of Middle East operations.

The port had been in British hands since it was seized by the East India company in 1839 to stop pirates attacking their ships on the way to India. When it was handed back to the new South Yemen 'People's Republic', Mad Mitch was given no more than a mere mention in dispatches while his superiors were laden with higher honours. His beloved Argylls were then threatened with disbandment. He resigned from the Army in order to be able to plead for the rescue of the regiment from extinction.

Willie Steen launched a petition in the Citizen, backed by the Express, and a million people signed it. At the end of 1968 it was presented to Parliament. Jack Webster was detailed to help to convey the petition, packed in 22 cardboard boxes, to the entrance of the House of Commons. Eight tail-coated attendants, walking two by two, carried the boxes inside with all due ceremony and placed them on the Clerks' table, piling them five feet high and all but obliterating the Mace.

Mad Mitch and the Duchess of Argyll (who had rallied massive support from Scots overseas) and Colonel Bertram Lang (the senior surviving officer of the South African War) watched from the public gallery as the Scots MPs in the House roared in triumph.

George Younger MP, a former Argylls officer (and future Secretary of State for Scotland), finally presented the petition, and paid due tribute to the Citizen for having gathered the signatures.

CHAPTER 33

Jackie Green knew it

IN OCTOBER 1968 THE *Daily Mail* ceased publication in Edinburgh. Under Ian McColl's charge the *Express* by then had reached its circulation apogee in Scotland. It was selling an average 630,000 copies a day, and 660,000 at peak times.

Two events probably contributed most to those sales peaks. It is a sad fact that newspapers sell most copies at times of disaster – and Jackie Green, Glasgow's best-known street-vendor, knew all about that. He would call attention to a disaster even if he had found just three lines in the paper about a flood in India. Unhappily, he had plenty of justification on the day of 19 November, 1968.

If you were to walk from the eastern end of Glasgow's Argyle Street in a straight line through what is colloquially known as 'The Hielan' Man's Umbrella' under the Central Station railway bridge and go as far as where Argyle Street meets the new Kingston road bridge, you will have covered the mile-long trail along which the city's three most disastrous post-war fires occurred. At the eastern end of that walk, 13 girls were trapped in the Grafton Gown Shop blaze in 1949; at the other end it meets Cheapside Street, where 19 firemen perished in 1960. In between, four blocks past 'The Hielan' Man's Umbrella', is James Watt Street, the scene of the third fire disaster, in 1968.

The four-storey furniture factory of B Stern and Co Ltd had bars on the windows of three of its floors, relics of its prior existence as a whisky bond warehouse. The owners had anguished over whether to remove them because they had experienced so many break-ins at their previous premises. Those bars were to make a prison for the occupants when fire erupted through the centre of the building. Only four escaped. The others screamed and beat frantically against the bars while horrified people in the street watched helplessly. Twenty two men and women, including the owner's brother, died.

The other predominant factor which sells newspapers is a murder trial, and no doubt the trial of Sheila Garvie contributed largely to another of those peaks.

When Sheila Garvie and her lover Brian Tevendale were tried at Aberdeen High Court for the alleged killing of her husband Max Garvie, Stuart McCartney headed our reporting team. What a tale was unfolded, of wild sex orgies she shared with her husband and then with her lover, of torrid love in an aeroplane, of bizarre parties at a nudist retreat the locals called Kinky Cottage. We can just imagine what some of today's tabloids would have done with it all.

What Stuart most remembered was Sheila Garvie's seemingly unwavering devotion to her lover. She told the court she would rather have killed herself than say that he had killed her husband: 'What Brian did was to protect me; I could not betray him,' she said. When they were both sentenced to life imprisonment they paused at the foot of the steps leading to the cells and embraced, and she said, 'I love you darling; I'm so sorry.'

Stuart McCartney asked Lawrence Dowdall, who was Sheila's defence lawyer, to find out if she would sell her life story to the *Express*. The two drove to Craiginches Prison in Aberdeen that evening and he waited outside until the lawyer returned with her answer. 'She said, 'Tell Mr McCartney I wouldn't talk to him or anyone else, not for a million pounds'.'

Stuart saw her again while she was serving her sentence at Cornton Vale women's prison near Stirling. After she had served two years there, the governor, Lady Martha Bruce (sister of the Earl of Elgin), allowed her a day's freedom on parole to see her children, who were being cared for by a housekeeper in a village in Lanarkshire. Stuart was alerted by one of his contacts, and he and photographer Tommy Fitzpatrick followed the housekeeper's car to Glasgow. He lost them for a time when the housekeeper took the children into Lewis' store in Argyle Street, and he had to call up reinforcements to watch all the exits. When the housekeeper and her charges emerged, Stuart and Tommy took up the trail again. It led to a clinic in Woodside Terrace at Charing Cross.

'As we stood near the fountain there, a couple of people arrived and, unbelievably, it was Lady Martha and Sheila Garvie,' said Stuart. 'I say 'unbelievably' because I didn't recognise her at first. Her blonde hair was darkened and I wondered if I had made a mistake. Then I saw that she was wearing the same kingfisher-blue suit she had worn at her trial. Her face lit up and she threw her arms wide in welcome as the two children ran to her. Lady Martha demanded to know my identity and how I had known of the rendezvous. Sheila just turned away. Then they all went into the clinic, and Sheila spent two hours there with the children.'

True to the message she had sent to Stuart from Craiginches Prison, Sheila Garvie had never uttered a word to any reporter; but Tommy Fitzpatrick had 'snatched' a photograph before his colleague approached the group.

If anyone were ever to write Sheila Garvie's luridly novelettish life story, the author of it would surely have had her leave prison after ten years to seek the man from whom she had parted with the words 'I love you, darling'. In real life, however, when she was freed, Sheila Garvie married someone else. That marriage failed, and she married a third time. When we last heard of her, Sheila Garvie had been left a widow.

One could not help but feel cheated. Did she have to spoil the ending of this story of star-crossed love?

To boast of how many editorial staff we could muster to make us supreme in the field would have been unwise at this time of disquiet in the industry about over-staffing, but that is what we did. It brings to mind Willie Merrilees, the pawky little Chief Constable of the Lothians and Peebles. One day he was a guest at a game of what the Americans miscall their 'football'; when he was asked by the radio commentator at half-time to contribute his views on the game he took the microphone and said, 'Man, you had mair men on that field than we had at Bannockburn.'

Perhaps we had not quite as many as that, but it was a formidable array. In Glasgow alone there were 23 reporters and 17 photographers, 19 feature writers backed by two photographers, 13 sports writers and a five-strong News Desk. Edinburgh had 14 reporters, six photographers and three sports writers. There were four reporters and two photographers and a sports writer in Aberdeen, and three reporters and a photographer and a sports writer in Inverness. Dundee had three reporters, a photographer and a sports writer. Ayr had three reporters and a photographer, Dumfries two reporters and a photographer, and there were reporters based in Falkirk, Stirling, Lanarkshire, Kirkcaldy, Dunfermline and Greenock. The grand total was 133 – and that did not include sub-editors, of whom there were more than thirty.

The climax of the Sixties for us was our 40th anniversary in 1968, and we had a glittering gathering of the great and the good to help us to celebrate. The Secretary of State for Scotland, Willie Ross, attended along with lord provosts and dignitaries of law and church and industry, and many toasts were proposed to our continued good health and success. All should have been bliss in our world. But it was not. There were storms ahead, and one of the crew was intent upon rocking the boat.

CHAPTER 34

The Father of his people

LIKE AN AMBASSADOR AT St James's Court coming to present his credentials, all stiffness and formality, so was the sub-editor who requested audience of Ian McColl in his office one day. He said it was his duty to inform the editor of his acceptance of the post of Father of the National Union of Journalists' Chapel. Furthermore, he announced that, whether or not it was acceptable to the editor, it was his intention to 're-establish industrial relations'.

Ian McColl told him that he noted what had been said, and the Father of the Chapel departed as stiffly as when he had arrived, to sit at his down-table desk. His name was Denny Magee.

We should have marked it well. But the election of a Father of the Chapel (branch) had never been regarded as momentous. Most journalists joined the NUJ as a matter of course or, if they were of executive rank or aspired to more gentlemanly company, they joined the Institute of Journalists, which concerned itself more with professional standards than with the living standards of its members. In any case, journalists were not given to industrial strife, and the preceding Father had never tried to stir the waters. Perhaps the phrase 're-establish industrial relations' was meant as a rebuke to what he considered a craven predecessor, and perhaps also we should have recognised it as ominous, but we did so only in retrospect.

Denny Magee was in his early forties, with prematurely grey long hair swept back from a thin face. His spectacles dangled on a gold (or brass) chain round his neck. No one was sure whence he had come to us. He was said to have a theatrical background, as a feed man to comedians, until television brought recession to the music halls, and he had sought a new role and found it in journalism. He had obviously learned the lines of that new role well, and since his arrival among us he had never fluffed them. On the other hand, since he had displayed no particular flair as a newspaperman, we would never be likely to ask him to play other than a bit part on our stage. If he realised this (and I believe he did), it gave him no concern: Denny Magee had brought his own script – he had come to rescue the serfs and give them a better life.

Some of the staff already had a good life, for Beaverbrook had a reputation for giving high rewards for high endeavour. Father Magee found his first adherents among those who had not. But he had a message with which he hoped everyone would identify – a message based on envy.

Basic wages and conditions for everyone in the business were agreed with the unions in Scotland by the Scottish Daily Newspaper Society, of which the Beaverbrook group was a member, and in London and Manchester by the Newspaper Proprietors' Association of which it was also a member. In Fleet Street, irresponsible production union chapels were holding their papers to ransom; there were exorbitant piecework deals, extra payments for work never done, 'ghost' casual workers added to pay sheets. Fathers of Chapels had offices of their own, and with no duties other than to their union they were able to determine who should be employed and who should not.

As Sir Max Aitken and his aides planned the future of the company after the old man's death, a series of 'productivity' settlements was negotiated with the craft union chapels. These were regarded by London management as 'most helpful', although the management were later to realise, wearily, that the promises of increased productivity would never be fulfilled.

Although by a process of attrition the craft union chapels at Albion Street had nibbled away territory here and there beyond what their basic agreements had given them, we had never suffered the same abuses as those in Fleet Street. But the 'productivity' deals opened up a distressing gap between the craft chapels and the journalists. Everyone in the editorial staff then came to know of the faceless fortunate who swept a caseroom floor of its metal shreddings and dross: if he did not go home each week with gold dust in his pocket, it was alleged that he was coining more than the basic level of a senior journalist. Myth or not, his was the image which epitomised disparity.

'Consider', said Father Magee, 'what others have wrought through strength. Have you not yourself the muscle to achieve just as much, were you disposed to use it?'

Reporter Jimmy Henderson, who kept a diary through this troublesome time, wrote about coming back to Glasgow from the Edinburgh office to find that the chapel which had been moribund was now in near-full membership, and about Denny Magee 'strutting around the office as father confessor and scourge of the bosses, with young journalists walking in awe of him'.

In 1968 Denny Magee decided to take his fight to the heart of the enemy. The opportunity came when the journalists' chapel in London initiated talks with the management towards an all-inclusive house agreement for its members.

Tom Blackburn had retired, and Sir Max had appointed John Coote, his loyal aide for eight years, to share the managing directorship with himself. John Coote went to the meeting with the London journalists' chapel to welcome them, planning to leave the negotiations to his deputy

John Dawson. He was astonished to see Denny Magee and his aides there, but he quickly regained his composure and in his speech he welcomed the inclusion of the Glasgow chapel representatives as 'observers'. He then prepared to take his leave, only to find Denny Magee blocking his path: he and his delegation were NOT there as observers, said Denny, but to take part in the negotiations.

No matter how often John Coote claimed that he had urgent engagements elsewhere and sought to pass, Denny Magee blocked his way, until John Coote eventually conceded and was allowed to make his escape. But when he left that room he had surrendered the Glasgow management case.

We in Glasgow could not afford the aspirations of the London journalists – a four-day working week, sabbaticals, and extra money for overtime (a concept foreign to most of us who had known and willingly accepted elastic hours as part and parcel of the nature of our job). The London chapel, however, was prepared to accept their Glasgow comrades within whatever concessions were to be won, and they were not to be side-tracked by any financial difficulties this might entail at Albion Street.

I now joined John Paterson at the London talks. I could sense an aura of inevitability already. My counterpart in London was Eric Raybould. Eric believed he had such rapport with the London chapel officials that he could influence them. He was wrong. Perhaps if John Dawson had been given some latitude he might have achieved a fair agreement – he was a most competent and impressive manager, respected and liked as a decent and fair-minded man. But while he could argue the demerits of the chapels' case, he could make no concessions himself. His brief was to hold the fort and yield not an inch – good-naturedly, of course.

This he did, but time after time the chapel delegates demanded to see John Coote. If they still received no satisfaction they would call a mandatory meeting of the full chapel which lasted until it so threatened the night's production that the chapel officials were recalled and their point at issue conceded either wholly or in part. Eventually they got the four-day week, and the sabbaticals, and everything else they demanded, and Glasgow fell heir to them – all because Denny Magee had faced down John Coote one day, and we had become party to all that was decided with the London chapel.

At Albion Street we began to be involved in disputes fabricated out of any pretext, and we never knew from day to day if the news we had to tell would reach our readers. 'Industrial relations' had been re-established – with a vengeance.

CHAPTER 35

Plastic flowers for heroes

THE PENTLAND FIRTH IS JUST 20 miles long, but it is as treacherous a stretch of water as is to be found in all the world. At Cape Horn the awesome waves come 60 feet high, one after another, but they come spaced regularly apart like ranks of disciplined storm troopers whose arrival you can time as if by a stopwatch. The Pentland Firth is not like that. When it is in the most evil of its wickedly unpredictable moods and it awakes its furies to rear up house-high, there is no time to draw breath after the arrival of one monster before its brothers crash down on top and climb over it.

Its seas were said to be more wicked than for twenty-five years when, on the night of 19 March 1969, the Longhope lifeboatmen left their little inlet harbour on Hoy Island in the Orkneys to look for a ship which had sent an SOS call from an imprecise position. The 2,600-ton Liberian freighter Irene had run out of fuel and was being driven helplessly, the captain knew not where. So the lifeboatmen set off, to keep a rendezvous with disaster.

The Irene piled up on rocks at Grim Ness, on the northerly part of South Ronaldsay, and a team of coastguards snatched the crew of 17 to safety on shore by breeches buoy. In the darkness one of the coastguards thought he glimpsed the Longhope lifeboat for a moment in the distance, 'and then she vanished under a huge wave'.

When we heard that the lifeboat was missing we flew Stuart McCartney and photographer Jack Middleton to the Orkneys. They arrived in Kirkwall to find the Liberian captain and his crew being cared for in the Royal Hotel. From Stromness a fishing vessel took our reporter and photographer the 17 miles across to Hoy island.

Stuart went at once to the home of Jack Groat, who was the honorary secretary of the lifeboat. A Daily Record reporter was already on the doorstep. He said he had knocked repeatedly without response, and that it was obvious there was no one at home. As he turned away, Stuart tentatively turned the door handle. It seemed to yield. He waited for a moment, then turned it. The door opened and he went inside to find Jack Groat hunched over his radio and his telephone, seeking news and knowing that it might only tell him that hope was surely gone. Stuart closed the door behind him and locked it in case the *Record* reporter should come back.

The man whose duty it had been to send off the lifeboat was

heartbroken. All the crew were his friends. Dan Kilpatrick, the coxswain, who was his boyhood chum, had with him in the boat his two sons, Jack and Ray, and the engineer, Robert Johnston, had his sons Robbie and James on board, too. 58-year-old Jimmy Swanson and bachelor Erik MacFadyen, who had volunteered to make up the crew, were not related to the others, but every one of them had been bonded like one family. Eight men in all.

Lifeboat crews are like that. You don't risk your life at a token 30 shillings (£1.50) for the first two hours and 7s 6d (37p) every hour thereafter if you are only doing it for the money.

When Stuart left Jack Groat two hours later the wind was driving rain along in sheets. In the darkness he went looking for a telephone kiosk in which to put together his story and call his office. Here one might recall that Stuart McCartney had sworn, soon after rejoining us in 1963, that he would never give an inch to the opposition. On this occasion, however, he was to give much more than an inch.

James Grylss was a young *Daily Mail* reporter on his first out-of-town assignment. He and Stuart are good friends today, but at that time they had not met before. Years later he told Stuart that he, too, had sought a telephone kiosk and had found the only one occupied. He crouched on the lee side of it for shelter to wait for its occupant to hang up and leave. But, he told Stuart, he 'heard this fellow inside telling the story of the lifeboat', and he listened and noted in shorthand what was being said, merged it with what he himself had gleaned, and then phoned in his story. 'And that was how I found out that I had helped to give a story to the *Daily Mail* for a second time,' said Stuart.

The Longhope lifeboat found and taken in tow...
but all inside her were dead
(Photo: *Evening Times*)

The news which Jack Groat awaited only confirmed his fears. The Longhope men were found by comrades of the Thurso lifeboat who had so often shared their rescue missions. She was wallowing 15 miles to the west from where she had last been reported seen. The 'T.G.B' – so named after her anonymous donor – was not a self-righting boat as later versions were. She was upside down.

When she was towed into Scrabster harbour and righted, everyone inside was dead. Dan Kilpatrick was at the chart table, the others below deck. Jimmy Swanson, the 58-year-old, was not among them; more than a year was to go by before the firth gave up its eighth victim, washing his body ashore on the coast of the mainland.

Kirkwall lifeboat brought the dead crew back from Scrabster to Hoy, escorted by the Stromness boat flying Dan Kilpatrick's Red Ensign at the stern. Robert Johnston, who had lost his father and two brothers, helped to carry the coffins ashore. The seven were brought to lie in state before their funeral at the little parish church at Walls which served the southern part of the island.

Admiral Sir Wilfrid Woods, a six feet former submariner who was chairman of the RNLI, and various other dignitaries, flew in for the funeral. They all crammed into the little hotel with the Press.

'I knew how distressed Dan Kilpatrick's widow would be, said Stuart, 'and I didn't want to intrude, but I asked the RNLI people if she would see me and, if so, whether I could have their sanction. As I expected, their answer was that they thought it best if she were left alone. But next day I was told she would be glad to receive me, and that the RNLI would appreciate if I saw her on behalf of all the reporters.

'At the door of her home Dan's little dog sat waiting for its master. This dignified woman who had lost her husband and two of her three sons, despite the burden of her grief, took my hand and said, 'How nice of you to come to see me'. On the walls of the house were the plaques which were testimony to the hundreds of people her husband had plucked from the sea. I did not stay long. After I left I called a mini press conference and told the others about the interview. I held nothing back for my own use – I owed that to Dan and his family and all the others.

'A reporter from *The Times* in London, Dick Sharp, had come with the RNLI entourage, and he and I were then asked if we would take floral tributes into the church and lay them on the coffins. I remember that all the flowers were plastic. No flowers grow in Orkney at that time of year. There was no one else there when we went into that little church. The coffins were laid out in a row, and on each there was a hat and a name and the medals which each man had won. But the last bier was bare, except for Jimmy Swanson's hat and his name.

'When we went to the church again for the service and sang that hymn for all who go to sea, 'Eternal Father, Strong to Save', I never felt so emotional in all my life'.

Just ten months after Longhope came another lifeboat disaster, and Stuart McCartney went north again. Jack Webster went too, because the lifeboat which was lost was Fraserburgh's and he knew and felt the town's sorrows more than most. As a young reporter with the *Press and Journal* he had opened an office there for the paper.

Seventeen years earlier, the town's predecessor lifeboat had taken a little company of yawls out of the grasp of a sea which had suddenly swelled up in anger, and after shepherding them over the bar into harbour it had itself been swamped by a freak wave. The crew of seven were pitched into the sea within sight of their homes, to swim for their lives.

Jack Webster had been among the crowd then – some of them relatives and friends – who ran to the harbour, there to see the crewmen drown, one by one, until only coxswain Andrew Ritchie was left for them to shout their frantic encouragement, until a bobbing chunk of flotsam hit him and sent him under. The youngest, Charlie Tait, survived – and he was the first to volunteer to man the replacement boat which the Duchess of Kent christened with her name.

Now, on 21 January 1970, a crowd was gathered at the harbour again, because the lifeboat *Duchess of Kent* had been gone too long since she went to help a little Danish shrimp fishing vessel, the *Opal*, thirty miles out to the north east. They shouldn't have been in danger, for the gale which swept the north in the early days of January had subsided, and the sun was even shining.

It emerged that the *Duchess of Kent* hadn't been needed at all. 'I only radioed my company to ask for a sister ship to send a spare pump,' said the skipper of the shrimp boat. 'I didn't ask for any other help.' But when he sent another message to say that his troubles had worsened, the owners alerted the coastguards and Fraserburgh's lifeboat was launched.

By the time she arrived at the *Opal* a helicopter had taken off an injured crewman and landed him in Lossiemouth; the Russian mother factory ship *Viktor Kingisepp* was standing by; one of her trawlers had a towline on board the shrimp boat; and a Shackleton plane circled overhead.

At 12.30 that afternoon the skipper of the *Opal* saw the lifeboat approaching in a sweep to come alongside. 'She seemed in no danger,' he said. 'I had started to take a radiophone call from Denmark when I heard an Eskimo among my crew shout out, 'She's gone over!' I ran to the side in time to see one of the lifeboat crew crawling up on to her hull.'

The one whom the Opal skipper saw clinging to the keel was the 44-year-old Second Engineer, John Buchan. He had been on look-out duty on the leeward side when the wave struck, and was later to say, 'I heard the cox shout 'Hold on, lads', and then this great lump of water rose up. It hung above us for what seemed a full minute and then it plunged down over us and turned the boat over as though it was no more than a cork. I didn't know if I was under the boat or out of it. But I found myself yards away from it and I swam and clung to the keel. The Russian trawlermen wrapped a rope round me and hauled me on board.'

A crewman on board the Russian factory ship Viktor Kingisepp took this picture at the very moment the killer wave struck the Fraserburgh lifeboat. In the foreground is the Danish shrimp boat Opal, and beyond her the dark shape of the lifeboat vanishing under the wave
(Photo: Press Association)

The crew of the mother ship *Viktor Kingisepp* lashed the stricken lifeboat to their vessel's side, scrambled down to try to save the trapped men, and for two hours they tried either to right her or to drain the water out of her in the hope that the men were safe inside a bubble of air. Then, at 3.15 pm, *Viktor Kingisepp* radioed that her crew were trying to break a way through the hull. Throughout these hours of confused language difficulties the only English-speaking link they had was the lifeboat's 2nd engineer, John Buchan, who was now on board the Russian trawler.

Throughout these hours, too, the six lifeboatmen's wives had waited by their radios, as they always did when the boat was launched. Stella Buchan's trawler radio was out of action, but she could hear the voices on an old radio in a corner of the lounge and, confused as they were, she knew that at least one of the lifeboat crew was safe.

Finally she heard her husband's voice. Not only Stella heard it, but all those listening at the harbour heard it, too. John Buchan's voice came amid crackling static in short and numbing sentences. 'Only survivor so far. Stop. Russian mother ship trying to right lifeboat. Stop. There were six men in the lifeboat. Stop.'

Once again a killer wave had destroyed Fraserburgh's lifeboat, and this one had taken five lives.

CHAPTER 36

Paddy is held for murder

THE CRIMINAL WE HAD COME to know so well as Stuart McCartney's underworld favourite was arrested for the umpteenth time. But this time it was not for safeblowing. Paddy Meehan was being held for murder. This was because Abraham Ross remembered only one salient thing when two hooded raiders broke into his home in Blackburn Place in Ayr and seized him and his wife Rachel and bound them and beat them so mercilessly that Rachel died twelve days later from her injuries. What pensioner Abraham Ross remembered was that their assailants had referred to each other as 'Pat' and 'Jim'.

When detectives began to question known criminals they looked in particular for a 'Pat' and a 'Jim'. Paddy Meehan admitted freely that he and a companion had passed through Ayr on the night of the crime on their way to Stranraer (more frankly, later, he conceded that their mission had been to blow a safe). His companion had been James Griffiths. With that, the police believed they had found 'Pat' and 'Jim'.

James Griffiths was a dangerous criminal who was wanted by the police in England. He had taken lodgings in the west end of Glasgow. Detectives who went to interview him there were met with a fusillade of gunfire, and one of them was hit on the back. The police sent in reinforcements. Griffiths went on firing from a window of the house, then escaped at the back of it and fled in a car which he seized at gunpoint from its owner. He managed to lose his pursuers, but in a crazy flight across the city he left a gruesome trail: he crashed the car, held up a bar to demand a brandy to sustain him, and shot and fatally wounded a newspaper vendor for no reason other than that he happened to be there. He then commandeered a lorry and drove to Springburn in the north of the city, where he holed up in a tenement flat and started to fire indiscriminately from a window. One bullet found its target in a child who had been playing in the street.

The siege could have lasted longer than the hour that it did, for Griffiths had two bandoleers of ammunition round his shoulders to replenish his rifle and he had a sawn-off shotgun as well. The nightmare was ended by Chief Superintendent Calum Finlayson. He and a colleague crept up the stairhead to the door of the flat.

'We didn't dare confront him on the stairhead,' he later told Jack Webster. 'One blast from that shotgun wouldn't have given us a chance.

But I opened the letterbox to look in. I think he must have seen me open it because he stopped and looked at the door. All I could see was a shadow. I really only meant to maim him, to disable him. I aimed at what I took to be his shoulder and I thought I had missed.'

But the superintendent had not missed. The bullet ricocheted from Griffiths' shoulder to the heart, and by the time the two policemen carried him down the tenement stair he was dead.

The police were convinced they had identified old Rachel Ross's murderers. 'Jim' was dead. But 'Pat' was brought to trial, protesting that they had the wrong man and offering to take a truth drug to prove his innocence. Paddy Meehan was found guilty on 2 October 1969 and sentenced to imprisonment for life. From a cell which he occupied – in voluntary solitary confinement – he was to go on protesting his innocence for seven years while the author and broadcaster Ludovic Kennedy and others campaigned for his release.

Compelling evidence of his innocence came when a criminal named Ian Waddell, awaiting trial on a charge, admitted to fellow inmates at Barlinnie Prison that it was he and his fellow criminal 'Tank' McGuinness who had committed the murder. Six months later, 'Tank' McGuinness was killed in a brawl, and the truth emerged. McGuinness had confessed his guilt for the murder of Rachel Ross to his solicitor Joe Beltrami: he and Waddell had chosen to use the names 'Pat' and 'Jim' in the Ross house that fateful night.

Paddy Meehan was released with a Royal pardon in May 1976. Waddell stood trial for the murder but, to the dismay of Meehan's supporters, Lord Robertson, the presiding judge, insisted on the possibility of Meehan's guilt, and questioned the wisdom of the pardon he had been granted. The jury took only one hour to acquit Waddell of the murder.

Another much respected judge, Lord Hunter, was then appointed in March 1977 to inquire into the Rachel Ross murder case. Lord Hunter did not presume Meehan's guilt; nor did he presume his innocence. Among the witnesses called by Lord Hunter was Stuart McCartney. Lord Hunter had cuttings of everything Stuart had written about Paddy Meehan. Stuart had no evidence of substance to give, but he had brought along a list of Meehan's convictions, of which Lord Hunter would have had a copy.

'I pointed out that Paddy had no convictions for violence except one,' said Stuart, 'when he did thirty days for bashing his brother-in-law during a family row.

'I met Paddy only once after that – he was in the double glazing business, of all unlikely things – and I spent a pleasant hour with him. The last time we spoke was when he telephoned me from a hospice in

Swansea to tell me he had cancer and had just two months to live. He died a fortnight later.'

Our own 'Big Name', Drew Rennie, then chose to leave us to set up in business for himself. Bafflingly (could the reason have been pique?) our London features department executives had never printed any of the series Drew Rennie originated, not even when Mark McCormack, impresario of the golfing greats, wrote about the champions under his umbrella. But we were not surprised to find that Drew acquired a big name elsewhere. It was in Chinese. He had gone to Hong Kong to take charge of public relations for the Royal Hong Kong Police.

The name given to him as adjunct to that of 'Chief Superintendent Andrew Rennie' was Ling Gai Lee: 'It means 'Man of Wisdom', and you can laugh that off if you like,' he told us. When he realised that nothing had been done to help the underprivileged Chinese, he remembered how his boxing champion friend Sugar Ray Robinson had started the Sugar Ray Foundation for the poor youth of Los Angeles, and so Drew founded Junior Police Call, which ultimately had more than 400,000 in its clubs. His work for the young Chinese was recognised with the award of the MBE.

The 'Dirty Dozen'

DENNY MAGEE WAS SAID to have boasted to other union officials that he would 'bring Beaverbrook to its knees'. No doubt he thought he could. A newspaper is one of the most perishable and thus most vulnerable of commodities: the loss of a single day's sale means a loss of revenue which cannot be recouped afterwards by further production – it is gone forever. So there is always pressure to avoid conflict and, should conflict occur, there is always urgency to settle.

At Albion Street there were 26 union chapels, several of which could cause harm if they willed it. In the machine room, machine operators and machine minders belonged to different unions. When there was conflict between them we never knew whose finger would be on the button.

Occasionally the process department elected to be militant, and then blank spaces – and apologies – would appear in pages where pictures should have been. Their union did not ban pictures which were in library stock, however, and I remember that after their rejection of a picture of Tony Lema which was meant to illustrate his golf series, Drew Rennie amazingly located in the library a photograph of that hitherto little-known golfer which had eluded an exhaustive previous search. The suspicious chapel officials sought to enlist support for a complete stoppage, and this was averted only because the other unions adopted an open mind about the validity of miracles.

On another occasion, when a crossword puzzle from London was rejected, we found a grid in the library and the addicts among us spent hours concocting clues to fit it. We had 'go-slows', too; the jesters said that several were impatient for these to end because they had never had to work so hard. On the whole the chapels had (so far) used their muscle sparingly. But if there was wounding to be done, Denny Magee had the opportunity to be first in the queue.

Night-shift sub-editors are the first link in the chain of newspaper production. If they stop working, everything is brought to a standstill. Denny Magee's bedrock of support was in that group of journalists who, in a morning newspaper, come in each day in the afternoon to receive the work of the reporters and writers, and to take duty in shifts until 3 or 4 o'clock in the morning. The full chapel membership was about 200; the night shift sub-editors accounted for about 30 to 40 at most. But with these as his shock troops Denny Magee conducted a war of nerves.

His strategy was no different from that of the Fleet Street guerrillas – to hold meetings at all inconvenient times and continue these until the ends had been secured. Any excuse served; even if an issue was readily disposed of, a chapel meeting 'for information' followed, the 'information' encompassing so much territory as to bring us to the brink of imperilling production.

We stuttered through 1969 and 1970 and into 1971 amid 'confrontations' which were so farcical that I suggested to him we seemed to be acting out a perpetual pantomime performance. We could never be sure whether the paper would come out in time – not even on the night of 3 January 1971, when we were telling of the most appalling happening in the history of Scottish football. At Ibrox Park 24 hours earlier, during the last moments of an Old Firm derby game between Rangers and Celtic, a barrier collapsed on the terracing and spectators fell forwards in a single pack; 66 of them died, with what others in the crowd heard only as one awesome gasp for breath.

It was particularly infuriating that most of the 'issues' raised latterly were not our concern but those of the *Sunday Express*. Some among us might have privately thought that our up-market sister was too snooty by far, and that when you worked for it as a casual on a Saturday it was akin to intruding on private happiness. But no one despised the money, not least Denny Magee and his chapel officials and other night shift sub-editors who regularly took duty on Saturdays. If Magee had held his meetings over *Sunday Express* disputes in *Sunday Express* time and thereby endangered their money, the revered Father would have been lynched.

He never to my knowledge directed his invective against me; he reserved that for the editor of the *Sunday Express*, Archie Freedman, possibly because Archie made no secret of the fact that he despised the FoC and treated him with such disdain on Saturdays that his ego was injured. But when I chided Magee for apparently conducting a personal vendetta, he replied, 'Oh, I don't hate Archie Freedman. I respect him. But he is our enemy. There is no good in an enemy.'

It was over a *Sunday Express* dispute that for the first time he went over the brink. I had no part to play in it; Archie Freedman, quite rightly, would not have countenanced participation in his province by anyone from the *Daily Express* editorial.

A *Sunday Express* reporter based in Edinburgh was dismissed. Archie had warned him several times about his conduct (an accepted routine before dismissal) but, crucially, he had not done so in the required presence of a union official, and so Magee had found A Cause. The reporter actually accepted a pay-off and resigned. But Magee refused to accept he had done other than resign under duress and that, in effect, he had been constructively dismissed.

The chapel meeting he called began – inevitably at the inconvenient time of 5 pm – on the night of 18 January 1971, at the *Citizen* end of the floor after the evening paper staff had left. As Magee fulminated against what he termed the editor's 'dictatorship' and 'bully-boy attitude', Jimmy Henderson proposed that since the dispute was primarily between the editor of the *Sunday Express* and one of his staff who was a member of the chapel, the meeting should adjourn to reconvene on the following Saturday. The motion was defeated by 43 votes to 19.

In a statement given to the chapel officials the General Manager, John Paterson, said that the disputes procedure was still open (which meant that the reporter remained suspended pending appeal), but Andrew McCallum, the deputy FoC, alleged that he had been told privately that the dismissal had already been endorsed in London. And so the meeting dragged on, interspersed by delegations trotting upstairs to talk to the general manager. At 7 pm, by which time production was already disrupted and the entire night's editions were in jeopardy, John Paterson's patience was exhausted, and he told the chapel officials that unless everyone returned to their desks by 7.30 pm they would be held to be in breach of their contracts and no longer employed.

At 7.30 pm, when the deadline passed, Andrew McCallum led the members out of the building and into the car park opposite to hear more declamatory speeches. One member did not go with them: Jimmy Henderson joined a group of us on the suddenly silent floor. We were to become castigated afterwards as 'The Dirty Dozen'.

We filed into Ian McColl's room. It was clear that all of us wanted to carry on with the paper. This of course would have been impossible without the goodwill of the printers. The caseroom overseer, Albert Tulip, took soundings and found there was no sympathy for Denny Magee and his men.

Thousands of copies were already lost. Time was pressing if the rest were to be saved, and inevitably much of the 'copy' we sent to the caseroom went there without adequate printing instruction. We need not have troubled. The lists of stock exchange prices for the financial 'City Page' were set in their normal form by linotype operators who could have done it with their eyes shut, and the same was true of the racing form and results. If Denny Magee could have seen the eager co-operation extended to the Dirty Dozen by the caseroom he would have been given seriously to think.

When we had put an edition together and put it to bed, several of us went to the hotel in the centre of the city where the annual Press Fund Ball was in progress. Our wives were waiting there, not knowing when or if their escorts would appear. We had been preceded by drifters from the car park meeting, but it was only when the street vendors appeared with that first edition that what we had done was borne in upon them. Several said to me, 'How COULD you? You've cost us our jobs.' It would have been pointless to counter that they had dismissed themselves. But although the atmosphere was cool there was no hostility and, with the support of our wives, we stayed defiantly until the last waltz and the traditional ending, with everyone singing 'Auld Lang Syne'.

The dismissed workers did not stay dismissed – the Dirty Dozen could not go on forever. The other chapels intervened to plead their case, and they were all reinstated without penalty while consideration of the suspended reporter's case was resumed. In the event he stayed dismissed – with his pay-off.

The Dirty Dozen all received a letter from Sir Max Aitken which ended: 'Needless to say, the management will protect you against any disciplinary action taken against you by any trade union authority.'

It WAS needless to say this in my case: I was a member of the Institute. But the promised protection could have been necessary for Jimmy Henderson, who had been a loyal member of the union for 19 years. He was summoned by the Glasgow branch of the union on 29 April to appear before a disciplinary inquiry to answer a charge of 'conduct detrimental to the interest' of the union and of his colleagues.

The bench of union officials who heard the case accepted his contention that the union's rules held that no industrial action could be contemplated except at the instigation or with the approval of the National Executive Council. He was acquitted. But Father Magee only retreated to gird his loins for the next contest.

On 21 April 1971, three months after the Dirty Dozen episode, Ian McColl was appointed editor of the Daily Express in London in place of the pedestrian Derek Marks. As his successor in Glasgow he nominated Clive Sandground, who had been his deputy.

A journalist censors his paper

CLIVE SANDGROUND WAS A very competent 38-year-old journalist, a most likeable fellow, gregarious and flamboyant, who wore a beard in winter and sheared it off in spring, and had a taste for outrageously loud tweeds. He was courageous, too: in boyhood, polio had claimed a leg as the price of his survival, but he made light of this. He had been one of our Dirty Dozen, and he was determined that if there had to be confrontation with Magee he would prevail. Since Magee, on the other hand, tended to misjudge the calibre of his opponent, the stage was set for battle.

Clive Sandground, editor in 1971, was to bear the brunt of the labour troubles. Here, on happier occasion, he meets the visiting Duchess of Kent

The first confrontation came when the editor sought to appoint someone of his own choice to an executive post. This entailed moving the incumbent to another position. The executive was an able and proud man who was prepared to resign (with compensation) rather than accept an alternative post. Magee disputed the editor's right to make the change, and Clive Sandground saw his authority as being directly challenged by the union. An acrimonious dispute, punctuated with several chapel meetings threatening production, ended only with the executive accepting an improved compensation payment. As a demonstration of his worth he immediately found a comparable position elsewhere.

On the night of 17 October, 1971, Danny Magee stopped the paper and earned dubious fame thereby. By that time he was titularly 'Night Features Chief Sub-Editor', a title which had been bestowed on him in the hope (which proved to be vain) that it would imbue him with a sense of executive responsibility. As such he had two night-shift sub-editors assigned to him. But his principal duty was to oversee the passage of the Hickey Diary page and the leader page through the caseroom.

The Opinion column on the leader page that night criticised the Government's failure to ban a party of Soviet and Czech Communists from entry into Ulster to attend a party congress – particularly because a planeload of Czech arms, bound for the IRA, had just been intercepted. Cartoonist Cummings had drawn a supporting cartoon portraying the Russian premier Brezhnev in the garb of a priest, carrying a satchel bearing the name 'Father O'Brezhnev, Missionary to Ulster', arriving in Belfast with a plane-load of tanks containing 'Czech shoes' and '25 Samovars to Falls Road', '16 Crates of Vodka to Londonderry' and '1500 Czech glasses to Belfast'.

Denny Magee found the cartoon 'inflammatory'. It was a belated discovery. He had left a hole in the leader page to accommodate the cartoon, as he often did when it was late in arriving from London, and when the page left the caseroom with the hole duly filled, it did so unsupervised by him.

It and all the other pages had already been cast when he summoned his chapel faithfuls and they decided to send a demand to editor Clive

Cummings Cartoon... censored by the Father of the journalists' union chapel...

Sandground that he allow space alongside the cartoon to carry a letter of protest from the unions. Clive Sandground rejected the demand, and the night-shift sub-editors voted by 29 votes to one to stop the paper. Since the pages were already cast and the plates were on the presses, ready to run the first edition, the only people who could stop the paper were the engineers. They agreed not to start the presses.

More attempts to secure the support of the other chapels, and more meetings of the NUJ chapel, followed. The one sub-editor who opposed Denny Magee was followed by another, and then three more. But the voting was academic: the presses remained silent.

Next day a full chapel meeting reversed the vote of the night-shift sub-editors, and deplored it. But Denny Magee had achieved what no other journalist had ever done: he was the first to have censored his newspaper. Thereafter he and his night-shift sub-editors were known to the other chapels as 'The Midnight Mafia'.

Three months after this, Clive compounded his tribulations by a singular lapse of discretion. He sent to London a report which, he told friends later, was a hypothetical exercise written at the behest of vice-chairman John Coote. He said he had been asked to estimate the numbers which a newspaper such as ours would have required to start from zero. The report had been written in August 1971. Now, five months after he had penned it, it caused dismay among his friends and provided eager fodder for his warring enemies.

John Coote was scheduled to arrive in Glasgow on 28 January, 1972, to address heads of departments and union leaders and present to them proposals to reduce staffs by voluntary redundancies. When Denny Magee called an emergency chapel meeting to impart 'vital information', the 100-or-so journalists summoned at 5.30 pm assumed that the 'vital information' concerned John Coote's redundancy proposals. The Father of the Chapel surprised everyone, however, by saying that he had come into possession of copies of confidential papers. The papers, he said, had been sent to London by the Editor; they contained his proposals for complying with the management's wishes for staff economies.

The FoC did not say how he had come into possession of them, but it was deduced that a copy had fallen into the hands of the London chapel. They listed 77 fewer people than the staff of 400, and the FoC went on to detail the proposed staff totals, department by department, in Glasgow and in all the district offices, and to compare them with the existing totals.

The fact that the papers were five months old did not lessen the impact of the FoC's 'revelations'. A young sub-editor at once moved a vote of no confidence in the Editor, and another sought to enlarge the condemnation to embrace the Editor and all his back bench executives. Jimmy Henderson, the thorn in the flesh of the FoC, offered an amendment which, 'while deploring the severity of the proposals', undertook Chapel action 'to effect economies to revitalise the paper'. It was lost amid the outcry. The original motion of no confidence in the Editor was then passed by 103 votes to 18.

Clive had been less than discreet in the memorandum he had written to accompany the assessment, although no doubt we could have agreed with the phrase 'a mob of surly clock-watchers' as applied to many of the Midnight Mafia. But too many who were well-disposed towards him saw themselves as candidates for dismissal in the appraisal. Clive disdained to make any peace overtures to his enemies (nor did he ever offer an explanation of the memorandum to other than his intimate friends), but he saw his position as having been undermined and felt obliged formally to offer his resignation. John Coote, just as formally, rejected it and Clive soldiered on with dignity.

It must have been an even more uneasy time. Not only did he have to continue to contend with the Midnight Mafia and with the staff's four-day week (that benison to the Chapel members which had been conferred by their inclusion in the company house agreement negotiations); there was John Coote's redundancy scheme as well. The scheme was part of the company's overall strategy; and it was flawed. The redundancies were truly voluntary – the Editor could not determine who should go and who should stay. The volunteers, moreover, were allowed to give notice of their intention to leave and then at any time over the next year decide the time of their going. The terms were generous, but the payment to anyone taking early retirement was much less so. The result was that few over the age of 50 volunteered to retire, but many of the younger staff elected to go.

In Fleet Street, able writers and sub-editors and executives had walked out of their jobs and into others immediately further up the street. The story in Albion Street was not very different. We had more than thirty acceptances in the first two days; those who accepted included men whom Clive would rather have retained, but could not.

Other ingredients in the overall strategy of John Coote and his aides were flawed, too. A massive £50 million investment included new Fleet Street presses, the benefits of which were invalidated by union insistence that they be run at a rate no faster than their aged predecessors.

John Coote was now replaced by Jocelyn Stevens. We came to call him Joss the Boss. If he knew this, he probably accepted the title with amused gratification. Jocelyn was a charismatic man. He was of impeccable pedigree – rich, Eton- and Cambridge-educated, well-connected and married to one of Princess Margaret's ladies-in-waiting. His grandfather, Sir Edward Hulton, was a press magnate of bygone years, but the grandson was already a legend in his own lifetime.

He had bought and transformed the genteel magazine Queen into one of required reading by the affluent young bright things of the age; and after he joined Sir Max Aitken in 1968 and became managing director of the Evening Standard, he changed that publication's image, too, and pushed it up market to its considerable benefit.

Several months after he had assumed office as Sir Max's deputy chairman he came to Albion Street and swept away the last vestige of the discredited redundancy programme. All those who had opted to take redundancy but had been allowed to stay, comfortably protected by the year's contract while they prospected for other jobs, were ordered to go, and he saw to it that they did, whatever the cost.

Clive Sandground left in January 1973 to become editor of the *Sunday Mail* and to spend a successful and happy decade there. Deputy editor Jim Middleton returned to Manchester and he was succeeded in that post by young John Ryan, whose rise through the ranks had been phenomenally rapid.

Thirteen years previously, John Ryan had been a copy-messenger doing a summer job while waiting to go on to university to study architecture. In the wee small hours one night he idly scribbled some pen-pictures of a few of the people around him, and left them lying around on the table. Ian McColl found them the next day and asked him about his ambitions. John said he wanted to become an architect.

'And if you happened to stay on in newspapers?' asked Ian.

'Then I would like to be a photographer,' said the copy-boy.

'Nonsense,' said Ian. 'You will make a good sub-editor' – and he moved him the very next day to the sub-editorial desks. The young man who had intended a career in architecture absorbed the lessons of sub-editing quickly and, in particular, displayed a remarkable flair for news page and feature page design.

When Clive Sandground left Albion Street he took with him the good wishes of many, and also a farewell payment which allowed him to buy a boat to sail at his holiday retreat in Portpatrick. He called it The Golden Handshake.

That he was well-liked was evidenced by the numbers who attended the service after his unexpected death in 1993. Among the tributes to him was one in the Newsletter of the freelance branch of the National Union of Journalists. It said, 'Members will remember him for his fairness as well as his sense of humour and adventure.'

One could only hope that the members of the Midnight Mafia who had sought to destroy him read it and felt, perhaps, a twinge of regret.

CHAPTER 39

A different war zone

IN JANUARY, 1973, IAN BRODIE, who had been a foreign correspondent, latterly in charge of the Foreign News Desk, was sent to replace Clive Sandground as the editor of the *Scottish Daily Express*. He was 36 years old when he arrived; when he left he was aged 37 going on about 70, having come into a war zone of a kind to which he was totally unaccustomed.

Ian had no sub-editorial or other production expertise and was therefore disadvantaged by dependence on others in this field, but he brought north with him someone who could compensate for this inexperience: Nick Morrison was said to be one of London's most adept young professionals. Unfortunately, on the day Nick Morrison arrived he took to his room, obviously ill, and left us four days later. The new editor, perforce (and most fortunately for him) then had to rely on the deputy editor, John Ryan, who had with good grace accepted the title of Associate Editor to accommodate the London nominee, Nick Morrison.

Ian Brodie

Ian Brodie was earnest, long and spare of frame and spare of words, rather withdrawn, in fact. His quiet demeanour contrasted with that of his extrovert and often openly confrontational predecessor, but that made no difference to the attitude of the Midnight Mafia. For them it was business as usual, and that business was mischief.

Ours was not the happy home it once had been. Morale had been sapped by ceaseless internal strife, and by the botched redundancy programme. Nor did it matter to the Midnight Mafia that the main family home in Fleet Street was not a happy place, either. In London, ever-rising costs and losses were a source of increasing concern not only to Sir Max Aitken but also to the banks to which he owed money.

The charismatic deputy chairman he had appointed in place of John Coote now sought to retrieve the company's fortunes with a radical new plan. Jocelyn called it the DX80. The concept envisaged a revitalised *Daily Express* – 'the newspaper of the 1980s' – aimed at capturing a more affluent and ambitious readership, and thus attracting more profitable advertising. The image he sought unfortunately called for a degree of uniformity which found little favour among those who had to present it, so Jocelyn brought his technicians to show us how to do it. The technicians produced a rigid formula. They might as well have been draughtsmen drawing the outlines of the prototype of a class of bulk carriers. They did not understand that whereas a magazine can conform to a pattern for issue after issue, news stories do not fit into a straitjacket. The formula had already been ill-received by the London journalists; we in Glasgow were a little more polite, but just as unconvinced.

In any case, soon after the launch of DX80, the IRA bombed the centre of London, killing one and injuring more than 250 of the citizenry, and this was no occasion for the presentation of the event in unyielding form. On our back bench that night, John Ryan threw the DX80 technique out of the window, and from then on we quietly began to depart from it as often as the news demanded.

By the end of 1973 the financial crisis had worsened. But if the bold Jocelyn saw himself as Sir Max's saviour, there were not many at Albion Street who believed the situation was such as to require a saviour. Denny Magee and his chapel aides could not be persuaded that what they were doing was imperilling us all. All warnings were dismissed as bluff; reports in the London press were disdained as scaremongering. The other chapels, as much cocooned in a time warp as was Magee's, gave as little thought to what was happening in our deep south.

The very worst scenario which most of them envisaged was the possible sale of the Citizen. But they had lived with that fear for a long time – unnecessarily long, as it happens, because the negotiations which had begun in the early 60s and had been seen as leading to a merger with the *Evening Times* had been dead in the water for some years past. Talks between Sir Max and Sir Hugh Fraser had actually continued to the stage where an agreement was drafted for their approval and signatures. However, Sir Hugh arrived at an accommodation with his in-house unions which encouraged him to continue independent publication of the *Evening Times*, and he withdrew from further negotiations.

Some thought also that if any of the *Express*'s operations was in danger, it was more likely than not to be Manchester's. In Manchester the industrial unrest had at one time had been even more prevalent than in Glasgow, but our North of England brethren were now singularly quiescent.

When the Manchester journalists' chapel, more aware of the real world (as perhaps all the unions there were), indicated that they would not pursue current claims in the house agreement talks, Jimmy Henderson wrote in his diary: 'I saw Denny Magee deliberately filibuster a meeting to cause production delay and the loss of 87,000 copies of the paper. I felt so angry and frustrated that I stood up on a desk to address the chapel. The mob were calling our Manchester colleagues cowards. I tried to show why they had withdrawn from further negotiations: they wanted to survive. Father Magee was holding the meeting entranced with tales of Beaverbrook lies and broken promises when I stood up. 'I've been 21 years with the paper,' I pleaded, 'and 25 years with the union. We have come a long way in that time, thanks to concerted action on pay and conditions. Now we are being greedy in the extreme. These stories in the London newspapers frankly frighten me.' But I was booed and howled down with derision.'

But if the workforce in Manchester was in less danger than we were in Glasgow, that was not only because it was presenting an amiable face. Our presses could not have coped with Manchester's print. Nor could we have undertaken their distribution commitments, whereas Manchester could cope with ours. This had been demonstrated when Albion Street was asked to print on New Year's Day and had refused to give up the traditional holiday: our readers in Scotland were supplied with a *Scottish Daily Express* printed in Manchester.

CHAPTER 40

Gorgeous Lord George

UNLESS OUR READERS HAD been subscribing also to the London-based newspapers they might not have guessed that we faced a mounting financial crisis. Normal reporting service went on as usual.

Probably the last major story out of our Albion Street home – and one of the most intriguing – was the life and times of Gorgeous Lord George. That was how George Pottinger was known to the civil service staff at St Andrew's House, the headquarters of the Scottish Office where he had charge of the Department of Agriculture and Fisheries. He truly was gorgeous, always elegant and immaculately attired. He was not really a lord, of course – the title had been conferred by the envious in derision – but he was tipped to become SIR George, at least, as the Permanent Under-Secretary at the Scottish Office – and probably would been so had he kept his slate clean. But George Pottinger loved the good life, and he met John Poulson, a 63-year-old millionaire architect who was engaged in building contracts for public works, and John Poulson gave him more of the good life in return for favours.

Gorgeous George was a minister's son, educated at the universities of Edinburgh and Glasgow and Heidelberg and Cambridge. He lived on an exalted planet, wining and dining at all the best places and with the right people. He was a member of the city's exclusive New Club, and was the only civil servant to belong to The Honourable Company of Golfers at prestigious Muirfield. His impressive house, the Pelicans (so named because the bird was part of the family crest) was designed by Poulson, and partly financed by him. It overlooked Muirfield.

When one of the Yard's fraud squad detectives, accompanied by an Edinburgh detective inspector, called at the Pelicans, Pottinger's wife telephoned to the clubhouse. George strode up the fairway, bounded over the garden wall and went inside to demand to know who had interrupted his dinner, which he had been taking in the company of two sheriffs and a judge.

The trial at Leeds Assizes of George Pottinger and John Poulson lifted the lid off corruption in public life. Involved in Poulson's web were MPs, councillors and local authority officials. Nearly 100 witnesses were called. Pottinger was charged with taking £30,000-worth of bribes in the shape of holidays, cars, Savile Row suits and help with the purchase of his palatial Edinburgh house. At the end of the trial both men were sentenced to five years in jail. George Pottinger's term was reduced to four years on appeal, but Poulson was later sentenced to seven years, this sentence to run concurrently with the first: he had paid out more than £500,000 to influence people.

The trial lasted 52 days. Stuart McCartney sat through it, travelling home at week ends when the court adjourned. After the verdict, the London reporters at the trial never understood how the Scots contingent had gathered so much detail about the life of Gorgeous George, and were so well-informed about how he himself viewed his life. George did not understand either. The reporters had never approached him when they all travelled home at week-ends. But one week-end a rail strike stranded everyone at Newcastle station to await a train to Edinburgh. They went into the station buffet where George was drinking a beer, and they invited him to be their guest at dinner in the nearby hotel.

George was gregarious, and he liked an audience. He accepted. Over dinner he was loquacious and talked freely about his influential friends and acquaintances. He had been offended by his arrest and trial. His dignity had been hurt. He felt he had been guilty only of indiscretion, if guilty of anything at all. The gifts he had accepted had been mere tokens of the friendship of a very rich man. What need had he of such baubles? He had a good salary, a good income from investments and from his books (he had already written three and was writing a fourth at the time, which was to be a history of the Medici family).

He thought that he should not have been tried along with Poulson in England (and many agreed with the view that an English court had no right to do so); he believed that in Scotland he would never have been charged at all, but if the unthinkable had occurred, he could have appealed. It would have been impossible for him to appear before three judges without his knowing at least one of them, and knowing him pretty well, at that.

His audience all carried, as part of their normal equipment, hand microphone recorders. One after another they asked to be excused, and went to the toilets to transcribe their recordings. When they reached Edinburgh they went to the Scotsman office, where they pieced together between fifteen and twenty of these recordings from which they wrote up their background stories.

Did George ever realise how much he himself had contributed to the reports?

'I believe the only thing he thought,' said Stuart, 'was that, as a class, journalists must have the weakest bladders in the kingdom.'

The Poulson case had a seismic effect on public life in Britain. It led to the resignation of the then Home Secretary (and Edward Heath's deputy Prime Minister) Reginald Maudling, and the jailing of the Newcastle city council leader, T. Dan Smith. Poulson died in 1993.

When George Pottinger came out of prison in 1978 he went to live in England, where he resumed his career as an author. He died there in January, 1998.

CHAPTER 41

We hadn't just cried 'Wolf!'

IN THE FIRST WEEKS of March, 1974, the disbelieving began to fear that they should have heeded the cries of 'Wolf! 'after all. Rumours were rife of financial collapse, of a change of editorship, of redundancies, of sackings. In fact, it had already been decided that the only way to save the patient's life was to amputate one limb: 1,800 jobs would have to be sacrificed in Glasgow, or 10,000 would have to go altogether.

How and when it was to be done was kept secret for several weeks. John Paterson, the General Manager, was the first in Glasgow to be told. As for myself, I could not but be aware that drastic action was impending, but John Paterson said nothing to me and he remained silent even in the company of his closest aides, Robin Stevenson and Ronnie Fowler, until the two were summoned to London to be told that Ronnie would take over management of the rump in Glasgow, under John Paterson's chairmanship.

Ian McColl then summoned to his London office John Ryan and Ian Brown, and told them that they were the key figures he had chosen to pilot the editorial reorganisation of the paper: John Ryan was to be Editor of the *Scottish Daily Express*, producing it in Manchester, while Ian Brown would be Editor in Scotland, in charge of news and features. Ian Brodie was one of the last among us to be told. In his case, it was to be told not only that there was to be no paper in Glasgow but also that there would be no place for him anywhere.

Denny Magee and everyone else found on March 16 that it was, indeed, no bluff, and that the threat was not to Manchester, nor just to the Citizen alone, when a statement was issued:

'In view of the speculation about the future of the Glasgow Evening Citizen, Beaverbrook Newspapers make the following announcement. The future of our newspapers in Glasgow is now for economic reasons under urgent consideration. Discussions with the Government are taking place and a meeting with union leaders has been arranged on Monday. There will be no statement before then.'

On Monday, 18 March 1974, it was announced that all three papers would cease to publish in Glasgow on 30 March, but that the *Scottish Daily Express* and the *Scottish Sunday Express* would be published from Manchester. Jocelyn arrived in Glasgow the following day to address a meeting in the City Hall. He and his deputy Tony Dyer braved a barrage of abuse and catcalls on the way. He told his audience that since the launch of DX80 a year ago there had been 56 interruptions in normal working, of which 40 had involved loss of sales. He could have added that responsibility for all but 16 of the 40 could be laid at the door of Denny Magee and his night-shift sub-editors.

Ten days before the closure it became known whom Ian Brown had selected to form his team in Glasgow. There was less certainty over who would go south. John Ryan foresaw difficulties in a smudged division of editorial authority; he decided not to accept the post in Manchester and refused to change his mind despite pleas by Ian McColl and further inducements from Jocelyn Stevens.

Ian McColl then appointed Jim Middleton (who was already in the Manchester office, to which he had returned in early 1973) as John Ryan's replacement. As aides he appointed two men from the back bench in Glasgow: Bill Merrifield and Ian Duff, who moved south with their families to set up new homes there.

Several sub-editors, however, then withdrew on learning that John Ryan would not be taking charge. I interviewed them one by one, and (as a precaution) interviewed some possible replacements too, and finally I promised that if any of those who went to Manchester were unhappy at the end of a year they could decide whether to stay or to take their redundancy. In the event one or two of them did indicate unhappiness at the end of that year and they had to be induced all over again. Jocelyn Stevens was furious, maintaining that I had made the promise without his sanction.

At the last NUJ chapel meeting to be held in Albion Street, Andrew MacCallum stood with a list of names on a paper he held in his hand. 'Welcome to Ian Brown's pawns,' he said.

The implication, said Jimmy Henderson, was that the fortunate ones were sycophants: 'But no one, including myself, protested as we watched the faces of our friends waiting to find out if their names would be read out. Some were in tears. Ian Brodie, too, in the tradition of the service, was going down with the ship. He was taking redundancy.'

Outside the editor's room was now another Wailing Wall, where sheaves of notices were posted telling of job prospects in so many places to which nobody wanted to go, and reporters and sub-editors jostled one another to take notes of any positions offered nearer home. For those who could find nowhere to go at all there was just one hope – the Action Committee which had been formed by the different chapels to try to stave off the shutdown was now seeking to print a newspaper as the 'true heritors' of the Express in Scotland.

Among the 1,800 were a blinkered few who to the very last could not accept the inevitable. The Father of one of the craft union chapels on the eve of closure was still pressing for a meeting with management in pursuit of a wage claim.

On the night on which we were due to print the last issue, not only in Tom's bar but in every hostelry for streets around there were more riotous wakes than could have been found the length and breadth of ould Ireland.

In the building itself there was chaos. A junior Citizen sports reporter sat weeping on the stairs. Girls from the telephone advertisements department, some so young-looking that their usual tipple could have been surmised as sweet sherry, lay prostrate where they had fallen. A photographer streaked naked through the editorial department and down to Tom's bar amid hysterical laughter and the clicking of cameras recording this souvenir of a memorable evening. But the real drama was in the caseroom.

John Ryan, loyally at work to the last as he had promised, schemed the front page and sent the layout to the caseroom copy desk. Under the shoulder of the lead story, which recorded Grand National Day race fever, he placed a news story with a double column heading and introduction. It was removed by the Action Committee. In its place they inserted a statement which claimed that they had been given first option on the building and plant, and had indications of Government help, and that they were now appealing for public support for a new paper they hoped to publish as the *Scottish Daily News*.

When Ian Brodie went to the caseroom he found almost thirty people, including several of the Midnight Mafia, and spillovers from the floor above, crowding around the front page forme. The shouting and the noise of mallets banging on steel tables was deafening. He tried to shoulder a way through but he was jostled away until he found himself penned behind a pillar from which he could only shout his protests and gesticulate.

John Ryan followed him downstairs. At the door of the department one of the caseroom overseers cautioned him, 'I'd not go in if I were you. There's mayhem in there.'

John Ryan got no further than his editor had done. Ian Brodie then telephoned to Ronnie Fowler to say that the page had been hijacked. Ronnie went to the machine room and ordered the presses to be stopped. Several of the staff in the machine room who had interpreted the Action Committee's action as a threat to their redundancy pay-offs heeded the order. But one press ran with the front page statement

Soon after Ian Brodie had gone back to his room the door, which had been unlocked, burst open to reveal a hysterical drunk in the clutch of several companions. He was yelling, 'I'll kill him, I will.' The inebriate was hustled away down the corridor.

It was now 10 pm. John Paterson and Ronnie Fowler were still seeking an accommodation with union officials over picture wire transmission to Manchester when they learned of the trouble in the caseroom. When Jocelyn Stevens was told, they were deluged with telephone calls ordering

John Ryan...
he was advised 'Don't go in there'

them to 'stop this anarchy'. Stop the anarchy? How does one immobilise plant which is operated by technicians unless you can manage to persuade them all?

Walter Bell, the recently appointed assistant works manager, said to Ronnie Fowler, 'Leave it to me.' Within ten minutes he reported that he had managed to have the plates removed from the solitary press. He then ensured that no more plates would be produced by removing the safety rods from the casters and hiding them in an air duct on the topmost floor of the building.

The single press which had operated produced about 3,000 copies. Ronnie Fowler instructed the despatch department overseer to ensure that none left the building, and none did, unless smuggled out as souvenirs.

Very few people went home that night; some could not have reached home anyway. At daylight scores were still milling around the building. *The Citizen* had been sold in the final weeks to Sir Hugh Fraser for £2.75 million. There should have been a final edition of our evening paper on that day. The print was cancelled.

Ronnie Fowler...
Jocelyn Stevens roared
on the phone 'Stop this
anarchy!'

The crowd outside the building included television and radio crews seeking interviews, and I went down as company spokesman to speak to them. I really did not expect any flak from Denny Magee's Mafia, had there been any among the crowd, but I did not see any of them. Their chairman-Father was now one of the Action Committee hierarchy, although it probably irked him to be of lesser status in that larger company of union leaders. Like several others he went on to pledge some of his redundancy money to work for the *Scottish Daily News*, that brave but foredoomed venture. In it there was to be no 4-day week and no restriction on working hours, no extra pay for overtime, no demarcation, no reward other than the satisfaction of working for one another.

Denny Magee is dead now, and perhaps from a distance it is possible to take a more charitable view of that strange man who infiltrated our ranks and brought such discord. I would like to have understood what impelled him. He obviously did not see himself at any time as a villain of the piece, because when I had taxed him with making a pantomime of our negotiations he advised me to be wary of the cast list – 'there could be misprints in the programme, you know.'

On the occasion that the chapel decided to honour him, I was asked, for whatever capricious reason, to make the presentation and I agreed. I described him as a caring father who had fed and clothed his children and wiped their runny noses – a Moses who had led them to the Promised Land of milk and honey – and he detected no irony and thanked me warmly.

But that was not his true self either. It was a role. Denny Magee was a dramatic actor manqué. Our misfortune was that he chose our stage on which to play the part. He never did bring Beaverbrook in Scotland to its knees as he said he would. The banks eventually did that. But what Denny Magee did do was to kick us, not once but many times, while we were struggling to get back on to our feet, and that is difficult to forgive.

I went out to the car park opposite 195 Albion Street with notes in my head of what I might say to the television crews, such as that there was no need of an inquest because there was no corpse – brave words like that – but I do not remember saying any of them, and truth to tell I was a bit choked emotionally.

I remember only that TV's David Scott, who had been one of my reporters when I was News Editor, asked me an obviously prepared question: Might not leaving Glasgow be seen as heralding the end of the operation in Scotland? I replied that if I had thought that I would not have been staying with my colleagues. It must have sounded like a planted question and answer contrived between us, although in fact we had had no contact. But I added one of the little bits still in my mind: 'And some day we'll be back to print in Glasgow.'

Epilogue

INSIDE THE BUILDING WHICH, three nights earlier, had housed such tumult, all was unnaturally quiet. We met in the Editor's room, which was now tenanted by Ian Brown. There came to my mind that imposing hierarchical array we had boasted at our pinnacle in 1968; now we could accommodate ourselves in one room without discomfort. Jimmy Henderson likened us to

Ian Brown... editor from 1974 (to 1986)

'a shipwrecked crew given another vessel in which to complete the voyage'.

Printing the paper in Manchester meant that Ronnie Fowler had to send 24 vans from Glasgow to rendezvous with another fleet of vans from Manchester. The drivers exchanged vehicles at Southwaite service station on the M6 south of Carlisle, and crossed the Border with their loads to follow pre-planned routes. Chartered planes took other supplies farther north.

Our Manchester contingent had given us an issue of the *Scottish Daily Express* as good as any of those in the past, and we were further buoyed to find that the dire prophecies of the Jeremiahs had been disproved. There had been no disruptions to production, and no transport boycott.

A few of those who had been unable to accept the grim reality of closure in Albion Street had made a last-minute gesture of defiance and were still sprawled that morning in sleeping-bags on the *Citizen* desks. Their unauthorised sit-in was promptly disowned by their own leaders; but as the squatters moved out, the leaders moved in.

Three days before the closure the 16-man Action Committee, led by Allister Mackie, Imperial Father of the Federated Chapel, had been given first option to buy the building, in which they planned to print their *Scottish Daily News*; they had also been given guarantees that no obstacles would be put in their way. John Paterson, our chairman, gave them a row of offices at one end of the third floor, with telephones, to launch their campaign to raise funds for the enterprise, to which the workers themselves had contributed £250,000 from their redundancy payments.

I was less conscious than others of their presence, having removed myself farther to the *Citizen* end of the floor to join the survivors of the *Scottish Sunday Express*; its Editor, Archie Freedman, was on the eve of retiring and his deputy, Fred Sillitoe, had agreed to edit the proposed *Scottish Daily News*. John Junor, the Editor of the *Sunday Express* in London, had asked me to edit the Scottish edition, but not to assume the title of Editor until Archie left.

The sports staff was intact, but there were gaps elsewhere, and no longer a pool of casuals to draft in on Saturdays, so I recruited two former colleagues from the closed-down Citizen – Jimmy Brough and Jimmy Donnelly – as well as Stewart McCulloch (Archie McCulloch's son) and features writer John Fowler.

For the next four years we sent news and features and sport for the Sunday paper during the week to Manchester, there to await the arrival on Friday evening of myself, Jimmy Brough, deputy sports editor Bill Moir, and a sports sub-editor. The four of us would then assemble the Scottish Sunday Express in Manchester, tearing chunks out of the English make-up; we changed so many pages that, at one stage, John Junor complained that we were 'disturbing the balance of the paper' (he also confided to one of his executives that he suspected me of being a closet Scottish Nationalist). We would travel back to Glasgow during the Saturday night, by car in summer and on the 1.45 am sleeper from Crewe in winter.

From time to time we learned how our 'neighbours' on the third floor, the members of the Action Committee, were faring with their company, Scottish News Enterprises Ltd. They had acquired the support (or rather, as events would later prove, the baleful influence) of the ebullient and controversial publisher Robert Maxwell, who pledged 50p for every £1 the workers contributed. They also had encouraging evidence of public sympathy in the form of various promises (yet to be fulfilled) of financial input; but there was no more than a disappointing trickle of money from the unions, who viewed the loss of 1,800 jobs locally as a lesser evil than a loss of 10,000 jobs nationally.

Sir Max Aitken reduced the asking price for the building from £2.4 million to £1.6 million; he also gave the Action Committee an unsecured loan of £500,000 and a secured loan of £225,000. He was accorded no vote of thanks: it was asserted that he had done all this only 'because there is no other buyer in sight'.

The Committee's most fervent hope lay in getting an outright grant of £1.75 million from the Department of Trade and Industry; instead, the Department gave only a loan of £1.2 million. Even this was hedged about by conditions, which included the requirement that the Committee must raise at least half of the capital for the venture 'from sources which had read and understood' the Department's own unhelpful report, which had itself cast doubt on the viability of the project.

At the end of September 1974 we of the old guard left the Action Committee in sole occupation of No. 195 Albion Street; Ronnie Fowler had found a new home for us in Park House, in the city's West End. Ian McColl returned to us in January 1975 as chairman in Scotland in succession to the retiring John Paterson. As a member of the main board he continued to fight our corner in London until he finally retired in 1982.

The *Scottish Daily News* appeared on 5 May 1975. Taking into account all the setbacks Allister Mackie and his group had encountered, and all the obstacles the Labour government of the day had placed in their path, it was no mean achievement, and even the ranks of Tuscany could scarce forbear to cheer. The 'splash story' featured a young girl who had been dragged out of a crashed car and at first given up for dead, but was now following a career as a model. It lent itself fortuitously to an appropriate front page headline: 'It's Great To Be Alive!'

But the *Scottish Daily News* only lived for six months; the last issue was on 9 November, 1975. The company had always been desperately short of funds and riven by acrimony among the Action Committee members over editorial direction; it was further bedevilled, and finally destroyed, by Robert Maxwell, who ousted Allister Mackie and imposed on the paper his own imperious and misguided will. The company collapsed with debts of £2.5 million. Those unfortunates who were thrown out of work by the closure did not all leave 195 Albion Street, however: deluded by Maxwell into believing that he was going to start a new evening paper from the plant, they sat inside the building (some of the most optimistic were to stay there for a year) until the liquidator, exasperated by Maxwell's evasions and excuses, decided to lock them all out.

The liquidator sold No. 195 Albion Street to George Outram & Co, owners of the *Glasgow Herald* and the *Evening Times*, for £875,000. He also auctioned the old plant, realising only a further £109,000. In total, the liquidator ended up with sufficient to pay only about 45p in the £ to the few preferred creditors with secured loans. One of those was the Government, which recovered about £580,000 of its £1.2 million loan. Another was Sir Max Aitken; he received a little over £100,000 of his secured loan of £225,000. The unsecured loan he had given to the Committee was lost, of course.

Ordinary shareholders received not a penny. Those included the workers themselves who had each contributed upwards of £600 from their redundancy money, and one could not help feeling sorry for some of them. Robert Maxwell, the principal ordinary shareholder, lost £114,000, and no one felt sorry for HIM at all.

Although during the six months existence of the *Scottish Daily News* we had been subjected to a barrage of taunts about 'deserting the Scottish scene', the *Scottish Daily Express* lost no more than 90,000 copies. But throughout that time we were ourselves having to watch every penny, to help the Beaverbrook company to survive. Alastair (now Sir Alastair)

Burnet, a former *Glasgow Herald* leader-writer and now political editor of *The Economist* and television pundit, was appointed Editor in London to take the *Daily Express* more up-market in the image of the (to many of us, already discredited) DX80 scheme. The change had no effect whatsoever on our fortunes; nor did the change from broadsheet to tabloid, which was effected by Roy Wright, Alastair Burnet's successor as editor, on 20 January 1977.

By that January of 1977 the financial hole in which we were floundering was deepening. The company had an overdraft of about £14 million and had to scratch hard to find the annual interest payment of £2 million. Rival newspapers reported that the *Daily Express* was 'sinking in a sea of debt'. Three suitors (or predators) were circling hungrily: Associated Newspapers, Sir James Goldsmith and Rupert Murdoch. Sir Max Aitken did not care for any of them, but he was now an exhausted man, having suffered several strokes.

A white knight then appeared, with no fanfare: Trafalgar House, owners of diverse interests far removed from our own, such as the Ritz Hotel in London and the QE2. Trafalgar offered £13,690,000. Sir Max Aitken accepted. Victor (later Lord) Matthews, who controlled Trafalgar House jointly with Nigel Broakes, then rode in to take the chair of the newspaper group. Sir Max's personal shareholding brought him just £1.2 million, and the honorary presidency of the company.

Thus ended, on 1 July 1977, Lord Beaverbrook's newspaper empire. Sir Max wrote to his colleagues: 'It is a sad time for us all and there is no more to say. Yours ever, Max.'

On my 65th birthday, in May 1978, I retired from the Manchester trail – and from the *Express* – taking with me a carriage clock inscribed 'From the directors, in appreciation of 49 1/2 years' brilliant service' (management could always count to the veriest fraction).

I also left with confused feelings. Whereas the *Scottish Daily Express* had exulted in a Scottish identity, our Sunday paper's ethos derived from John Gordon, who famously said that his paper would be recognisable and acceptable 'as readily in Dublin as in London', and this formula was followed rigidly by his successor John Junor. I had known and liked John Junor since the 1930s, but I found his straitjacket uncomfortable to wear, being ever impelled to tilt the sacred 'balance' and ever irked to find that I could not do so with impunity.

In July 1980, at the end of a three-year modernisation programme financed by loans and grants, the *Herald* and the *Evening Times* began to print at 195 Albion Street.

Nine months later, on 26 April 1981, George Outram & Co. launched from there the *Sunday Standard* in a bid to capture Scotland's Sunday paper middle ground which the *Sunday Express* had dominated for so long. It was just in time to forestall Lord Thomson of Fleet, who had planned a rival broadsheet from the *Scotsman* stable.

John Ryan was recruited to plan the design of the new paper, and a formidable array of noted writers of the day was assembled to fill its pages. The first issue sold 380,000 copies. It was a false dawn, a novelty sale. But it was estimated that a steady sale of around 175,000 copies a day would be enough to see the venture viable.

The new paper won no fewer than 18 British press awards; but however good the content and presentation, a paper's livelihood depends on advertising revenue, and the *Sunday Standard* had a basic weakness: it had not been thought necessary (and this, moreover, in an unstable market) to give the venture an advertising direction of its own, separate from the rest of the group. After a little more than two years, the battle was given up; on 31 July 1983 the *Sunday Standard* came out for the last time.

Throughout this period, the Express newspapers group was assuming the first of a series of different forms. Victor Matthews, who during his tenure fought several successful battles with union militants, added the Daily Star to the stable in July 1978, and in February 1982 he piloted a demerger from the Trafalgar group, marrying the Express newspapers and the Trafalgar magazine subsidiary Morgan Grampian as 'Fleet Holdings'; in the process he summarily dismissed Jocelyn Stevens, who was opposed to the plan. Matthews then sold Fleet Holdings in October 1985 to David Stevens (Lord Stevens of Ludgate), the chairman of United Newspapers, for 20 times its original value, and retired to the Channel Islands with an estimated personal profit of £8 million to add to his already considerable fortune.

In June 1995 the Labour peer Lord Hollick came into the picture, bringing with him television and other interests, and United Newspapers became United News Media; Lord Stevens stayed on as chairman but executive control was exercised by Lord Hollick.

But two months before that, the prophecy I had uttered on impulse in the car park opposite 195 Albion Street on the day of the closure in 1974, that 'some day we'll print again in Glasgow', came true. On 20 March 1995 the *Scottish Daily Express* started to come off presses which the company had rented from the *Sunday Post* at Port Dundas, Glasgow.

We had a celebration breakfast at the Town House in Glasgow, and although I did not see any of the 1928 'midwives' there, it was a cheerful occasion, and champagne made a pleasant change from cups of tea.

On October 5 1996 the 'Seven Day Express' was started: not the *Daily Express*, not the *Sunday Express*. It was now simply (and wasn't that, after all, just what all Beaverbrook's Scottish army had called itself?) – The Express!

Acknowledgements

THESE, IN ALPHABETICAL ORDER, were my Good Companions along the way, to whom I am most grateful:

David Aitken
William (Bill) Bryson
Ronald (Ronnie) Burgess
James (Jimmy) Donnelly
Ian Elder
Ronald (Ronnie) Fowler
James G (Jimmy) Henderson
William M (Bill) Johnston
Philip D Mackie LVO
Magnus Magnusson KBE
Mamie (Baird) Magnusson
Ian McColl CBE
Farquhar McKechnie
Stuart McCartney
Andrew (Drew) Rennie MBE [died, 29 December 1996]
John Ryan
Robin Stevenson
Jack Webster

and

Margaret, my wife, whose patience and understanding helped to make the book possible.

Special additional thanks are due to three of the Good Companions who helped me to drive the book towards completion:

Ian McColl would have a major role in any story which concerned Beaverbrook's newspapers. I was fortunate enough to be able to draw on personal knowledge acquired during a long and valued friendship. Some day, I hope, Ian will tell the story of the fateful times in Beaverbrook history which he spent in the Editor's chair in London and on the company board.

Magnus Magnusson revelled in the challenge of helping to sub-edit the text. He scrutinised every fact, every spelling and every date, and insisted on 'correct punctuation' and on changing every 'that' to 'which' when it was being used as a relative pronoun.

Jack Webster used his kindly whip unsparingly to spur me to further effort whenever my energies flagged.

Index

Some other books published by **LUATH** PRESS

Old Scotland New Scotland

Jeff Fallow

ISBN 0 946487 40 5 PBK £6.99

'Together we can build a new Scotland based on Labour's values.' DONALD DEWAR, Party Political Broadcast

'Despite the efforts of decent Mr Dewar, the voters may yet conclude they are looking at the same old hacks in brand new suits.' IAN BELL, *The Independent*

'At times like this you suddenly realise how dangerous the neglect of Scottish history in our schools and universities may turn out to be.' MICHAEL FRY, *The Herald*

'...one of the things I hope will go is our chip on the shoulder about the English... The SNP has a huge responsibility to articulate Scottish independence in a way that is pro-Scottish and not anti-English.' ALEX SALMOND, *The Scotsman*

Scottish politics have never been more exciting. In *old Scotland new Scotland* Jeff Fallow takes us on a graphic voyage through Scotland's turbulent history, from earliest times through to the present day and beyond. This fast-track guide is the quick way to learn what your history teacher didn't tell you, essential reading for all who seek an understanding of Scotland and its history

Eschewing the romanticisation of his country's past, Fallow offers a new perspective on an old nation. 'Too many people associate Scottish history with tartan trivia or outworn romantic myth. This book aims to blast that stubborn idea.' JEFF FALLOW

Notes from the North
incorporating a Brief History of the Scots and the English

Emma Wood

ISBN 0 946487 46 4 PBK £8.99

Notes on being English
Notes on being in Scotland
Learning from a shared past

Is it time to recognise that the border between Scotland and England is the dividing line between very different cultures?

As the Scottish nation begins to set its own agenda, will it decide to consign its sense of grievance against England to the dustbin of history?

Will a fresh approach heal these ancient 'sibling rivalries'?

How does a study of Scottish history help to clarify the roots of Scottish-English antagonism?

Does an English 'white settler' have a right to contribute to the debate?

Will the empowering of the citizens of Scotland take us all, Scots and English, towards mutual tolerance and understanding?

Sickened by the English jingoism that surfaced in rampant form during the 1982 Falklands War, Emma Wood started to dream of moving from her home in East Anglia to the Highlands of Scotland. She felt increasingly frustrated and marginalised as Thatcherism got a grip on the southern English psyche. The Scots she met on frequent holidays in the Highlands had no truck with Thatcherism, and she felt at home with grass-roots Scottish anti-authoritarianism. The decision was made. She uprooted and headed for a new life in the north of Scotland.

She was to discover that she had crossed a border in more than the geographical sense.

Loving her new life and friends in first Sutherland and then Ross-shire, she nevertheless had to come to terms with the realisation that in the eyes of some Scots she was an unwelcome 'white settler' who would never belong. She became aware of the perception that some English incomers were insensitive to the needs and aspirations of Highland communities.

Her own approach has been thoughtful and creative. In *Notes from the North* she sets a study of Scots-English conflicts alongside relevant personal experiences of contemporary incomers' lives in the Highlands. She gently and perceptively confronts the issue of racial intolerance, and sets out conflicting perceptions of 'Englishness' and 'Scottishness'; she argues that racial stereotyping is a stultifying cul-de-sac, and that distinctive ethnic and cultural strands within Scottish society are potentially enriching and strengthening forces. This book is a pragmatic, positive and forward-looking contribution to cultural and politicial debate within Scotland.

Notes from the North is essential reading for anyone who is thinking of moving to Scotland and for Scots who want to move into the 21st century free of unnecessary baggage from the past.

An Inhabited Solitude: Scotland – Land and People

James McCarthy

ISBN 0 946487 30 8 PBK £6.99

'Scotland is the country above all others that I have seen, in which a man of imagination may carve out his own pleasures; there are so many inhabited solitudes.'

DOROTHY WORDSWORTH, in her journal of August 1803

An informed and thought-provoking profile of Scotland's unique landscapes and the impact of humans on what we see now and in the future. James McCarthy leads us through the many aspects of the land and the people who inhabit it: natural Scotland; the rocks beneath; land ownership; the use of resources; people and place; conserving Scotland's heritage and much more.
Written in a highly readable style, this concise volume offers an understanding of the land as a whole. Emphasising the uniqueness of the Scottish environment, the author explores the links between this and other aspects of our culture as a key element in rediscovering a modern sense of the Scottish identity and perception of nationhood.

'This book provides an engaging introduction to the mysteries of Scotland's people and landscapes. Difficult concepts are described in simple terms, providing the interested Scot or tourist with an invaluable overview of the country... It fills an important niche which, to my knowledge, is filled by no other publications.'

BETSY KING, Chief Executive, Scottish Environmental Education Council.

Wild Scotland: The essential guide to finding the best of natural Scotland

James McCarthy

Photography by Laurie Campbell

ISBN 0 946487 37 5 PBK £7.50

With a foreword by Magnus Magnusson and  striking colour photographs by Laurie Campbell, this is the essential up-to-date guide to viewing wildlife in Scotland for the visitor and resident alike. It provides a fascinating overview of the country's plants, animals, bird and marine life against the background of their typical natural settings, as an introduction to the vivid descriptions of the most accessible localities, linked to clear regional maps. A unique feature is the focus on 'green tourism' and sustainable visitor use of the countryside, contributed by Duncan Bryden, manager of the Scottish Tourist Board's Tourism and the Environment Task Force. Important practical information on access and the best times of year for viewing sites makes this an indispensable and user-friendly travelling companion to anyone interested in exploring Scotland's remarkable natural heritage.
James McCarthy is former Deputy Director for Scotland of the Nature Conservancy Council, and now a Board Member of Scottish Natural Heritage and Chairman of the Environmental Youth Work National Development Project Scotland.

Rum: Nature's Island

Magnus Magnusson

ISBN 0 946487 32 4   £7.95 PBK

Rum: Nature's Island is the fascinating story of a Hebridean island from the earliest times through to the Clearances and its period as the sporting playground of a Lancashire industrial magnate, and on to its rebirth as a National Nature Reserve, a model for the active ecological management of Scotland's wild places.

Thoroughly researched and written in a lively accessible style, the book includes comprehensive coverage of the island's geology, animals and plants, and people, with a special chapter on the Edwardian extravaganza of Kinloch Castle. There is practical information for visitors to what was once known as 'the Forbidden Isle'; the book provides details of bothy and other accommodation, walks and nature trails. It closes with a positive vision for the island's future: biologically diverse, economically dynamic and ecologically sustainable.

Rum: Nature's Island is published in co-operation with Scottish Natural Heritage (of which Magnus Magnusson is Chairman) to mark the 40th anniversary of the acquisition of Rum by its predecessor, The Nature Conservancy.

Blind Harry's Wallace

William Hamilton of Gilbertfield

ISBN 0 946487 43 X   HBK   £15.00
ISBN 0 946487 33 2   PBK   £7.50

The original story of the real braveheart, Sir William Wallace. Racy, blood on every page, violently anglophobic, grossly embellished, vulgar and disgusting, clumsy and stilted, a literary failure, a great epic.

Whatever the verdict on BLIND HARRY, this is the book which has done more than any other to frame the notion of Scotland's national identity. Despite its numerous 'historical inaccuracies', it remains the principal source for what we now know about the life of Wallace.

The novel and film *Braveheart* were based on the 1722 Hamilton edition of this epic poem. Burns, Wordsworth, Byron and others were greatly influenced by this version 'wherein the old obsolete words are rendered more intelligible', which is said to be the book, next to the Bible, most commonly found in Scottish households in the eighteenth century. Burns even admits to having 'borrowed... a couplet worthy of Homer' directly from Hamilton's version of BLIND HARRY to include in 'Scots wha hae'.

Elspeth King, in her introduction to this, the first accessible edition of BLIND HARRY in verse form since 1859, draws parallels between the situation in Scotland at the time of Wallace and that in Bosnia and Chechnya in the 1990s. Seven hundred years to the day after the Battle of Stirling Bridge, the 'Settled Will of the Scottish People' was expressed in the devolution referendum of 11 September 1997. She describes this as a landmark opportunity for mature reflection on how the nation has been shaped, and sees BLIND HARRY'S WALLACE as an essential and compelling text for this purpose.

'Builder of the literary foundations of a national hero-cult in a free and powerful country'.
ALEXANDER STODDART, sculptor

'A true bard of the people'
TOM SCOTT, THE PENGUIN BOOK OF SCOTTISH VERSE, on Blind Harry.

'A more inventive writer than Shakespeare'
RANDALL WALLACE

'The story of Wallace poured a Scottish prejudice in my veins which will boil along until the floodgates of life shut in eternal rest'.
ROBERT BURNS

'Hamilton's couplets are not the best poetry you will ever read, but they rattle along at a fair pace. In re-issuing this work, the publishers have re-opened the spring from which most of our conceptions of the Wallace legend come'.
SCOTLAND ON SUNDAY

'The return of Blind Harry's Wallace, a man who makes Mel look like a wimp'.
THE SCOTSMAN

On the Trail of William Wallace

David R. Ross

ISBN 0 946487 47 2 PBK £7.99

How close to reality was *Braveheart*?

Where was Wallace actually born?

What was the relationship between Wallace and Bruce?

Are there any surviving eye-witness accounts of Wallace?

How does Wallace influence the psyche of today's Scots?

On the Trail of William Wallace offers a refreshing insight into the life and heritage of the great Scots hero whose proud story is at the very heart of what it means to be Scottish. Not concentrating simply on the hard historical facts of Wallace's life, the book also takes into account the real significance of Wallace and his effect on the ordinary Scot through the ages, manifested in the many sites where his memory is marked.

In trying to piece together the jigsaw of the reality of Wallace's life, David Ross weaves a subtle flow of new information with his own observations. His engaging, thoughtful and at times amusing narrative reads with the ease of a historical novel, complete with all the intrigue, treachery and romance required to hold the attention of the casual reader and still entice the more knowledgable historian.

> 74 places to visit in Scotland and the north of England
>
> One general map and 3 location maps
>
> Stirling and Falkirk battle plans
>
> Wallace's route through London
>
> Chapter on Wallace connections in North America and elsewhere
>
> Reproductions of rarely seen illustrations

On the Trail of William Wallace will be enjoyed by anyone with an interest in Scotland, from the passing tourist to the most fervent nationalist. It is an encyclopaedia-cum-guide book, literally stuffed with fascinating titbits not usually on offer in the conventional history book.

David Ross is organiser of and historical adviser to the Society of William Wallace.

'Historians seem to think all there is to be known about Wallace has already been uncovered. Mr Ross has proved that Wallace studies are in fact in their infancy.' ELSPETH KING, Director the the Stirling Smith Art Museum & Gallery, who annotated and introduced the recent Luath edition of *Blind Harry's Wallace.*

'Better the pen than the sword!' RANDALL WALLACE, author of *Braveheart*, when asked by David Ross how it felt to be partly responsible for the freedom of a nation following the Devolution Referendum.

The Bannockburn Years

William Scott

ISBN 0 946487 34 0 PBK £7.95

A present day Edinburgh solicitor stumbles across reference to a document of value to the Nation State of Scotland. He tracks down the document on the Isle of Bute, a document which probes the real 'quaestiones' about nationhood and national identity. The document ends up being published, but is it authentic and does it matter? Almost 700 years on, these 'quaestiones' are still worth asking.

Written with pace and passion, William Scott has devised an intriguing vehicle to open up new ways of looking at the future of Scotland and its people. He presents an alternative interpretation of how the Battle of Bannockburn was fought, and through the Bannatyne manuscript he draws the reader into the minds of those involved.

Winner of the 1997 Constable Trophy, the premier award in Scotland for an unpublished novel, this book offers new insights to both the academic and the general reader which are sure to provoke further discussion and debate.

'A brilliant storyteller. I shall expect to see your name writ large hereafter.'

NIGEL TRANTER, October 1997.

'... a compulsive read.' PH Scott, THE SCOTSMAN

The Great Melnikov

Hugh MacLachlan

ISBN 0 946487 42 1 PBK £7.95

 A well crafted, gripping novel, written in a style reminiscent of John Buchan and set in London and the Scottish Highlands during the First World War, *The Great Melnikov* is a dark tale of double-cross and deception. We first meet Melnikov, one-time star of the German circus, languishing as a down-and-out in Trafalgar Square. He soon finds himself drawn into a tortuous web of intrigue. He is a complex man whose personal struggle with alcoholism is an inner drama which parallels the tense twists and turns as a spy mystery unfolds. Melnikov's options are narrowing. The circle of threat is closing. Will Melnikov outwit the sinister enemy spy network? Can he summon the will and the wit to survive?

Hugh MacLachlan, in his first full length novel, demonstrates an undoubted ability to tell a good story well. His earlier stories have been broadcast on Radio Scotland, and he has the rare distinction of being shortlisted for the Macallan/Scotland on Sunday Short Story Competition two years in succession.

'... a satisfying rip-roarer of a thriller... an undeniable page-turner, racing along to a suitably lineactic ending, richly descriptive, yet clear and lean'. Katrina Dixon, THE SCOTSMAN.

Over the Top with the Tartan Army (Active Service 1992-97)

Andrew McArthur

ISBN 0 946487 45 6 PBK £7.99

 Scotland has witnessed the growth of a new and curious military phenomenon – grown men bedecked in tartan yomping across the globe, hell-bent on benevolence and ritualistic bevvying. What noble cause does this famous army serve? Why, football of course!

Taking us on an erratic world tour, McArthur gives a frighteningly funny insider's eye view of active service with the Tartan Army - the madcap antics of Scotland's travelling support in the '90s, written from the inside, covering campaigns and skirmishes from Euro '92 up to the qualifying drama for France '98 in places as diverse as Russia, the Faroes, Belarus, Sweden, Monte Carlo, Estonia, Latvia, USA and Finland.

This book is a must for any football fan who likes a good laugh.

'I commend this book to all football supporters'. Graham Spiers, SCOTLAND ON SUNDAY

'In wishing Andy McArthur all the best with this publication, I do hope he will be in a position to produce a sequel after our participation in the World Cup in France. CRAIG BROWN, Scotland Team Coach

All royalties on sales of the book are going to Scottish charities, principally Children's Hospice Association Scotland, the only Scotland-wide charity of its kind, providing special love and care to children with terminal illnesses at its hospice, Rachel House, in Kinross.

Poems to be read aloud

Collected and with an introduction by Tom Atkinson

ISBN 0 946487 00 6 PBK £5.00

This personal collection of doggerel and verse ranging from the tear-jerking *Green Eye of the Yellow God* to the rarely printed, bawdy *Eskimo Nell* has a lively cult following. Much borrowed and rarely returned, this is a book for reading aloud in very good company, preferably after a dram or twa. You are guaranteed a warm welcome if you arrive at a gathering with this little volume in your pocket.

This little book is an attempt to stem the great rushing tide of canned entertainment. A hopeless attempt of course. There is poetry of very high order here, but there is also some fearful doggerel. But that is the way of things. No literary axe is being ground.

Of course some of the items in this book are poetic drivel, if read as poems. But that is not the point. They all spring to life when they are read aloud. It is the combination of the poem with your voice, with all the art and craft you can muster, that produces the finished product and effect you seek. You don't have to learn the poems. Why clutter up your mind with rubbish? Of course, it is a poorly furnished mind that doesn't carry a fair stock of poetry, but surely the poems to be remembered and savoured in secret, when in love, or ill, or sad, are not the ones you want to share with an audience.

So go ahead, clear your throat and transfix all talkers with a stern eye, then let rip!

TOM ATKINSON

LUATH GUIDES TO SCOTLAND

South West Scotland
Tom Atkinson
ISBN 0 946487 04 9 PBK £4.95

The Lonely Lands
Tom Atkinson
ISBN 0 946487 10 3 PBK £4.95

The Empty Lands
Tom Atkinson
ISBN 0 946487 13 8 PBK £4.95

Roads to the Isles
Tom Atkinson
ISBN 0 946487 01 4 PBK £4.95

Highways and Byways in Mull and Iona
Peter Macnab
ISBN 0 946487 16 2 PBK £4.25

NATURAL SCOTLAND

The Highland Geology Trail
John L Roberts
ISBN 0 946487 36 7 PBK £4.99

WALK WITH LUATH

Mountain Days & Bothy Nights
Dave Brown and Ian Mitchell
ISBN 0 946487 15 4 PBK £7.50

The Joy of Hillwalking
Ralph Storer
ISBN 0 946487 28 6 PBK £7.50

Scotland's Mountains before the Mountaineers
Ian Mitchell
ISBN 0 946487 39 1 PBK £9.99

Walks in the Cairngorms
Ernest Cross
ISBN 0 946487 09 X PBK £3.95

Short Walks in the Cairngorms
Ernest Cross
ISBN 0 946487 23 5 PBK £3.95

SPORT

Ski & Snowboard Scotland
Hilary Parke
ISBN 0 946487 35 9 PBK £6.99

SOCIAL HISTORY

The Crofting Years
Francis Thompson
ISBN 0 946487 06 5 PBK £6.95

MUSIC AND DANCE

Highland Balls and Village Halls
GW Lockhart
ISBN 0 946487 12 X PBK £6.95

Fiddles & Folk: a celebration of the re-emergence of Scotland's musical heritage
GW Lockhart
ISBN 0 946487 38 3 PBK £7.95

FOLKLORE

The Supernatural Highlands
Francis Thompson
ISBN 0 946487 31 6 PBK £8.99

Tall Tales from an Island
Peter Macnab
ISBN 0 946487 07 3 PBK £8.99

BIOGRAPHY

Tobermory Teuchter
Peter Macnab
ISBN 0 946487 41 3 PBK £7.99

Bare Feet and Tackety Boots
Archie Cameron
ISBN 0 946487 17 0 PBK £7.95

On the Trail of Robert Service
GW Lockhart
ISBN 0 946487 24 3 PBK £7.99

Come Dungeons Dark
John Taylor Caldwell
ISBN 0 946487 19 7 PBK £6.95

Luath Press Limited

committed to publishing well written books worth reading

LUATH PRESS takes its name from Robert Burns, whose little collie Luath (*Gael.*, swift or nimble) tripped up Jean Armour at a wedding and gave him the chance to speak to the woman who was to be his wife and the abiding love of his life. Burns called one of *The Twa Dogs* Luath after Cuchullin's hunting dog in *Ossian's Fingal*. Luath Press grew up in the heart of Burns country, and now resides a few steps up the road from Burns' first lodgings in Edinburgh's Royal Mile.
Luath offers you distinctive writing with a hint of unexpected pleasures.

Most UK bookshops either carry our books in stock or can order them for you. To order direct from us, please send a £sterling cheque, postal order, international money order or your credit card details (number, address of cardholder and expiry date) to us at the address below. Please add post and packing as follows: UK – £1.00 per delivery address; overseas surface mail – £2.50 per delivery address; overseas airmail – £3.50 for the first book to each delivery address, plus £1.00 for each additional book by airmail to the same address. If your order is a gift, we will happily enclose your card or message at no extra charge.

Luath Press Limited
543/2 Castlehill
The Royal Mile
Edinburgh EH1 2ND
Telephone: 0131 225 4326 (24 hours)
Fax: 0131 225 4324
email: gavin.macdougall@luath.co.uk
Website: www.luath.co.uk